P9-CEM-798

TOO GOOD FOR HER OWN GOOD

———— ✳ ————

TOO GOOD
FOR HER
OWN GOOD

---

*Breaking Free from the
Burden of Female Responsibility*

CLAUDIA BEPKO
&
JO-ANN KRESTAN

1817

HARPER & ROW, PUBLISHERS, NEW YORK

*Grand Rapids, Philadelphia, St. Louis, San Francisco
London, Singapore, Sydney, Tokyo, Toronto*

FIRST EDITION

Designed by Helene Berinsky

Library of Congress Cataloging-in-Publication Data

Bepko, Claudia.
    Too good for her own good: breaking free from the burden of female responsibility/Claudia Bepko, Jo-Ann Krestan.—1st ed.
        p.   cm.
    Includes bibliographical references.
    Includes index.
    ISBN 0-06-016365-8
    1. Women—Psychology. 2. Responsibility. 3. Self-respect. 4. Interpersonal relations.
I. Krestan, Jo-Ann. II. Title.
HQ1206.B365   1990
155.6'33—dc20   89-46071

90 91 92 93 94 DT/RRD 10 9 8 7 6 5 4 3 2 1

To the Memory of Patricia Webb

CONTENTS

———— ✳ ————

PREFACE AND ACKNOWLEDGMENTS

---- ✳ ----

In 1985 we published a text on the family therapy of alcoholism. That book, *The Responsibility Trap,* was the outgrowth, for both of us, of several years of public and private practice with addictive families.

Addiction is a great teacher. From it we learned about the process of change, and we began to understand more about the effects of unbalanced gender rules in families. We came to believe that addiction was a metaphor for the ways that stereotypes of maleness and femaleness deprive both men and women of their full humanity. Addiction, eating disorders, phobias, depression, codependency—all began to make some larger sense as metaphors for unworkable gender arrangements. We found that our work with alcoholism could be generalized to all families.

As therapists who had begun our work from a feminist perspective, we learned even more directly from addiction how the larger social rules that apply to women have a deep impact on the ways we think and feel about ourselves. Many of the serious problems all women face are a product of the ongoing impact of those rules.

This book represents our effort to share the insights we've gained in a useful and direct way. It represents our understanding of gender issues and of aspects of family treatment, and it represents a philosophy of change. It reflects our commitment to helping women, as well as ourselves, achieve more rewarding and balanced lives.

Many of the ideas in this book aren't new ones. We've drawn on the work of the major figures in family therapy, particularly Murray Bowen and his feminist interpreters and critics, and we've integrated the ideas of many thinkers who've written about the social predicament of women.

But we've also told the stories of many women, friends and clients, whose comments have helped to shape our particular understanding of the dilemmas of being a woman. Those stories speak for themselves. It's paying careful attention to women's own words and experience that helps us understand that "breaking free" continues to be the major work of women's change.

This is also a book that may be of interest to men. From it, men can gain an understanding of the rules that affect their relationships with women. Certainly they'll learn how to change those rules. And they might also identify with many of the descriptions of "goodness" because, as we suggest, men too suffer from conflicts and misunderstandings about who's responsible for what.

In the process of talking about women's "goodness," we try to provide a broader context for thinking about behavior that is currently referred to as codependent. We hope we've provided a perspective that suggests that codependency may be a form of being too good, but that not all "good" behavior is necessarily codependent. Rather it's adaptive, it's behavior we've been taught "works" if you're a woman.

We've tried to integrate useful ideas with useful suggestions for change. You'll find exercises throughout the book that are designed to help reinforce the ideas we discuss—they're designed either to enhance or to start you on a process of change. Some of the exercises may be more powerful than they look. Don't hesitate to discuss them with a trained therapist or counselor if you feel you'd like to go further with them than we take you here.

Finally, we've been concerned not to "label" women's experience in any way. We've given names only to processes and to principles; we've named ideas about change. It's been our intention to convey respect for the conflicts we all encounter as women without resorting to a need to categorize or pathologize us for having them.

We began this book one month after making a major geographical and professional move that relocated and dislocated our lives. It felt at times that we were writing in the face of almost insurmountable odds—we were living through some of the more dramatic effects of change.

One of the women whose story we tell in this book says that only her friends "get her through." What's true is that, had it not been for the support of our friends during a time of major transition and upheaval, this book might not have been written. So we consider this piece of work a truly collaborative effort. We have many people to thank.

Our gratitude first goes to Harriet Goldhor Lerner, who helped give birth to this book by sharing her editor, her knowledge of the pains of book writing, her humor, and her ongoing authorial and emotional support at all phases of the project. Not only has she offered inspiring direction and advice, but she kept us going more than once when the struggles of collaboration felt insurmountable. She has read the manuscript at many stages, including in proposal form. She tolerated frantic calls early in the morning and late at night. She is a truly generous and nurturing friend who has made our writing lives much easier than they might otherwise have been.

Other friends nurtured us and this project in countless ways. We thank our friends Jeff and Marsha Ellias-Frankel, Dorothy Smith, Jenny Hanson, Mary Nolan, Barb Schnurr, Betsey Alden, and Charlotte Look for both technical and emotional support. Each read the manuscript at a moment's notice, some more than once, and all gave helpful comments that required a great deal of their time and attention. Each also routinely fed us wonderful dinners, housed us when we traveled, and otherwise supported us emotionally as we tried to cope both with change and with the demands of a writing schedule. Further, Jo-Ann is grateful to Walt Marz for teaching her bass fishing as a meditative art during the worst of the pressure.

Mary Caplan, Terry Kelleher, Lois Braverman, Ellen Fox, Beth Anderson, Barbara West, Susanne Mastropietro, Madeline Muise, and again, Jeff and Marsha Ellias-Frankel, among others, took the time to discuss the ideas in the book at length and to lend some of the wisdom of personal experience to their development. Each has made significant contributions to the thinking that shaped our work. Each helped immensely to add life and color to concepts that might otherwise have been less accessible.

No acknowledgments would be complete without thanking the many women who have been our clients over the years, particularly those who gave their permission to have their words and stories included in this book. Much of the energy that went into this project grew from our deep respect for and identification with their struggles. Our work with each of them has added immeasurably to the richness of our lives.

If nurturing friends are an asset, a nurturing editor is a writer's blessing. Janet Goldstein has been a friend and supportive presence even at points when things were in grave danger of not coming together. She helped to shape the form and content of the book from the beginning and worked with us closely to restructure and refine it into its present finished state. She taught us a great deal about good writing and throughout was enthusiastic, nurturing, firm. Along with our agent, Joy Harris, she dealt adeptly with our egos and our various crises of confidence. She challenged us to do our best work and for a year became the new standard of "goodness" in our lives. We're very grateful to have the chance to work with her.

Finally, we need to acknowledge one another, at the very least for our mutual perseverance with a collaborative experience that was challenging in its better moments and harrowing at its worst. Those harrowing times notwithstanding, Jo-Ann is to be thanked for her humor, her energy, her skill at responding to and capturing the drama of people's stories, and her often brilliant flashes of insight into the core issues behind a problem that she then translates into powerful descriptive prose. Claudia is to be thanked for her ability to maintain her vision of the forest as a whole while each tree was planted, uprooted, replanted, transplanted. She is to be acknowledged for the exceptional clarity of her thought and writing, her personal triumph in allowing her wit and warmth to surface differently in this book, and her uncompromising commitment to excellence.

These acknowledgments don't and can't really respond adequately to all the people, including our families, who had a part to play in making this book a reality. They don't really express the true depth of our gratitude. We love all the people in our life a great deal and hope that that energy extends itself to all those who will read this book.

———————— ❋ ————————

PART ONE

THE PROBLEM
WITH GOODNESS

1

THE WOMAN'S CODE
OF GOODNESS

—— ✳ ——

Our friend Janet had a dream. It came during a period of greater than usual stress.

"As the dream began I was trying to completely renovate a building, a major apartment building. I was doing the whole thing by myself. The next thing I knew, I had to go to Africa for a business conference. I didn't know where I was supposed to go, to Capetown or Johannesburg. I was uneasy, frightened. My best friend just kept telling me, 'Get on the plane and go. You can do it, somebody on the plane is certain to know.' Then the dream shifted to home. I was trying to get Jimmy to bed. I kept saying to myself, I have to get this child to sleep. But Jimmy was screaming, he wouldn't go to bed. He screamed, and then Adam started yelling at me because Jimmy was screaming. Finally, I started screaming. I just put my hands over my ears and screamed. The screaming was real. Adam woke me up. I realized I was dreaming, or screaming, the story of my life."

Janet is a woman who worries continually, never feeling good enough about who she is or what she does. She ministers to her family, she does her best to be there for her many friends, and she pushes herself to achieve more and more in her business. What seems obvious to us is totally hidden to her: She's too good for her own good. Yet her response is to try frantically to do and be better. When we try to tell her what a good person she is, she says, "Yes, but you don't see me when I get mad.

"A few nights after the dream I woke Adam up at four in the morning. I was feeling overwhelmed, and I hadn't slept at all. I said to him, 'You've got to give me more help. I can't get up this morning and, if I don't get up, you won't know what to give Jimmy for breakfast or what to pack in his lunch.' Adam looked at me and said, 'You must be depressed or something.' For a minute I thought, maybe that's the problem. I'm just crazy. Then I got mad. I said, 'I'm not crazy or emotionally disturbed, damn it, I need more help. You've got to do more!' He turned over and said, 'I'll try.'

"You have to understand, in my family, being good meant doing what was expected. If you complained, there was something wrong with you. It still feels that way to me. When I do anything for myself I say to myself, 'this must be bad.' When I get mad, I feel crazy. If I need anybody or want anything for myself, I feel bad."

"Does anything that you do ever make you feel good?" we asked her.

"I only think about how good I am as a mother. But it doesn't run through my head to think I'm a good person. Like in the dream, I'm always feeling panic that I can never do enough, never get it done. Sometimes I get furious about all this pressure that's on me. Yet I know if I express that, I'm going to make more work for myself. So I just keep doing what has to be done. I feel I have a moral obligation to see that certain things are taken care of."

"Doesn't Adam help at all?" we keep asking her. "Certainly he would do more if you did less and expected more from him."

"Sometimes it's hard for me to look to Adam for emotional support or help. It's hard for me to trust that it will really be there. Often I'll send Jimmy to Adam for something, and he'll run back saying, 'Daddy's too busy, Daddy doesn't want to do it.' Adam is busy. But sometimes it's just hopeless with men. One day I was entertaining people from his office. I was getting ready and he was out playing tennis. When he got back, I asked him if he would make the coffee. He said, 'I don't know how to make coffee.' So I said, 'Well, then, go down and put the wash in the dryer for me.' He said, 'I'm not sure which clothes go in which load.' A few days later, I'd decided I'd had enough so I showed him how to make the coffee. The next morning I waited for him to do it. He put the coffee in the pot without a filter, so what did I get for my efforts? Grounds in my cup. I get angry and then I feel bad, sorry for him.

"On days that I'm particularly busy with work, sometimes he'll push himself to do things he wouldn't ordinarily do. He likes it that I'm competent. And when I work I feel very competent—it's much easier than the rest of my life so the tendency is to work all the time. You can get a lot of positive strokes for working."

"But does that make you feel good about who you are?" we ask again.

"Well, I think I have a good life. I do many of the things I want to do. I love my work and I enjoy my family. When I finished graduate school and took on a new career I felt wonderful about myself. But truthfully, since that dream, I keep wondering what price I've paid. There's little time to think. You can't even count on having any time to yourself when you finally get to bed. You never know when you're going to feel a small hand on you in the night saying, 'I need you.' The week when I had the dream I did think I could just leave them all and move away. I'm just so tired."

As it does for Janet, when you're a woman, being good comes almost by instinct. It could be said that to be a woman *is* to be good. Goodness consists of all those small things you do each day from the time you plant your feet on the floor. The gestures are simple, and because they are you barely notice them and neither does anybody else. You give, create, work, plan, design, clean, organize, straighten, put yourself out, try hard, and expect yourself to be there emotionally for men, children, bosses, coworkers, employees, friends, parents, your church, stray cats, and the rest of the world at large.

But do all these acts of goodness make you *feel* good about who you are? Hardly. Chances are that the most familiar emotion in your life is that sinking one in the pit of your stomach that tells you that you haven't done it quite well enough, that you're not quite acceptable as you are. For many of us, no achievement and no amount of selflessness permits the luxury of self-satisfaction. *To be good is to KNOW that you're never good enough.* A woman's work is never done. Tomorrow you'll try harder.

It seems the more we try to be competent, emotionally responsible, hard-working, and successful, the more we are rewarded with self-doubt, guilt, and greater conflict in our relationships. When we added the world of work to our work world at home, our reward *was* to have been a stronger sense of self. Yet what most of us experience in reality amounts to a sense of exhaustion and the nagging feeling that there must be "something wrong," something else that we're looking for, something more that we should do.

Clearly, as women, we've been operating with some false ideas about what makes us feel good. Clearly we're doing things, on scales large and small, that seem to be against our own best interests. Most of us would change things if we weren't so confused. Our dilemma is that doing good rarely leads to feeling good, and we just aren't sure what new choices would make a difference in our lives.

TOO MUCH OF A GOOD THING

Janet's story is not unusual; her nightmare is a familiar one. We hear her story in our practice as family therapists; we hear different versions of her dream in our women's therapy groups. Single career women, older women, lesbian women, women who achieve enormous financial and professional success—none are immune.

In fact, we've come to realize that most women operate in a powerful state of trance—a hypnotic Code of Goodness that pervades our relationships, our sense of who we are, and even our dreams. The powerful suggestions of that trance keep us unconscious of the ways that our behavior is always focused outward on what other people think, want, or need. Confused by our state of trance, we often forget to be the major characters in our own life stories.

In 1963 Betty Friedan inspired the beginnings of revolutionary change in women's lives with the publication of *The Feminine Mystique*. In that book she discussed "the problem that has no name." This problem, as she defined it, was women's yearning to have the freedom to pursue their own dreams as whole and separate people. It was the yearning to free themselves from the prevailing social norms about what a good woman is and does. Friedan jogged our consciousness about how deeply enslaved we were by other people's definitions of femininity.

Janet is a product of the revolution. She has had an opportunity to pursue her dream. She is educated, traveled, sophisticated, successful in business. And yet her nightmare speaks to her sense of being still burdened by an almost overwhelming sense of responsibility for those outside, beyond, other than herself. She believes that it is always her responsibility, her "moral obligation" to be good. As a child, being a "good girl" might have meant doing what was expected by others. But as an adult, being a good woman to Janet means always doing what's expected *for* others. Inevitably that means doing too much, trying too hard, feeling driven to do everything perfectly. Any impulse to act in her own interests leaves Janet feeling anxious, guilty, and ashamed.

In fact, most women still suffer, in more disguised forms, from "the problem that has no name." While outwardly their lives may be changing, inwardly women still feel trapped by a deep conviction that their lives are only on loan to them, borrowed from creditors, all those external arbiters who set the standards for goodness and to whom they then feel responsible. The fact that many women now work in the world doesn't prove that they're any less trapped. It only means that they work harder while the voice of their inner experience still goes unheard.

In the addiction-conscious eighties, our society gave this trance of female responsibility a new name—codependence. Codependence is really a different name for Friedan's Feminine Mystique. It describes the ways that many women behave in their attempts to feel and think of themselves as good. As therapists who have specialized in working with addiction for most of our careers, we've seen the concept of codependency reach and help many women who feel trapped and even harmed by their goodness, whether or not they've been affected by addiction.

But as the codependency movement has become more generalized, we've become concerned about the ways that the codependency label may further our society's tendency to be woman-blaming. The names we give to problems shape our ideas about what to do about them. If Janet were labeled a codependent she might wonder why behavior that she views as "moral obligation" is considered bad. And she wouldn't know what to do instead. Just as psychiatric labels that are applied to women—like masochistic, narcissistic, hysterical—are demeaning and devaluing of women's experience, the name codependence has a subtle blaming quality to it. We've seen too many women adopt the label codependent only to feel that they're sick for doing what they've been socialized to do. Codependency can sound like an indictment of who women are rather than how they behave. It implies that they love too much, that they make foolish relationship choices, that they are controlling, intrusive, martyrs. It tells them that they need to be improved.

While we use the concept of codependency in our work, we believe that it's important to develop ways to think about our experience as women that allow us to understand codependent behavior within a broader perspective. Part of the work of this book is to talk about codependency and the "problem that has no name" in newer ways. Janet and women like her don't need improvement. In fact, Janet is too much of a good thing. What she needs is to wake up from the trance that prevents her from living comfortably at the center of her own life. She needs to feel good rather than be good.

UNDERSTANDING THE TRANCE
THE WOMEN'S CODE OF GOODNESS

To be in trance means to be unconscious of the rules that drive you. It means to be affected by your environment without even knowing it. *MS* magazine played on this notion quite effectively years ago when it coined the term "click" experience. The "click" was a trance-breaker. Whenever a woman realized that she was being demeaned or devalued, whether in the media or in personal interaction, her heightened awareness "clicked." She shared the offensive experience with others. Women's collective consciousness was raised.

But we've not totally awakened from trance yet. We're now used to recognizing the overt signs that we're being treated unequally by others. But we're less conscious of the ways that our own feelings and behavior reflect hidden rules about goodness. Women have been hypnotized to believe certain things about themselves, to define good behavior in very specific ways. In our women's therapy groups, we try to create "click" experiences that address these deeper levels of trance.

One night in group, we saw a striking example of the ways that women need to "appear" good. Margot, the focus of the group work for the evening, is a proud woman, the wife of a prominent businessman. Margot's told us often that she believes that women should have power, but only in an indirect way. "Rule with an iron hand in a silken glove," she tells us. In other words, take charge, but not in a way that makes it look like you're taking charge. Already, she's said a great deal about her prevailing beliefs about how to be a good woman.

In the middle of our meeting this evening, Margot remembers that she needs to make a phone call and excuses herself to leave the room. Surprised, because it's so unusual for Margot to interrupt a group session, we ask if there's a problem. She says, "Not a problem, really, I need to remind the two girls (both are teenagers) to call their grandmother and wish her a happy birthday before it gets too late in the evening."

A tall, always elegantly dressed woman who is somewhat imposing at her full height, Margot stands, ready to leave the room. She is somewhat disconcerted when we say we think she should forget the call and let the kids remember their grandmother's birthday by themselves. As the unofficial authority figures in the room, we as therapists have set a new standard for good behavior. Margot is now in a bind. She needs to appear and to feel accommodating. But she wants to make that call.

Margot begins to challenge us. It's clear that she wants us to tell her it's good to call her children. We stand firm. She tries to coax us into giving her "permission." "But my mother is eighty-one. She'll be devastated if the girls don't call." We won't budge from our position. The more she pressures us, the more we stand firm. Either Margot needs to maintain her good "appearance" and give up the call, or she needs to take off the "silken glove" and openly disagree with us. She leaves the room to make her call.

When she comes back, everyone in the room shifts anxiously in their seats. Someone finally asks Margot if she's angry. The final blow to Margot's beliefs about being a good woman has been struck—a woman should never "appear" angry. Another group member says, "Margot, you swept out of this room like a Spanish galleon under full sail." At this point, Margot begins to sob. It looks like she may really be shaking with rage, but she doesn't yet admit to herself or to the group that she's angry.

From experiences like this one we learned along with our clients how deeply embedded certain messages about goodness can be. We learned how difficult it can be for women to give up their focus on other people. We learned that women's efforts to be good often leave them feeling pained and uncomfortable with themselves.

THE CODE WOMEN LIVE BY

Over the years of work with the women in our practice, we've been able to define more clearly the "rules" for women's behavior. The rules are there, hidden in experiences like Margot's or Janet's. Janet talks about feeling compelled by "moral obligation." And it's true that most women unconsciously feel these rules to represent "ethical standards of conduct" for their behavior.

We've identified what we believe are five major hypnotic rules at the core of the Code of Goodness:

BE ATTRACTIVE: A woman is as good as she looks.

BE A LADY: A good woman stays in control.

BE UNSELFISH AND OF SERVICE: A good woman lives to give.

MAKE RELATIONSHIPS WORK: A good woman loves first.

BE COMPETENT WITHOUT COMPLAINT: A good woman does it all and never looks overwhelmed.

You'll recognize how these rules operate for Margot. She's trapped by the Be a Lady injunction. She must appear "nice" and in control at all times. She must also dress well and take care of the relationships of all the other members of her family. Janet can't escape the Be Unselfish rule and she has also to Be Competent without Complaint. The two of us have our own troubles with the code, as you'll see in later chapters. Claudia works especially hard to Be Unselfish, and Jo-Ann must always Be Competent and Make Relationships Work. As we go on, we'll find that all of us are affected by all the injunctions in various ways at different times.

THE PURPOSE OF THIS BOOK

This book is designed to help wake you from trance, to help you rewrite the rules of goodness. It's designed to make you conscious of the ways that you're too good for your own good and to give you new strategies for achieving balanced relationships with the important people in your lives and with yourself.

In Part One, we'll talk more specifically about the impact of the Code of Goodness. We'll look at why these rules have had such a powerful effect on our feelings and beliefs, and we'll describe the consequences of those rules for ourselves and our relationships. In Part Two, we'll propose a new definition of goodness and suggest a step-by-step process of change for achieving it. Finally, in Part Three, we'll look at the dilemmas of goodness in many different types of relationships and suggest further directions for change.

Our hope is that reading this book will move you closer to a recognition of the value of your own inner life, and closer to the freedom to live your dreams rather than dreaming nightmares about your life. We can change our beliefs, our expectations, and our feelings, and we can behave in ways that enhance our well-being rather than denying it. We can awaken from the trance of goodness as whole and responsive women who can comfortably live at the center of our own lives. The words of one woman only hint at the sense of freedom that giving up goodness has created for many women who've undertaken the work of change:

"For years, no, really all my life, I tried to be good. In fact, I *was* good, so good that I really couldn't understand why people weren't better to me. My birthday never seemed to get remembered—that's just a metaphor I guess. I was always fixing myself to make myself more acceptable. If I got recognition at work, then I felt somehow I wasn't doing enough at home. I tried so hard and yet I rarely felt good.

"Now, by other people's standards, I guess I'm not so good anymore. I've gained a few pounds. I've left nursing to go back to art school, and I've stopped letting my husband run our marriage. My mother's worried —seriously. She keeps saying to me, 'What happened to my good girl?' I just don't fit the mold anymore.

"But you know what? For the first time in my life I'm beginning to feel good about myself. I feel more alive and I feel more real. It's not every day and it's not perfect. It's just that I feel more in charge of my life and, to myself, I seem to make much more sense. I know that I really am my own person now and nobody can take that away. Some days I really feel, deep inside, that I'm a good person, that I'm lucky I'm me."

2

LIVING THE CODE

----- ✳ -----

Women's Ways of Being Good

What's your image of a good woman? We might have answered that question more easily twenty-five years ago. In those days families aspired to the mythical Father Knows Best status that they saw portrayed on television. Women didn't have much difficulty knowing their place. The Code of Goodness was reinforced in a more or less uncomplicated way by the media, advertising, and the arts. Images of women being good were consistent. Women were mothers, women were wives, women were self-sacrificing and virtuous, and did good for others. While many women didn't fit the mold, they certainly knew what it was.

Often, the most powerful reinforcers of the Goodness Code are the romantic dramas we see in the movies. One of the most appealing images of women to dominate our cultural consciousness has been the one in which a "good" woman tames a "bad" man. The scene that comes to mind is Katharine Hepburn floating regally down the Nile on the back of an old river boat in *The African Queen*. Hepburn, in this classic 1951 film, is a virginal, hymn-singing missionary in Africa who boasts an almost unassailable purity and goodness of character. To her initial distaste, she's dependent for safe passage on Humphrey Bogart, who plays the "river rat" who drives his dilapidated vessel down the river in the face of continual danger. He is unwashed, uncouth, and drunk most of the time. Katharine enjoys high tea and he drinks gin.

Her goodness prevails, however. They become lovers, and he cleans up and drinks tea with her. He liberates her passion. Together they overcome the German enemy, shoot rapids in the Nile, and outwit the crocodiles. What we never do find out is what happened after they get back to dry land.

The appeal of this story, repeated with almost endless variations in other films of the time, is the image of the good and gentle woman of latent passion softening the edges of the harsh, uncivilized male who requires only the love of a good woman to change him. It's a story about the good woman as savior and tamer of the boyish independence of men. It's a story about the male's renunciation of adventure for love. The plot line may be an archetype that still has particular appeal to women struggling with men who are drug or alcohol abusers, or who are somewhat irresponsible in other ways. The message is deeply rooted in our psyches: We women can save men from themselves if only we are good enough.

Another popular movie image of a good woman adds children to the equation. Those of us who were raised as Catholics found particular pleasure in the character of Maria in *The Sound of Music*. What could be more appealing than a young, high-spirited nun who falls in love with a militaristic older widower and leaves the confines of her convent to care for him and his children in the shadow of the Second World War? In this story, the character Maria is almost supernaturally good and nurturing. She sings to the children and is always sweet and good-natured. She comforts the pain of the lonely, bereaved Captain Von Trapp and, like Hepburn, she softens her man's harsh and rigid edges. She transforms him into the archetype of the good father, strong but gentle, kind and sensitive, both with his children and with her.

The archetypal woman in these stories is a male fantasy come true. She is moral, even virginal, yet lusty and loving. She mirrors a man's preferred images of himself: either rough and tumble all-man adventurer/hero or strong, solid patriarch. She understands his pain and is a good mother to his children. She plays either mother to his own boyish acting out or daughter to his strong paternal domination.

Today these same images of goodness often seep into the media in more subtle ways. We can see the ugly man loved on Broadway in *The Phantom of the Opera,* and we're drawn to J.R. in "Dallas" despite his tough exterior. Surely, the hero of *Raiders of the Lost Ark* is a modern parallel of Bogart in *The African Queen*. Clearly women are still meant to tame men in some way.

These highly romantic images of goodness still affect us; they are part of the hypnotic pull of trance. They are idealized views that bear little resemblance to the real experience of women. Rather, they don't tell the story from a woman's perspective. But they do tell us something about the rewards and power of goodness. They tell us that a good woman at least wins love.

Today we more often know what goodness is for women by being presented with images of what is bad. If anything, in today's movies, such as *Fatal Attraction* and *Broadcast News,* we see women who clearly violate the Goodness Code—women who are sexual, women who depart from traditional norms of mothering, women who overtly want power. The attitude conveyed about this "new" woman is ambivalent. The images are certainly not romantic ones, and it's still not clear that they reflect women's perspective on their own experience. They point out that giving up goodness has its price.

In our modern culture any definition of goodness for women may be contradictory and unachievable. But the reality of women's life experience as we see it each day in our offices, women's chronic guilt, their depressions, addictions, burnout, and stress, their continual feelings of being torn between many conflicting choices, tell us that the mandate to be good still operates in deep and powerful ways.

Keeping in mind the historical images of good women that color our thinking, we need to look in greater depth at the injunctions that influence the way we feel about ourselves, the messages that shape our beliefs about being good.

HOW WE LIVE BY THE CODE

The first three injunctions of the Goodness Code form the bedrock of our sense of femininity. They define what it means to be female. While many of us probably feel some freedom from the more obviously traditional aspects of these hidden rules, old messages that seemingly had more impact on our mothers than on ourselves have a lingering hold in our subconscious. We may have changed our behavior in many of these areas, but the fact that we often feel mysteriously bad in spite of these changes is a signal that the code is still in effect.

In this chapter, we'll explore the underlying structure of these first three injunctions, understanding that every woman is affected differently by their dictates at different points in her life.

BE ATTRACTIVE
A WOMAN IS AS GOOD AS SHE LOOKS

"Beauty knows no pain" is the motto of the Dallas Cowboys Cheerleading Team. The phrase evokes images of women standing outdoors in freezing weather for hours with few clothes on. It stirs in us visions of smiling young women carefully looking their best to entertain the crowds. It reminds us of the sacrifices most of us are willing to make to look good and hence to please.

The ages-old injunction to women to Be Attractive really hasn't lost any of its power. More than any of the other rules of the Goodness Code, this first one puts a woman's focus on someone out there. It tells her to "work" at looking good for someone else's pleasure and approval. Rarely do we think about what feels comfortable and enjoyable to wear. Rarely do we stop to appreciate our own unique appearance. Rather we struggle painfully to match the contours and style of the "perfect female." And we feel uncomfortable and somehow at a disadvantage when we can't achieve the ideal.

These days we aren't concerned only about our looks, we're concerned about our "image." Many successful women are paying specialized "image consultants" to create a look that specifically suits them.

As an advertising executive explained to us, "I work among all these high-powered people, but in our private moments we're all running to 'consultants' to get our 'images' straightened out. I feel a weakness about having gone for a 'makeover,' but I guess I'm still doing all the things I have to do to be a perfect woman."

For many women, self-image becomes almost totally identified with body image. If they look good, they are good. But if, in their own estimation, they don't measure up, they may experience some serious and painful feelings of self-loathing. As psychologist Rita Freedman describes it in her book *Bodylove,* a woman may be more focused on looking good than on *feeling* good. A sense of achieving external approval becomes more important than a feeling of internal satisfaction with one's physical experience of the self.

So we see that women today are no less affected by this injunction than the women of our mothers' generation. But some new pressures have been tacked on. The career woman who goes to an image consultant knows she needs to look feminine but also needs to "look the part" that she hopes to play in the corporate or professional world. While she dresses for power and success, she also has to portray the image of the trim and fit. When people look at her, they should know that, in the midst of her demanding schedule, she finds time to run five miles, get to her gym to work out, or, at the very least, stand in her bedroom exercising with Jane Fonda.

While the power of the injunction to Be Attractive really hasn't changed much over the decades, what does change about it are the standards that tell women whether they're living up to it successfully. That change in expectations is most noticeable when it comes to our weight. Women have to be considerably thinner than they did fifty years ago to be considered attractive. It seems that our society wants to see less, not more, of women.

For many of us, weight continues to be the battleground on which the war for self-approval is fought. Eating disorders are one of the most prevalent problems that mental health professionals encounter. And diet books, diet centers, exercise machines, and health spas consume much of our hard-earned money. While some of this focus represents more a concern with health than with weight as such, our mass preoccupation with the size of our bodies reflects our ongoing struggle to control the way we look and, by extension, how much we're valued by the external world.

One client of ours was asked to present a major talk at a prestigious national convention. Apart from working tirelessly on her speech for months, she also prepared by going on a liquid diet and losing thirty pounds. When she talked about her reasons for doing this, she said, "I didn't want what I had to say to be discounted because of the way I looked."

A friend who is a successful composer tells us, "I feel I've failed miserably at all attempts to be attractive, but I keep on trying. I feel the pain of not looking the way one is supposed to look . . . that's *thin,* of course, thin, thin, thin."

Another friend, Barb, is an attractive academic who had outpublished the men in her department but nevertheless lost her job. Shortly after, a man she was involved with ended their relationship. Her friends were uncomfortable and withdrew from both of them. On the phone, as she was describing these losses, she said disgustedly, "Oh, I know what you're going to say. But I *am* being good to myself. I eat healthy foods, I cut down on fat, I exercise. My life is filled with activity. Don't tell me not to be hard on myself. I'm doing all the right things."

Barb extends the Be Attractive injunction to include remaining physically fit and taking care of herself. When she hears "Be good to yourself" she thinks "Take care of your body." Part of her discouragement is that she believes that if she could only take good enough care of herself, things would work out.

A focus on looking good can be an enjoyable expression of how we feel about ourselves inside. But this focus becomes a problem when we begin to think that how we look is a yardstick for our value as a person. Many women who *are* strikingly attractive feel valued *only* for their physical attractiveness, and many women who are very attractive don't feel it. Often women who achieve a great deal disqualify the value of their accomplishments because they don't feel attractive and that's their real standard for success.

We may extend the rule of attractiveness to include our homes, our children, our husbands, our cars. Somehow we feel we are failures if our living space and the people we live with don't conform to perfect standards of neatness, organization, and visual appeal. When you panic at the thought of anyone coming to the door before you've vacuumed, dusted, cleaned the bathrooms, and set a perfect vase of flowers on the dining room table, you're being driven by the Be Attractive injunction.

The most problematic quality of this first rule of femaleness is that as much as we try to change our appearance, often nothing we can do will make us acceptable in either our own eyes or in keeping with the standards someone else has set. In other words, we may try to control aspects of our physical selves that simply can't be controlled. "Beauty may know no pain," but the message that we're only as good as we look is painful. It's the first in a series of hypnotic suggestions that tell women there's something wrong with the way they are.

The Be Attractive injunction comes into play most when we:

- Dislike looking at ourselves in a mirror.
- Don't believe them when other people tell us we look good.
- Spend more time, before a professional or work commitment, focused on what we'll wear than on the task at hand.
- Get complaints or comments from other people in our lives about the amount of time or money we spend on cosmetics, clothes, diet books, exercise.
- Feel that the appearance of other people or things such as husband, lover, home, or children is a reflection on us.

- Feel envious and uncomfortable whenever we're with another woman who is attractive and knows it.
- Do things to our bodies that are harmful in the interest of making them look better.
- Feel we don't look right or we can never achieve certain goals in life because we don't "look" the part.
- Feel that we're not lovable and desirable because we're not attractive enough.

BE A LADY
A GOOD WOMAN STAYS IN CONTROL

A woman who came for therapy at age twenty-five for help with her overly compliant behavior brought in a report that had been written about her in nursery school.

Her mother had proudly saved the report as evidence of her "goodness" as a child.

> Mary has shown the ability to play alone in the doll corner with the most grown-up patterns of behavior—proceeding through a whole day with her family of dolls, imitating a mother precisely. . . . Mary seems very mature emotionally and seldom cries when things do not suit her. She is always pleasant and cooperative and unusually helpful toward other children. . . . She works industriously long after her contemporaries have finished—a little perfectionist. Mary is very independent in caring for herself, dressing and undressing easily and even lending a hand to those less capable. There is a sweet, motherly quality about her. When things do not please her she tends to withdraw from the situation rather than to stand up for herself.

Mary was four years old when this description of her perfectly ladylike behavior was written.

The caution "Remember to act like a lady" issued forth from our mothers' lips more often than we might have preferred to hear it. Most likely, our mothers heard it even more often from their own mothers. Seen as an extension of the injunction to Be Attractive, being a lady can be thought of as another way of keeping up appearances, of presenting a certain image to the world.

"Ladiness" is grounded in a rather rigid code of behavior that varies only slightly according to ethnic or cultural values. Basically, if one is a lady one observes certain rules about propriety and decorum. Those rules are always related to the *absolute necessity of remaining in control.*

We tend to blame our mothers when we think about the ways we were taught to be a lady. Family therapist Ellen Berman writes in an essay, "I am trying to find something to wear for giving an important talk, a task taking only slightly less time than writing the talk. When I find the dress I want, my first thought is, My mother would have liked this dress. The thought fills me with pleasure." In counterpoint she also writes of a woman who buys a dress that her mother would hate. That woman too says, "The thought fills me with pleasure." [1]

The rules start out innocuously enough in girlhood. We are first taught as little girls that girls don't chew gum. Or little girls don't climb trees. Later on, ladies never cross their legs, and they always wear white gloves to church. Ladies wear clean underwear whenever they go out because they might be in a car accident and end up at the hospital where somebody might *really* see what's underneath.

But as we approach adolescence and adulthood, the principles of being a lady become more focused and more dangerous to our evolving personhood. In the interests of our not causing discomfort to the others in our lives, we begin to force ourselves into a mold of submission.

A lady always controls her impulses. This means that a lady doesn't get angry. She is not competitive, loud, or aggressive. A lady doesn't argue. A lady backs down. A lady doesn't challenge or show strong emotion. A lady looks desirable but doesn't permit herself sexual desire. A lady is calm, kind, patient. A lady soothes the egos of others while quietly controlling and submerging her own. A lady is always in control of herself yet never seeks power for herself.

Most of us, in our more liberated states of mind, don't give much thought to the ongoing power of these impossible rules of restraint. We may deny their hold on us until we step too far over the line. Think about the reactions you stirred up the last time you were very angry or very upset. You were probably told you were overreacting or that you should "calm down" and stop being hysterical. When was the last time you heard a man being called hysterical if he was angry or upset?

Or maybe you remember the last time you were told you were "too much" of something. One woman tells us that she's been described cumulatively over the years by various people as too serious, too competent, too intense, too demanding, too confident, too threatening, too smart, too aggressive, too independent—for her own good. Recently she developed an interest in theater and took a class in being a clown. Then somebody told her that she was *too* funny. She wants to start a "Too Club" for women who feel that no matter what they do they're too much of something for somebody.

DON'T EAT, DRINK, OR BE MERRY

The rules about controlling ourselves are most potent in terms of our responses to food, alcohol, sexuality, and intense emotion. The injunction to Be a Lady dictates that a woman should not express too much passion or strong emotion. A woman who indulges in excess in any of those areas is certain to be thought of as "bad."

In our lectures we sometimes tell the Greek myth of the Bacchantic Maidens, women who lived in the forest and tended to eat and drink to excess; they were priestesses of Dionysus, the god of wine. As the myth goes, when they drank wine, the Bacchantes became crazed women and went whooping through the forests in an excess of lust and violence. They became so crazed that they made love collectively to Pan (who didn't mind, apparently) and went on to murder animals and eat the raw meat with their bare hands. Their gravest crime was to murder their own husbands while the husbands were dutifully worshipping in the temple of Orpheus, the god of the underworld. (What the husbands were doing consorting with the underworld, we don't know.)

We like to share this story because it reflects a very primitive terror of a woman's going out of control. In fact, this myth involves all three requirements of being a lady: Control your appetites, control your sexuality, and control your emotionality. Even though excesses of eating, drugging, sex, and violence may still be more typical of male behavior, the myth instructs us in the ways we tend to vilify and fear women who show any signs of similar impulses.

As we discussed earlier, the fact that we are a culture obsessed with dieting and weight is a vivid reminder that we must, as women, control our appetites. And controlling our appetites is a metaphor for controlling all our impulses, a metaphor for limiting any desire to have something for ourselves.

Holding one's liquor has long been considered a sign of manliness. But societal attitudes toward women who drink are highly judgmental and punitive. The same double standard applies to sexuality. Promiscuity for a man has always been a somewhat accepted code of behavior, whereas, for a woman, active sexual behavior is viewed as selfish and suspect. The myth of the passionate virgin who should please a man but frown upon sexuality for her own pleasure still dominates our culture.

Alcohol use and sexuality have also been historically connected for women.[2] In early Roman times, proof of alcohol use was presumptive evidence of adultery. A woman could be automatically put to death if a husband or other male family member thought he smelled liquor on her breath. It was assumed that if she'd been drinking she must necessarily have been sexually unfaithful as well. Wine-loosened inhibitions were implicitly connected with out-of-control sexuality. And a good woman should not ever be out of control.

DON'T GET MAD

Perhaps the real fear buried in the myth of those bad maidens was a terror of women's anger and of their emotional intensity when those emotions aren't under control. We all know the epithets that get hurled at a woman when she's angry and shows it. "Don't raise your voice." "You're too aggressive." "Pull yourself together." Surely a lady doesn't have a mouth like a truck driver.

In other words, a lady can't even be appropriately assertive without feeling bad or being treated badly. If a lady gets too upset, she goes to a doctor who will give her tranquilizers that will help get her back to being calm, kind, and patient. If she gets too emotional, somebody will undoubtedly tell her to stop being hysterical. If she does get angry, she'll have to show it by crying. If she cries, somebody will tell her to calm down.

A woman's feelings are particularly forbidden in a work setting. It would be unbecoming to show emotion, and the job might not get done. Work and feelings don't mix. As one woman told us, "I never get emotional in a work setting. It's seen as being too feminine."

LADIES DON'T HAVE NEEDS

Finally, a lady doesn't have needs. She never expects and tries not to ask for nurturing, attention, affection for herself. These feelings in a woman make others uncomfortable. The danger in a woman's becoming uncontrollably needy and emotional is that she might not be able to function for others. Her family, marriage, relationship, or friendships might not withstand the strain. The rules about not being "needy" often get played out in our relationships without our even being aware of it. We're so entranced by the Goodness Code that we do our best to quell our own feelings, and we feel upset with ourselves for having them besides.

One night in our therapy group, we asked the women to role-play a situation we had been discussing in which one of them had felt shamed by her husband for feeling needy. Jane volunteered to play herself asking her husband to spend time with her. Pat volunteered to play Jane's husband. Without any coaching of Pat, this is the way the drama unfolded.

Jane begins by explaining that, in this scenario, she and her husband haven't talked in eighteen days. He's been angry, and the only thing he's said to her is, "Bring me coffee."

JANE: I can't believe another whole day has to go by without my spending time with you. It's so depressing. I really want to be with you. I can't stand not talking.

PAT/HUSBAND: What's depressing? I'm here.

JANE: I know.

PAT: You're behaving like your mother, hysterical. Always this depression, this unhappiness, for God's sake.

JANE: I feel so needy, and so crazy. . . . Life is just so scattered, I don't feel grounded. I can't sleep at night and I wish that we could go away together—you know, just run away.

PAT: You know I can't get away. I'm backed up at the office, and I just can't do it—you know that.

JANE: I know, I understand. But I just can't help the way I'm feeling. My life is centered around you. You're the most important thing to me. My work consumes so much time, and it just doesn't matter. . . . Everything that matters is here.

PAT: But I *spend* time with you. We live together. I don't know what you need from me. . . . I'm here, damn it. . . . You keep saying you need me but I'm right here. . . . What do you want anyway?

JANE: I just don't know why I'm feeling this way. It's so upsetting. I know you're here. *(Jane begins to cry.)*

PAT: Oh God, here you go again.

JANE: I just don't know why I feel this way. I don't know what's wrong with me. I'm just crazy.

PAT: There you go again. I just can't deal with you when you're like this. . . . Calm down, make sense!

JANE: I know I have to do more things, keep more busy. I have to make more contacts, I have to call someone else. . . .

Five minutes later after Pat/Husband has tried continually to tell Jane not to have her feelings, Jane delivers her last line:

JANE: Go to hell!

The group applauds. The applause is not just because Jane finally got angry, but because Pat, as the husband, gave a cameo performance of the lines they all know so well.

Ladiness is alive and well, whether we are always conscious of it or not. And every time someone tells us to "make sense, be in control, calm down," we feel more crazy and somehow bad. The problem with the Be a Lady injunction can be summed up eloquently in the words of one woman's letter to her mother:

> You know what I remember you telling me—I remember you telling me proudly that other adults told you I was very "poised" for a child. And I remember you talking with pride about knowing you were better heard on the Board of Education because your voice was well modulated—that's how a lady speaks. So where's the *passion*, Mom? Where's the life energy? Looking good, being acceptable—it's not enough. I feel like you cheated me. Now I cheat myself. I am so much more than poised and articulate, and I deserve to be all of who I am.

The Be a Lady injunction comes into play most when we:

- Feel uncomfortable about getting angry. When we do we may cry or simply get quiet rather than express it.
- Protect other people from our real feelings.
- Don't allow ourselves to sit and have a good cry. If we do, we do it alone.
- Find it hard sometimes to let go and enjoy sex. We're careful about how we dress because we fear looking seductive. Really desiring or lusting after someone makes us feel bad.
- Have a hard time enjoying sensual pleasures such as massage, hot baths, time spent alone enjoying a forbidden movie, our favorite food.
- Feel constricted about our bodies. We sometimes can't enjoy dancing, playing athletic games, activities that require that we express ourselves physically.
- Shy away from competitiveness in work or sports.
- Back down when challenged. If somebody says jump, we ask how high. We tend not to join an argument and if we do we lose gracefully.

- Never allow ourselves to holler, scream, yell, or throw an occasional dish.
- Have difficulty challenging or questioning authority figures, particularly doctors, therapists, or those who have the status of expert on *our* emotional or physical health.
- Feel that the worst experience we could have would be one in which we went out of control and somebody saw it happen.

BE UNSELFISH AND OF SERVICE
A GOOD WOMAN LIVES TO GIVE

CLAUDIA GOES TO THE BEAUTY PARLOR

The year was 1989. I had recently moved to a small, rural town in New England, and I decided to try a new beauty salon for a haircut. The hair stylist, Mona, was an affable, chatty woman who was interested in people's families. I told her that I had two younger sisters and described my household growing up as so woman-dominated that even the dog was a female. I joked that my father had always felt a little uncomfortable and outnumbered by that. In the mirror I could see Mona shaking her head as if she couldn't understand it. "Why should he be uncomfortable? With all those women in the house, he gets better service, right?"

Mona had voiced openly what many of us still believe unconsciously —that to be unselfish and of service form the core values of our female lives.

Jo-Ann calls this the rule of "Never take the biggest piece of cake." It might equally have been listed in the Be a Lady category, because what it refers to is her mother's reminder to her, as she left home for a friend's birthday party, that she was not *ever* to act as if she felt entitled to something for herself. This would be unladylike. This would appear selfish. No one should ever catch her wanting something, even if it was only cake.

The lessons to Be Unselfish and to Be of Service are the most powerful that women learn. Most of us don't even question the implicit assumption that we are not entitled to want anything for ourselves. We learn that the other person's happiness is more important, that the other person's needs take priority, that our most important role in life is to give of ourselves to others. Culturally, the model for a woman's role and identity is that of mother. Our entire sense of ourselves is to be structured around the behavior of nurturing and selflessly giving to a dependent, needy other.

The lessons of history in this regard are compelling. When we read about "famous women" in our textbooks, we tend to see stories about Florence Nightingales and Clara Bartons—not women of power but women of sacrifice, women who help. If one grows up Catholic, one learns to revere women as Sisters of Charity, Sisters of Mercy, hand-maidens of the Lord.

To Be Unselfish and to Be of Service are the dominant definitions of "good" for a woman. And they are no less compelling in our complex liberated and modern world. The symptoms are simply more subtle.

If you're a good woman, you don't expect to be paid well for your work. If you finally do demand more money, it's with an apology. You worry about being "fair." You don't overtly seek power. If you do, you feel guilty or sorry that you've undermined someone else. You rarely try to work situations to your own advantage. You would be horrified if someone thought of you as ruthless. You get angry for other people but never for yourself, and you work harder in their best interests than in your own. If you're a good woman, when you allocate your time, most of it goes to everyone else. You can never think of yourself as wanting wealth, freedom from caretaking, any life-style that would seem unlady-like—that is, focused on yourself. If you happen to be with a partner who achieves those things and you are along for the ride, that's accept-able. But it's hard for you to just take your life into your own hands, because your life often feels like the property of someone else, someone to whom you are being kind, unselfish, and of service.

One woman had a history of severe asthma. She describes how she felt about its limiting her in the early days of her marriage: "I always felt I didn't have the right to be sick, so I'd make myself sicker by pushing myself to do more than I really could. I had to because I just felt I wasn't living up to what I was supposed to do as a wife and mother. I felt terrible that I couldn't go out to work too. They'd fre-quently rush me off to the hospital where I'd nearly stop breathing. I'd be close to death and my sister would lean over the bed saying, 'Offer it up, offer it up.' She was very religious—she meant for me to offer up my pain as a sacrifice to God."

Psychoanalyst Karen Horney called behaviors like these "self-effac-ing." [3] They constitute one of the dominant neurotic styles that she identified. To be self-effacing is somewhat like the description "masochistic" that is frequently applied to women. The terms imply that women have a pathological need to hurt or act against themselves. But most of us are neither masochistic nor self-effacing as a chosen style—we're simply being unselfish as we've been taught to be. Horney rightly taught us that we experience conflict whenever we don't *want* to do what we think we *must* do to be valued. The injunction to Be Unselfish is a powerful one, yet it challenges a woman's psychological survival. It would be unusual for her *not* to experience deep conflict about it. Many women fight the rule, but others simply give in.

CLAUDIA'S POETRY CLASS

If the symptoms of goodness are more subtle these days, so are the effects. Not long ago I attended a poetry-writing workshop at a popular New York City university. In the class there were women and men, but more men. The instructor asked each person to talk about why he or she had come. The differences in the comments were dramatic. Uniformly the women, myself included, said: "I don't really know if I have any talent at this. I thought a class would help me to take my writing more seriously. I need to learn more." But the gist of the men's comments was: "I came because I need a wider audience for my work."

Does this story represent a fundamental difference in the male and female psyches? Or is it the case that women have been so conditioned to be attuned to others that they experience profound discomfort at any focus on their own experience? Here the men take for granted that their creative work is valuable and worthy of attention. They feel entitled to be heard. The women, in contrast, wonder whether it's alright to do creative work at all, to do it *seriously*. They feel shy and inadequate about it. They seem to fear imposing themselves on the world. They seem to fear expressing a self.

The suppression of our creative power is a serious effect of the rules of unselfishness and service. As a composer friend says, "To be an artist is not compatible with being a woman by definition. The whole point of creative work is to let yourself go enough to pick up whatever falls out of your right brain before it disappears. If you're always paying attention to everybody else, that's hard to do. You can't comfortably have a 'career.' A woman's not supposed to blow her own horn, and, if you're an artist, in this country anyway, you have to do it. You have to write your own bio and market yourself. Women aren't supposed to do those things."

In fact, it's hard to do many things when we pay so much attention to others. Sometimes we deprive ourselves in small, seemingly insignificant ways. One evening Sue came to group feeling particularly depressed. Sue was an incest survivor who overcame her addiction to alcohol only to marry a man who had been physically abusive to her. She finally left this relationship and got involved in another, and the new relationship forced her to think about what it would mean to have her emotional needs met.

"I always feel terribly deprived. I suppose it's because of my childhood. I'm always *wishing* other people would give me attention or support or whatever though I'd never ask for it. But when I did ask Joe to go with me to a lecture on incest and he said no, I felt rage. It had been very hard for me to ask. Now I'm just depressed. Sometimes I just feel so empty."

It was suggested that since she felt so deprived and needy, it would be positive for Sue to give something to herself. She said she loved flowers, so her assignment was to stop and buy herself as many as she could afford on the way home. The assignment meant that she was to lavish some attention on herself.

But she couldn't, she reported at the next group session.

"It just didn't seem justifiable," she said. "It's not even that I don't have the money. It just seemed frivolous and as if, how can I just do something like this for *myself?* I bought a small plant instead. A plant was OK because at least it wouldn't die. I think I live with some 'rule' in my mind that it's somehow selfish for me to do anything for myself."

But the group was not appeased. They hammered at the issue for most of that session. By the following week, Sue had bought herself flowers. In such small ways are the lessons of selfishness and service relearned.

The Be Unselfish and of Service injunction comes into play when we:

- Feel envious and uncomfortable about the fact that another woman thinks of herself as entitled, or acts entitled to, money, freedom, attention, recognition, power.
- Feel angry that other people don't seem to be aware of what we need or want because we feel we can't ask for it directly.
- Put aside our own agenda when someone else wants or needs anything.

- Have a hard time saying no.
- Handle our anxiety in social situations by helping the host or hostess to serve the food or clean up.
- Feel in conflict about a career choice because we think we need to do something that's of service, but would rather work at something else that is either more enjoyable or more lucrative.
- Feel guilty about buying things for ourselves, and then work extra hard to make up for it. Or we can't buy something for ourselves without bringing home something for someone else as well.
- Feel good about ourselves *only* when we're doing things for other people who need us.
- Resent it that other people take time for or spend money on themselves because we can't permit ourselves to do either.
- Ignore any impulse to do creative work because we feel we're not really good enough at it to justify taking the time.

The first three injunctions of the Code—Be Attractive, Be a Lady, and Be Unselfish and of Service—define the qualities of the ideal and "good" female. Think for a moment about how you measure up to these standards of being a woman. Do you question your attractiveness? Do you feel guilty that you're not more giving to people? Do you tell yourself on a daily basis that you shouldn't be so angry, upset, sexual, sad, happy, intense, selfish?

There is a positive value to be found in every injunction. It's healthy to enjoy our appearance. It's positive at times to exercise self-control. It makes us feel good, and can even boost our immune systems, to be helpful and generous to others. The important question to ask ourselves is, Why are these behaviors important—because we choose them or because we fear how we'll feel and what people will think if we don't? If you feel bad any time you fail to achieve these qualities perfectly, it may be a signal that you're trapped by the Code of Goodness. You may be too good for your own good.

3

LIVING THE CODE

------ ✳ ------

Women's Ways of Doing Good

The first three injunctions of the Code of Goodness dictate "good" qualities of female character. They tell us how we're supposed to act, how we're supposed to *be*. The last two rules of the code describe what we're required to *do*. Make Relationships Work is an injunction about the work of love. Be Competent is an injunction about the work of managing everything else. The two rules are related. Since taking care of relationships is primary for a woman, when she takes on a job or a career her relationship work comes along with her. In other words, competence for a woman means being a juggler of career and family, and it means doing it while maintaining her appearance, remaining calm, and being perfectly in control. These two rules require that women be superwomen without complaint.

JENN COMPLAINS

Jenn was a tall, wiry woman with such enthusiastic energy that she seemed to burst into a room like a diver into water. She was always eager for debate about whatever current issues dominated the news. But when the conversation became more personal, Jenn grew quiet. Sometimes it seemed there were two Jenns: the charming, engaging woman and a more private, guarded one.

When Jenn started therapy at age thirty-two, she was suffering from bouts of terrible anxiety. The fear had started when she realized she wanted to divorce Alan. Her complaints about the problems with Alan echoed the concerns many women feel about their marriages. Alan wasn't emotional or responsive enough. She felt alone. All he did was work.

To add to the problem, Jenn thought of herself as underutilized professionally. She had been an honor student in college, but she still worked as an administrative assistant. Because she contributed so much less financially to the marriage, it was a continual struggle for her to feel that she was a worthwhile and valid person in her own right.

Jenn's anxiety seemed related to her realization that she didn't want to make her relationship work. She felt guilty that she wanted to leave Alan. Because her sense of herself was so negative and because she thought of herself as so "bad," Jenn's first therapy assignment was to go home and make a list of the qualities that she believed would make her a "good" woman. When she came back the following week, she described a strong reaction to the exercise.

"When I thought about the idea of being a 'good woman,' I got really upset and thought about the years of not wanting to be a woman, of just wanting to be a person. I wanted me to be a person and I wanted a man to be a person. I just wanted equal people. I didn't want to have a distinction. You know, I like to dress in an oversized man's sweater and jeans. To me it's sexy because it's suggestive—you really don't know what's underneath. But also it does cover me up, and I think that this covering up is indicative of me not being able to say what's underneath and define what a woman *is* and how I feel about myself as a woman."

Though Jenn could acknowledge her difficulty with the work of defining *herself*, she realized she had routinely taken on the work of making her marriage right. That same week she'd gone to a lecture on women and their relationships, and it had made her angry.

"I went to a presentation by a woman writer yesterday. The theme was love, intimacy, and relationship. I was sitting there, and she was talking about women coming into their own as individuals and the *work* that they have to do with themselves and the *work* that they need to do in community with other women. Then she talked about the *work* that needs to be done with the men in our lives. And I found myself getting so angry. It's *us* who always have to do the *work*. I'm so mad at us always having to do the *work,* when I have a husband who still doesn't get that he has any work to do.

"I sat there thinking, why aren't there men in this audience listening to this? And there weren't. There were maybe five men in the entire room. So I was angry—not at her, just at the issue. Ever since I left that lecture I haven't been able to let go of it. I don't want to have to make excuses for Alan, to say he's a man and he was socialized not to have feelings.

"It's like this article (she makes a face and pulls an article out of her bag from which she begins to read): 'Can You Small Talk? Women who have better marriages become skilled at getting their men to talk.'

"It's really not an appropriate title," Jenn explains. "It's a very nice article about how women can do the work of involving men in their lives, teaching them to open up and be articulate. And it finally sunk in (here she dramatically drops the article to the floor as if handling something dirty) why they don't write these articles for men. It's *our* job to keep lovely healthy bodies, perform like twenty-year-olds in bed (she is numbering the sanctions on her fingers), dress beautifully, keep a healthy emotional attitude, keep our spiritual sense going, be calm and serene, and now go to *work* and earn money besides."

It seemed that Jenn was coming out of trance. She realized she was getting tired of the "work" of love. It soon became clear that a good part of Jenn's focus in therapy would be to redefine what it meant to *her* to be a woman. She would need to look at the ways that the Code of Goodness had shaped her beliefs, and she would need to do the work of taking off the baggy sweater that "covered her up" in order to define more clearly for *herself* who was underneath.

MAKE RELATIONSHIPS WORK
A GOOD WOMAN LOVES FIRST

The injunction to Make Relationships Work defines the place of love in our lives; it defines love *as* work—the work of taking care of others. For a woman, the word "relationship" really means "I give to you." As one friend of ours realized recently, "I learned in my family that it was 'selfish' for a woman even to think about being single. I began to actually fear wanting to be by myself. The idea that a woman must always be giving to someone was so strong—SELF was the worst four-letter word I knew."

Historically women have been viewed as sustainers of the family unit. Not only were they to raise and nurture children, but they were to care for home and hearth, creating for their male providers a safe, pristine haven from the cruel, immoral world. Women were to be strong and responsible for the emotional and physical needs of their families, but they were also to stay dependent and without the economic means to be solely responsible for themselves. In other words, women have traditionally had a great deal of responsibility but no real power.

Out of necessity, women became relational experts. We've developed the capacities to be sensitive, intuitive, generous, nurturing, and focused on the emotional and physical comfort of others. "Never hurt anybody" seems ingrained in our psyches. These skills are put to the service of everyone but ourselves, as it rarely occurs to us to nurture our own well-being.[1]

Ironically, this capacity for emotional responsiveness is vulnerable to attack when others are angry. For example, we are expected to be sensitive, yet are often accused of being "too sensitive." And our sensitivity to others sometimes works to our own disadvantage. We're often more likely to protect another's feelings and to act in his or her interests rather than to act on our own behalf if the two happen to conflict.

Relationships are maintained partly through ritual, and for the most part it's still a woman's work to make the customary rituals of family and relational life happen. We still visit the sick, bury the dead, and often prepare the seder for Passover without help. We shop for gifts, remember birthdays, plan parties, send cards and thank-you notes. That is, we tend to take care of the small, endless details that ease life's difficulties and ensure the continuity of our relationships. We observe rules of propriety and decorum in ways that are never expected of men. Women may do it less these days, but it's hard to imagine a man reading Emily Post or Amy Vanderbilt. Sustaining the etiquette of living is a part of women's work.

One of the areas that seems most resistant to the changes of the women's movement is the expectation that a woman maintain her male partner's relationships with his family. Somehow along with an intimate relationship a woman tends to inherit the job of sending birthday cards and gifts to *his* mother, father, siblings, aunts and uncles, nieces and nephews. *He* may never have done it himself, but we're somehow unable to avoid doing it for him. It violates every principle we've ever learned about how to make relationships work.

Caring for our partner's family sometimes extends to the job of dealing with the health problems of *his* aging parents. If we don't physically do the work, we're often the ones dealing with doctors or searching for a nursing home.

We sustain many different types of relationships and assume ours is the primary responsibility to do so. When it comes to children, the responsibility is usually intensified. The school nurse still calls us even if we have a career that's as demanding as our partner's. If our child is unhappy or has a problem, we feel it's our fault. Women are still the primary consumers of therapy for their children's problems. And therapists often still reinforce the idea that women are to blame for those problems by asking us to do all the work of change.

Our responsibility for relationships often doubles at certain points in our lives. Locked in what's referred to as the "sandwich generation," many of us may be caring for aging parents at the same time that we're caring for growing children. When women's place of employment was only in the home, this job was less fraught with complications, if not less emotional stress. Women were at home to do the physical caring and nursing that's often required.

Finally, if we're divorced and remarried to a man with children, we assume responsibility for his children as well as our own. The new family we inherit becomes ours to make whole. We often become a go-between, trying to mediate relationships between two other people in our lives who can't get along, like our husband and his son or our mother-in-law and *her* son.

WHERE DID I GO WRONG!

The most insidious effect of the Make Relationships Work injunction is to make women believe that there's something wrong with them if a relationship doesn't work. Not only do we need to succeed at relating, we often need to do it according to the norms that define what a "normal" relationship is.

If we choose any "alternate" life-style, if we're a single mother, if we have an intimate relationship with another woman, if we have a commuter marriage, or only live with a man rather than marrying him, we often feel a nagging sense that somehow we're doing something wrong. We have a hard time letting go of ingrained assumptions about what a "good" relationship should be. We have a hard time deviating from the norm. Any attempt to create a new definition of a "good" relationship for ourselves seems to put us at odds with the standards of goodness. As much as we try to fight it, we often still feel a little "bad."

A lesbian client says, "I'm not in conflict with my life-style choice, but it still hurts me that my kids have to hear me called names on the playground. I still wonder when I've met someone new who seems to like me if they'll reject me when they 'find out.' The conflict comes not within me but in my relationships with other people who I fear will judge me."

Our tendency to feel responsible for a relationship is heightened when that relationship fails. We know that if there's a problem with an intimate partnership, we're the ones most likely to get help for it, because we're the ones most likely to feel it's our fault. We often stay in relationships long past the time that they're viable, not just for economic reasons or out of concern for our children, but because we think that if we can just "do the right thing" the relationship will work. We'll try any number of "right things." To admit defeat is an indictment of ourselves as bad.

The message that we're inherently responsible guarantees that many of us who might prefer to pursue our own careers or other interests feel guilty when we do unless all our relationships are working perfectly. The sad reality for most of us is that, no matter how much we achieve, no matter how much recognition we're given in the world of "other work," we secretly feel inadequate if we're a single parent or even, at times, if we're simply single. We feel like a failure if we've been divorced, if our kids or stepkids are having problems, if we've had a falling out with a friend, if our mother seems disappointed in us, if our colleagues don't like us though they may respect us, if our sex life isn't great. For a woman, "goodness" has everything to do with how well we do the work of relating.

In fact, we expect perfection of ourselves when it comes to our relationships, and we rarely do stop to question our own assumptions. It never occurs to us to expect other people to share half the emotional burden. We seem to believe on some deep level that we won't be loved ourselves unless we succeed at the work of loving. We just keep asking, "Where did I go wrong?"

The Make Relationships Work injunction comes into play most when we:

- Know there's a problem in a relationship and assume it's our fault.
- Feel guilt that our child has a problem or doesn't achieve in the way we'd expect him to.
- Feel we're always the one to raise problems for discussion.
- Feel we can't leave a relationship even though it's not satisfying.

- Feel guilty and inadequate about conflicts or negative interactions.
- Don't expect the other person to work as hard as we do at resolving a problem.
- Do more than our fair share of the work.
- Give more than we get.

BE COMPETENT WITHOUT COMPLAINT
A GOOD WOMAN DOES IT ALL AND NEVER LOOKS OVERWHELMED

Jenn's complaint about relationships wasn't limited to her frustration with the work of love. She also felt, like most women, that her double role as wife and worker ended in an unfair division of labor.

"Let's face it," Jenn said, "when most men get home from work they don't do anything. It's not fair. I've always worked, and I've always done more than my share around the house."

If women in our mother's generation had the somewhat paradoxical pressure to be responsible for caretaking everyone while still being dependent, at least economically, today's woman knows that being competent means taking financial responsibility for herself *along with* taking care of everyone else. Sociologists such as Arlie Hochschild in her book, *The Second Shift,* tell us that women still assume the dominant share of household responsibility in spite of their vastly increased participation in the work force. And beyond what they actually *do,* they're the ones most likely to be *thinking* about what needs to be done. They're the captains in the war on household chores—men simply report for their orders.

The woman today who achieves financial and professional success has no wife to sustain the emotional and physical environment. She does this for herself, and in most cases she does it for the rest of her family as well. She has to create her own safe haven from the demands and pressures of the working world—except that, for her, there is no real haven from the working world because home is a work world too.

Family therapist Monica McGoldrick writes, "Somehow women never seem able to find wives, or at least I never have. A nanny or a secretary or a housekeeper may sometimes be a partial replacement. But they can always quit and leave you holding the bag. Their commitment is for a specific job, not for the whole you." [2]

COMPETENCE AS AN IDEAL

The dilemmas of the Be Competent injunction are complex. The injunction creates an ideal of a "perfect" woman, an ideal that most of us can never hope to achieve, one that perhaps we shouldn't hope to achieve. Understanding the Be Competent injunction makes us all too aware of the impossible bind of being a woman. As one woman told us, "I think of my mother-in-law as a Renaissance Woman. She has an incredible job, she dresses to the nines, has an incredible body, is a great cook, a fabulous hostess, and never looks overwhelmed. She's always composed, and she was my ideal about what a successful woman is. In all arenas she looks like she has everything handled and takes care of everyone else at the same time, and anything short of that is failure. So it's not OK for me to say, I have a really responsible job and when I get home I'm exhausted and so I don't cook."

As a way of exploring this new ideal for women's behavior, we recently asked a group of professional women attending a workshop, "What makes you feel that you're good?" The responses were remarkably similar: "I'm good when I act competently, when I'm not overwhelmed, when I'm not acting overly emotional. I am what I do, and I'm good if what I *do* is good." When we asked them what piece of praise from somebody else would make them *feel* good, the response was, "You're competent, you work hard."

Competence has become the new standard of excellence for women. It speaks to the unlimited capacity to do it all well and without help and without ever feeling or showing that you're vulnerable. Notice that the responses of the women in the workshop commented on two aspects of this injunction: I must *do* something well, *and* I must handle everything that there is to be handled without seeming overwhelmed or overly emotional. The modern stress of a woman's role is not so much in coping with the practical problems of taking on more work; it's to look like she's bearing up well under the strain.

Competence is not just a matter of how well a woman juggles. It's more than a matter of handling the child-care problem, getting Johnny to his baseball game when you have a meeting in Chicago, "sequencing" your pregnancies in the interests of your career,[3] or responding to your friend's crisis when you also have to be available to take care of your mother who's in the hospital. It's a question of "taking care" of all those details and never acting vulnerable, needy, or overwhelmed.

One friend tells us, "It's a great criticism to be caught looking flustered. I force myself to work against this message; sometimes I work hard to *make* myself complain. Because I can go for just so long looking like I'm holding it all together and then, like this morning, I put my head in my hands and cry at the kitchen table. Then, sometimes if we're out with people, I think, good, we're going to this social situation so I have to keep quiet. If somebody got too close to me I might complain. I hold it together and then I get hives, I'm short with the kids, I hate my husband. . . . I love what I'm doing, it's just that I'm doing too much."

Among women who choose not to "do it all," women who stay home with children, there have been different casualties. Because the injunction to Be Competent has become a new standard of goodness, women feel bad when they fail to embrace it even as they live up to all the other injunctions:

"Nobody has any respect for mothers who stay home. They think we sit home and watch soap operas all day. When I go to pick up the baby from nursery school, you can tell the mothers who work from the ones who don't—the ones that don't wear sneakers and jeans. For the most part the working mothers and the nonworking ones don't talk to each other much. At home, during the day, you don't have too many people to relate to because everybody else is at work. And, I'll tell you, when you go out to a party you never really come out and tell them you stay home unless they come out and ask you. I'll sit there and think to myself, I've got to get a job so people will respect me. You don't feel like you're contributing anything if you don't work."

In professional circles, women "network" to find sources of support in their career climbing. But we rarely seek or get support for or help with the emotional strains of added responsibility or even the strains of being a nonworking mother at home. The Be Competent injunction is one that further reinforces our tendency to act as if our own emotional lives come second, or third. In the words of one psychiatrist, "The lives of women attempting to live up to the current cultural ego-ideal have become juggling acts, competitive juggling acts at that, with many women seemingly caught up in the competition to keep ever more events, objects, people, and careers in the air. . . . Is it to be overlooked that, to successfully carry off this automatic identity switching, a woman no longer knows what it is to be and feel like a human being?"[4]

This double-edged job, competence, affects even women who are unmarried and don't have children. A man goes to work and does his job.

A woman goes to work, and part of her job will always involve dealing with the emotional impact of the relationships between people in the work setting as well as with the task at hand. Her job will always involve dealing with the impact her work choices have on the important relationships in her life.

Nancy, a plumber, says of working with her male boss, "I've always been the one to say 'How do you feel about how we're working together?' He'll talk about it like he's indulging me in this kind of quirky thing I have to do because I'm female. But it's not that I'm just taking the responsibility for the emotional process between us. It makes the work go better."

Nancy goes on, "I feel like I have to worry not just about being good at the trade, but that I have to balance all possible things, being a homeowner, a daughter, a lover, all of it. The other piece is to have to balance work with how much time I have for my friends. And then those of us who are women moving into jobs that haven't been open for women before, we have to be good not just for ourselves but for all the women who come after us."

Women have come a long way in terms of their freedom to involve themselves in the affairs of the world. The women's movement gave us choices that were often unheard of even in our mother's generation. But because we're still burdened by the dictates of goodness, choice has often been difficult for us. Sometimes rather than traveling a road leading to greater empowerment and self-respect, we've merely heaped more responsibility and more exhaustion on ourselves. We've become too busy to notice how we feel. Some of us have adopted other people's standards for goodness and success—we're driven by the need to prove our competence, prove our worth, and we forget to pay attention to what we enjoy.

We forget that we have choices still. Often our work, our competence, isn't a form of self-expression so much as it is a way of conforming to yet another set of external dictates about what makes us good. In the process, many of us have acquired power, but we haven't necessarily achieved satisfaction.

The Be Competent injunction comes into play most when we:

- Are perfectionists and feel like a failure if we don't handle everything perfectly at all times.
- Never assume it's an option not to pursue professional "success" as defined by others.

- Feel worthless and inadequate if we haven't achieved something we consider important.
- Always assume we have to handle everything without help.
- Think of it as "help" when our partner does pitch in around the house, rather than thinking of it as being his/her appropriate job to take a share of the work.
- Assume that the primary responsibility for taking care of the children is ours even though we work as many hours as our partner.
- Find ourselves being short and irritable with people who disrupt or interrupt our work agenda.
- Set rigidly high standards for ourselves and tend to be equally rigid in our expectations of others.
- Find we have little time for friends, recreation, or taking care of our physical needs because we're too busy working.
- Feel that taking time off is not an option.
- Feel that anything we may do—entertaining, gardening, decorating our home, painting a picture—doesn't "measure up" to some standard.
- Feel like a failure because we have to say no.

THE CONFLICTING PRESSURES TO BE GOOD

The major difficulty with the five injunctions to be good is that they frequently conflict with one another. If a "lady" is never competitive, how exactly does she achieve success, the pursuit of success being, in fact, a competitive venture? If a woman is never to be emotional, how does she make relationships work? Emotions are part of who she is and part of what people need to know about her in relationships. If a good woman is unselfish, how does she justify pursuing individual achievement? If a lady is compliant and never challenges or acts with authority, how does she demonstrate competence? If a good woman is to take care of everyone emotionally, how can she free her energies to focus on her own projects?

In essence, the harder we try, consciously or otherwise, to live up to the dictates of the code, the worse we're likely to feel about ourselves. The code represents an impossible set of expectations that have been generated over the centuries with the effect of depriving women of their own definitions of themselves and their own inner sense of worth. We all suffer the effects of these injunctions, some more visibly than others. They follow us throughout our lives. Over time, unless we challenge them, they rob us of ourselves. We all become Jenns, hidden beneath our clothes, uncertain of the shape of our own female identity.

4

IF I'M SO GOOD,
WHY DO I FEEL SO BAD

———— ✳ ————

Basic Female Shame

"I spent a lot of years not wanting to be female. I wanted to be called a boy's name—Jeff instead of Jenn. I felt bad about this, I thought I had a terrible problem. But the truth was there never was anything to appreciate about being female in my family. I cleaned while my brothers watched TV. It's not what you do but who you are that matters, and I wasn't a boy."

These feelings of Jenn's tell us a good deal about her baggy clothes. Jenn was trying symbolically to hide herself from the world. She dressed to be indistinct, almost as if to cover up the femaleness that she thought of as so unworthy. Her clothes protected her from being seen, and they covered up any vivid expression of herself.

"I need to hide out. You don't understand how much I wish I could disappear. When I go out I often hope that I don't run into anyone who knows me. When other people look at me too closely I feel like they see 'failure' written all over me."

Jenn hid behind her baggy clothes because of her pervasive feeling that something was wrong with her. Those feelings started in childhood when she learned in countless small ways that males were valued more than females. The feelings intensified as she struggled to embrace the Code of Goodness and felt like a failure at it. Even though her marriage was meeting few of her needs, she felt guilty that the work she did to make it better didn't help. Jenn felt unattractive, she felt unaccomplished. She had little sense of her own worth.

Why does Jenn feel so bad about herself? Why do women in general have pervasive problems with self-esteem and depression?[1] Why do we try so hard to be good and then feel even worse when we realize that we can't or don't want to live up to the injunctions of the code?

WHY WE NEED TO BE SO GOOD

In general, all people are motivated to be "good" by a need for approval. That need is intensified when someone implies that we're not acceptable as we are.

Jenn got the message that females were less valuable in her family. But messages about the innate inferiority of women have been part of the larger social fabric for centuries. Aristotle, writing in the fourth century B.C., believed in the basic inferiority of women: "The female is a female by virtue of a certain lack of qualities. We should regard the female nature as afflicted with a natural defectiveness."[2]

Women are afflicted. Women are defective. Women fall short. Women are *less than* men. The messages are like subtle hypnotic suggestions, and we are not always conscious of them. We know that the feminist movement represented the beginnings of a struggle to overturn those messages, to claim our rightful equality with men. But sometimes this struggle to enter a man's world heightens our pain. It makes us more aware of how shamed we've been. And it's hard to fight a basic cultural assumption that you are of less value when that message continues to be reinforced on a daily basis.

The messages may be less overt today than they were in the days when women were burned at the stake as witches, for instance. But when we're slighted at a meeting or passed over for a job that's given to a man, when we're left with the dishes to clean up or the children to watch because our partner is doing more important things, when we are sexually harassed, or sometimes abused, when we're left in poverty because of a divorce that reminds us how little access we have to financial resources, when we're told in countless ways that who we are doesn't count because we aren't male, we get the message that we're less valuable than a man—that something is wrong with us. And on a daily basis, some of us forget to notice those messages and we begin to sink back into trance, we forget to remind ourselves of our own worth. We sink into a state that we aren't even aware of. It's a state that we call basic female shame.

EXPLORING WOMEN'S SHAME

In their book *Facing Shame,* Merle Fossum and Marilyn Mason define shame as "an inner sense of being completely diminished or insufficient as a person." If a woman is affected by a sense of shame, she may feel "bad, inadequate, defective, unworthy, or not fully valid as a human being."[3]

We all experience shame at different levels and to different degrees of intensity. But it's the "not fully valid as a human being" feeling that is part of the collective legacy of womanhood. Often our female shame is hidden to ourselves because we unconsciously *assume* that a woman has less value than a man and we rarely stop to think about it.

Guilt and shame are frequently confused, but they're really two very different feelings. Guilt refers to an infraction, a breaking of the rules; guilt results from something one does. Shame, on the other hand, refers to a falling short, a limitation. Ernest Kurtz makes the point that guilt results in a sense of "wickedness," of being "not good." But shame results in a feeling of worthlessness, of being "no good."[4] So that Jenn, for instance, might feel guilt if she acted selfish because that would violate the Goodness Code. But she feels shame that no matter how good she is, she's never as important as her brothers. She feels shame that no matter what she does her marriage doesn't improve. She feels shame about being who she is, and much of her trying hard to be good in life will be an attempt to hide her feelings of inadequacy so that she won't be exposed as lacking.

Most of the cultural messages about the basic inferiority of women (think, for instance, about the fact that for many decades women weren't considered competent to vote) are messages that shame women for being women. Human beings suffer from a kind of existential shame for the human condition which is the recognition of their own limitation, the recognition of the fact that they're not divine. Women suffer from a second shame because they're not seen even as fully human. If men can't be as good as gods, women can't be as good as men.

It's been a tradition in literature and in some religious dogma, just as it is in the early biblical story of the Fall, to see women as the root of all evil—as man's obstacle to becoming godlike. This attitude, that men can aspire to be godlike and powerful and that women or their female qualities only get in the way, has serious consequences for our entire culture. It leads to a rejection of those qualities that are viewed as innately "female"—qualities that have to do with being emotional, nurturing, full of feeling.

It's no wonder that a major injunction of the code is Be a Lady—stay in control and don't express feelings. In our society's emphasis on qualities like autonomy, competitiveness, strength, aggressiveness, and acquisitiveness, we've developed the tendency to see all feeling as weak and shameful. We devalue those more feminine, feeling parts of our characters. If we can control or deny feeling, we experience ourselves as more competent and in charge. We have the illusion that we can achieve perfection.

SHAME AND THE DYSFUNCTIONAL FAMILY

There is a growing recognition among mental health experts that dysfunctional families teach by shaming. A dysfunctional family, loosely defined, is one that's dominated by conflict and anxiety. Family members don't get their basic needs met, and they find themselves doing whatever they have to do to survive. There's little time or energy available in such a family to respond to or to value people's feelings. People don't feel safe or secure. Such an unsafe environment sets the stage for or maintains serious problems like addiction and abuse.

Someone who grows up in a dysfunctional family develops a "shame-bound" identity.[5] In other words, people whose families ignore their developmental needs and who are repeatedly shamed for those needs end up feeling bad about who they are.

Though men and women may be equally shamed in a dysfunctional family, the underlying lessons that they learn are radically different. Women are shamed for not knowing their place. If they acquire more aggressive, "masculine" characteristics, they're shamed for being unfeminine. They are shamed for not being "good" and nurturing caretakers. They are shamed for not living up to moral standards not required of men.

Men, on the other hand, are shamed for acting like women. They're called "sissies" or "girls." The message is clear. It's uncomfortable to be shamed at all, but the most awful way to shame a man is to accuse him of being like a woman, that is, emotional, full of feeling, soft, vulnerable.

THE BELIEFS THAT RESULT FROM FEMALE SHAME

Kate, a woman who came for therapy because of her chronic depression, told a powerful story about feeling shamed. In the beginning of her marriage, at a point when she was in her early twenties, she went with her husband to a large professional meeting on the West Coast. She had never been to a conference like this, and the new situation made her uneasy about how she would "measure up" with her husband's colleagues.

"The second evening we were there we had to go to this cocktail party. I was taking forever to dress so I told Joe to go downstairs without me.

"When I was sure I looked OK I went downstairs. I opened the door to a crowd of about three hundred men and walked alone into the ballroom. I was one of the few women there. It was as if all the men turned to stare at once. Some of them had had too much to drink. I walked through the ballroom looking for Joe. Men started calling and yelling to me. One guy came up to me and started teasing me for looking so 'serious.' He kept asking me what the matter was, why I couldn't smile. The more I tried to avoid the attention, the more uptight I got. Other men started teasing me too. They told me to smile, be fun, stop acting so serious. At that moment, part of me kept thinking I *should* be smiling, I should be acting more sociable. Another part of me just knew that I couldn't. I finally raced back upstairs to our room, locked myself in the bathroom and burst into tears. I never did find Joe until later in the evening."

This experience might not have felt shaming to another woman. But for Kate it triggered many painful feelings of not measuring up. "My father had always told me I was too serious. He didn't like the fact that I was so studious. I had always felt very awkward in social situations. I never felt like I wore the right clothes, I never felt attractive enough. I *was* a serious person. I couldn't laugh and be flirtatious with men like other girls my age. It just didn't work for me to be that way, and yet I knew that made me lacking somehow. I knew that's how a woman was supposed to be. When those men started calling at me it was like being hit with every inadequate feeling I ever had about being a woman. Joe never really did understand why I got so upset."

Two things had happened for Kate. The first was that she had been shamed in her family for not being "feminine" in a way that was pleasing to her father. But the second was that, over time, she had internalized the injunctions of the Goodness Code. She believed on some level that if she were a good woman, she would behave according to the expectation that she be flirtatious and playful. It never occurred to her that the men were being intrusive and rude, that in effect they were harassing her. It never occurred to her to be angry or to question her father's disapproval of her. Aware that she just couldn't live up to those particular expectations, she felt a burning shame. In the ballroom, people "saw" her being inadequate. At that point, she was too flooded by self-consciousness and too upset to question the code.

In therapy Kate needed help to challenge her own beliefs. She needed to change the "I'm inadequate because I'm serious" belief to "I'm great because I have such a lively, intense mind." Having made that conscious shift in her beliefs about herself, Kate wouldn't be vulnerable to shame in the same way. We can imagine that a more aware Kate would walk through that same ballroom and be politely assertive or even yell back at the men who caused her so much pain the first time. Clear that other people don't truly have the power to define her value as a person, she'd also feel more secure in her marriage and more valuing of her own unique ways of being female.

THE VOICES IN OUR MINDS

Most of us have a well-developed set of negative beliefs about ourselves. Those beliefs are good road maps to the areas where we feel that we fail to measure up. We often internalize other people's voices and shame ourselves when we're not "good." Kate's greatest area of shame was focused in the Be Attractive part of the Goodness Code. Be a Lady and Make Relationships Work were close seconds for her. She described a part of her mind that she called a "broken record" of voices that said things to her like "What's the use? They stare at me because I'm so serious and unfeminine. I probably make Joe ashamed too. He's probably embarrassed about how I look. If I were as good as other women, like his sister, I would want to please him. I wonder if he's glad he married me."

The "broken record" was really a recording of all the underlying beliefs about goodness that Kate had internalized, had absorbed from the air around her. They kept her in a perpetual state of shame.

Each of us has a different set of messages that we give ourselves.

We've each inherited our own favorite collection of songs from the chorus of shaming voices that sing to us from our families and from the world at large. Here are some other examples of dominant beliefs that influence the behavior of many of us:

- No matter what I do, it's never enough.
- He or she is unhappy, and I caused it.
- I'm selfish.
- I enjoy myself too much.
- If someone else hurts me, it's my fault.
- I can't say what I think because it might hurt someone.
- I feel bad if I'm angry.
- I'd better not say no.
- It's bad to like sex so much.
- I have to take care of him (or her).
- I'm not desirable because I'm not attractive enough.
- I'm not "good enough" as I am.

TO BE SEEN AND NOT HEARD

The heart of shame is the pain of exposure. Kate was deeply traumatized by the experience in the ballroom because she was "seen" as inadequate, seen as a "failure" by the many men who watched with such amusement as she struggled to please them. Kate felt she had been caught wanting approval. She had dressed carefully, trying to be as attractive as possible. When the teasing started, instead of walking firmly away, she hesitated. In her hesitation, everyone saw her vulnerability. She was caught *trying* to live up to the Goodness Code, and she also felt exposed as a failure at it.

When we overfocus on our clothes and on our bodies, it's often a cover for a feeling of being unacceptable as a person. Kate often talked about not wanting to look at herself in a mirror after she'd had any kind of intense personal contact with someone else. She didn't want to know what they'd seen. On one level she feared that they'd seen an undesirable face or an undesirable body. But her real fear was that they'd seen an undesirable self.

Shame is most painful when we feel exposed to ourselves. We often feel ashamed when we're brought face to face with our own need for approval. Often our internal shame is triggered by the shaming behavior of someone else.

Janice is a very beautiful woman who never questioned her attractiveness. But what she really wanted was to be valued for her competence. Specifically she wanted to publish her research on Chinese literature. One evening at a lecture she happened to meet a man who was a well-known scholar in her field. They talked for a while, and he asked her to lend him the manuscript she was working on. Flattered, she gave him the copy she had with her in the car.

He called the next morning to tell her how much he liked her work. He even offered to give her an introduction to his publisher and suggested they meet that afternoon for a drink to talk about the manuscript. Janice was thrilled and called to tell her best friend about it. As it turned out, the scholar didn't have much to say about her manuscript, but he did ask her to have dinner with him that evening. He told her how attractive she was, and he also mentioned that he'd been curious about her work because he was writing a book of his own.

Janice felt like a fool. She was exposed, if only to herself, as wanting approval for her competence and of thinking she had gotten it. The man was clearly more interested in a sexual encounter than in her thoughts about Chinese literature. She had no way of knowing whether any of his reactions to her manuscript were valid or whether it had all been a ploy.

What was exposed for Kate and Janice was their desire to be valued. They felt shame both about their failure to measure up to the Goodness Code, and they felt shame about being "caught" trying. But the shame of exposure is often most intense if somebody else notices, or even when we ourselves notice, that we don't *want* to live up to the code. The most shameful secret any of us may carry is the awareness that we don't always *want* to be good. It's a secret that's hard to admit to ourselves and that we hide carefully from other people.

A friend says, "When my marriage failed, I failed. The worst part of it was that I was the one who wanted to end it. I couldn't admit that to myself for a long time. I felt terribly disloyal. Bill would accuse me over and over of not loving him, and I would act insulted and fight him and make accusations back. But it was true, and I had to hide it from myself. I was ashamed for being selfish and abandoning him. I was ashamed for not loving him anymore. It wasn't even that I *couldn't* make it work. I *didn't want to*. He provided well. He didn't abuse me. But I wasn't happy. What was wrong with me for wanting more? It was a long time before I even talked about these feelings with any of my friends."

HOW WE COMPENSATE FOR SHAME

To counteract our sense of shame we often try harder to be good. Shame binds us to the Goodness Code. Each of us has a dominant strategy for avoiding shame.

DOING TOO MUCH FOR OTHERS

The Goodness Code is actually a prescription for female shame. It sets unrealistic standards that we can't possibly meet. The code prescribes doing for others, being responsible for others, acting in the interests of others. It's as if the Goodness Code is societal leverage that shames women into being too responsible. Being too responsible becomes the dominant definition of being good.

When we live by the code, we make a statement to ourselves that we're not important. We feel ashamed about our unimportance. Feeling unimportant, we focus even more on others. We take on their feelings, their needs, their expectations. We caretake, we protect, we make excuses for, we take responsibility for. We are endlessly available. We become acutely attuned to every unmet need of others, while allowing ourselves to be deaf and blind to what *we* want. We do too much for them and too little for ourselves.

We may overfunction at work. We take on too much responsibility, more than we can really handle, and we don't ask for help or let anything go. We assume that the more we do, the more valued we'll be. We become overly focused on achievement as if nothing else will prove our worth. We begin to act as if our work is who we are.

One client said, "After a while I began to realize that I was driving myself crazy trying to be perfect, trying to do everything they wanted me to do because I so desperately wanted to feel that I was special. People would say to me, 'Stop doing so much.' But I realized that I couldn't because giving up all that overwork was like giving up the hope of being loved."

And so long as we can keep all the balls in the air at once we avoid shame. But silently we may be suffering. We don't set limits or let people know what we really think. We do all this to feel good, to be approved of, and ironically, since we can never do it perfectly, we end up feeling worse. Adherence to the code gives us only the *illusion* of overcoming shame. In the end, overdoing for others doesn't make us feel good; it only makes us feel exhausted. And we end up feeling more and more vulnerable to the judgments of others about our own value.

Yet if we *don't* do too much we feel terrible too. As Sarah said, "If I ever take care of my own needs in a work situation, like the time I gave up some of the executive committee work for the church board I had been so involved with, I feel terrible. I have a crisis of questioning my decision. Usually I can't even check it out with anyone, because I can't talk about it. It always seems so shameful to admit that maybe I don't *want* to be superwoman and take on all the work."

HURTING OURSELVES

While being too responsible for others always has indirectly damaging consequences, sometimes we compensate for shame by being overtly hurtful to ourselves. We may not exercise, go to doctors, or let ourselves rest and relax. We may become so emotionally upset that we actually hurt ourselves physically. We may become trapped in relationships where we are physically or sexually abused. Shame keeps us there, and we are also ashamed of being there. We may become involved in some compulsive or addictive behavior as a way to numb or purge our feelings. We may overwork in a way that causes us extreme physical or emotional stress.

Deidre told us, "I had periods when I'd starve myself and periods when I would eat. They called it a combination of bulimia and anorexia. For me, being in control, of my emotions especially, meant not talking about anything, not about how I felt, not about my body, not about the alcoholism in my family. Part of what happened for me was that when I didn't eat I'd feel good about being in control of my body. Then when I did eat I felt ashamed. That shame was my trap, like a prison, and one of the ways to expel it was to eat and throw up because then I could flush it down the toilet along with anxiety and every other feeling.

"I thought I didn't need anybody or anything. When I did ask for anything, I felt disgusting. I just always felt really crazy. At times I'd actually have dreams about asking for help and in them I'd just feel stupid, because in my family you're supposed to know everything. And if you didn't, you didn't ask about it, you just didn't do it."

During her work in therapy, Deidre had begun to see a clear connection between her shame for having needs and the attempts to control her shame by controlling her body. She'd throw up or not eat to counteract the shame. Like Kate, who fled from the abusive situation at the conference further convinced of her basic inadequacy, Deidre had never questioned the negative messages she'd heard about her valuelessness. Like many of us, both women believed that their needs and feelings were inherently shameful. Their strategies for coping inadvertently hurt them further.

This "shame trap" is critical to our understanding of women who fail to leave battering situations or who seem to "put up with" other abuse. These women feel such a sense of failure and inadequacy that they can't imagine change is possible.[6] The more they're abused, the more ashamed they feel, and the more ashamed they feel, the more they're trapped by the abuse. They get caught in a vicious cycle of worthlessness and fear that they feel helpless to escape.

The same trap gets constructed in less visible ways for those of us who pursue relationships with unavailable or very distant people. We're drawn or attracted to them because they represent the goodness, the charm, the attractiveness, the competence, the virtue that we want and feel we lack in ourselves. We almost sense that we'll achieve value *through* them. We feel that if we can only gain *their* love and approval, we'll overcome our own shame.

Once we're focused on the man who won't make a commitment or the lover who isn't really there for us, it becomes almost impossible to stop pursuing the relationship because we'd be faced with feeling all the deepest pain of our sense of worthlessness. And yet in our "unrequited" pursuit, our shame and lack of value to them is reinforced almost daily. In our struggle to be valued by somebody else, we inadvertently further shame ourselves.

SILENCE AS THE VOICE OF SHAME

While some women overtly hurt themselves, others simply withdraw. As Deidre said, "What had to be controlled was my emotions." Women who feel as Deidre did may become silent participants in life, fearful of expressing what they truly feel and who they truly are. These are the women who are "too polite" to interrupt, the women who always feel that what others have to say is more important and significant than their own views. They compensate for their shame by leaving themselves out.

Silence in women is at the heart of the Be a Lady injunction. We've been taught, like children, to be seen and not heard. We've been assigned the role of caretakers; therefore our voices should be well modulated so as to provide the silence in which others may express their needs and thoughts.

Because of the negative attitude toward feeling and emotion in our society, we've been constrained from expressing ourselves. A woman's mode of self-expression is to speak the language of feeling. When we stay silent, we reinforce the belief that feelings are somehow suspect, that "woman's talk" is of little value and importance.

In her book *Writing a Woman's Life,* Carolyn Heilbrun writes about the ways that women have been constricted in literature from writing the truth about their lives. The real pain and emotionality of those lives has been consistently discounted. It's devalued both as truth about women's experience and as a valid form of literary expression. As an example of the effects of such suppression of our experience she writes, "Forbidden anger, women could find no voice in which publicly to complain; they took refuge in depression or madness."[7] She points out too that when women do try to write their true experience, they're criticized for being too "strident" or too "shrill."

The silence that expresses shame is most powerful and most damaging when we fail to speak up for our rights and when we fail to talk about the fact that our rights have been violated. Ironically, one of the dominant reactions of women who have been sexually abused or battered is to become silent and to fail to speak about it. They hold inside a belief that somehow they are responsible for their own abuse. They feel so shamed by having been abused that they silence and thus shame themselves further with their secret.

Jo-Ann recalls the silence of one woman who had been sexually abused by her brother:

"Linda spoke so softly in the first few sessions that I could barely hear her. On an instinct, because this was years ago and we didn't ask as routinely then, I questioned whether anyone had ever abused her sexually. Something about her quietness gave me a hint. Slowly, she began to tell me the story of ten years of being repeatedly violated by her older brother. As she talked, her voice got louder and louder, stronger and stronger. The change in her, her giving up her silence, was so dramatic, I'll never forget it."

Women have difficulty being assertive and direct because of the power of the Be a Lady injunction. But even more powerful than the injunctions themselves is the promise, rarely fulfilled, that if we are only good ladies, if we speak softly and don't say things that are better left unsaid, maybe we will finally get approved of, accepted, wanted, loved. Or at least we may avoid having to feel more shame.

TAKING PRIDE IN BEING GOOD

Finally, as a way of compensating for shame, some of us embrace goodness, and we begin to take a kind of false pride in our capacity to "measure up" to the demands of the Code of Goodness. Karen Horney talked about the "idealized images" of self that we construct to avoid our own awareness that we don't perfectly meet some external standard of goodness that would protect us from hostile rejection or shame.[8] We tell ourselves, for instance, that we're perfectly honest, perfectly giving, perfectly kind and free of anger. We come to take particular pride in our unselfishness, our caring behavior, our competence.

When we force ourselves to obey the code rigidly and can't accept any suggestion that we're less than perfect in those areas, we develop an illusory idea about who we truly are and what we truly feel. In the process, we may judge others harshly for their failures to be good. Often we relieve our own shame by subtly shaming others. And often if we live up to the code in one area and not in another, we feel shameful and fraudulent if we're seen as "good" at all. We think in extremes—either we're perfect or we're worthless and bad.

We have to be or to appear perfect because we need to feel safe from the disapproval that would make us feel more ashamed. When we take too much pride in being good, we are deeply offended by any feedback from other people that we're less than perfect. We demand that other people maintain the image of us that we see of ourselves. We may get defensive if our partner tells us we've hurt him. We may get silent and withdrawn if someone notices us feeling needy or upset. In the process, we deprive ourselves of knowing our true feelings and of accepting ourselves as we are. We're incapable of being "a little bad."

The Goodness Code becomes a prison, and we force ourselves to stay within its narrow walls. Otherwise, the shame feels too overwhelming. If at any point we have to acknowledge a mistake or a failure to be good, or even a faint wish to break out of prison, we feel shattered and guilty. Our response is usually to step up our attempts to be good or to punish ourselves in some way for being bad.

THE CYCLE OF SHAME

Pamela had been fired from her job. She had directly challenged her boss's decision on a budget item. Her first response was to feel absolutely furious. Her next was to consume an entire chocolate cream pie.

Pamela's daughter, who as an adult had developed a talent for being critical of her, said, "So, you got fired and now you're going to have to live with that. And, by the way, when are you going to handle your weight problem?"

It was hard to tell whether Pam was most ashamed about challenging her boss, about losing her job, or about eating the pie. But the shame about weight was consistent. She said, "I tell myself that my size is not within the normal range of female size—it's not even under consideration as a female form. By size, I think I don't just mean my weight. I often feel too pushy, too opinionated. Like I'm trying to be 'too big,' stepping out of line. That's probably why I lost my job."

Pam understood that by "size" she meant not just physical appearance but power. Her experience was that the more she expressed herself and her opinions, the less acceptable she became. Her daughter seemed to make the same connection, implying that in some way Pamela had been "too much."

To compensate for feeling so bad about herself after she was fired and went on her food binge, Pamela tried harder to be good in other areas. Shortly after she lost her job, her sister was hospitalized. She left her own home and went to stay with her sister's family to help out.

Although a visit was in order and would have been helpful, Pamela overdid, staying three weeks when a few days would have been enough. Her sister criticized her for the way she handled things. At home Pam's husband was angry that she was gone so long.

But other people told her what a wonderful sister she was. She was, in fact, so good to her sister that by the time the three-week visit was over, she did feel much better about herself. Unfortunately, she got so exhausted that she went on another food binge.

Shame always makes us work harder at being good because the appeal of goodness is that it temporarily relieves shame. Pamela talked about having a constant chatter in her head about her violation of the Be Attractive rule. It went "I shouldn't have eaten that. I'm so fat already. I'm never going to get anywhere. This is terrible." The chatter stopped temporarily when she became a "good sister," when she obeyed the injunction to Be Unselfish. But being so unselfish left her own needs unmet, and she started to feel empty. The emptiness led back to the food, and the food would temporarily and falsely relieve the emptiness. But then the chatter would start again and she'd need to resort again to being good.

Let's look at the cycle[9] Pam went through more carefully because it's critical to understanding our responses to shame. Pam asserted herself at work and was shamed for it. She was fired. Her daughter shamed her further. She tried to relieve the feelings by bingeing on pie, a response that ultimately made her feel worse because her "basic shame" was all focused in her failure to live up to the Be Attractive injunction. In another effort to feel better, Pam went to her sister's and overfunctioned for three weeks. While she could temporarily feel "good" about her unselfish and generous behavior, she so overfocused on her sister that she ignored some of her own needs. So again she felt bad. This time she went back to her other solution, which was to overeat.

Once again, Pam becomes vulnerable to overfunctioning, in an endless cycle of attempts to deal with her underlying sense of shame. The problem with her solutions is that rather than making her feel good, they only add to her bad feelings about herself. "I'm not attractive enough, I'm selfish, I'm too aggressive, pushy, strong for my own good." Notice that all her shame-bound beliefs are statements about the ways she feels she fails to live up to some *external* standard of goodness. Pam doesn't challenge the beliefs, she simply tries to cope with the bad feelings they arouse.

As is true for most of us, Pamela's feelings included generous doses of anger, guilt, anxiety, humiliation, and depression, all the feelings we have when we fail to meet either other people's demands or our own unrealistic expectations of ourselves. Her determination to control those feelings rather than to challenge and explore them led her to go out of control in another area. For example, if she had been directly angry with her boss when he fired her, she might not have felt compelled to eat the cream pie. And if she had challenged her daughter's criticism, she might not have felt compelled to move in with her sister's family for three weeks.

As Pam talked more in therapy about her underlying feelings, and as she shared them with other women who had similar feelings about themselves, she felt less driven to be good. Given voice, feelings like anger and guilt lose their power. Overcoming shame involves facing our negative feelings squarely and, by expressing and challenging them, empowering ourselves to be accepting and to think differently about who we are. As we face the feelings and beliefs that drive us, we can begin to write new rules for ourselves. We can face the demon shame without an automatic retreat into goodness or into behaviors that punish us for feeling bad. Ultimately, our shame is only as deep as our secretiveness about it.

✳EXPLORING YOUR BELIEFS ABOUT YOURSELF

Our unconscious beliefs create shameful feelings. When we're caught in trance, we're not aware that at least some of our good behavior is designed to fight and control shame.

The following exercise is designed to help you become more conscious about the shame-bound beliefs that affect you. Spend some time filling in the blanks of these open-ended questions. Don't give a lot of thought to your answers—write down the first thing that comes to mind.

The thing I've done (or do) that makes me feel most awful about myself is . . .

The one thing about myself that I could never tell anyone is . . .

If I'm honest, the thing I most hate to do for _____ is . . .

If people knew what I was really like they would see that . . .

Deep down, I believe what's true about me is . . .

I think people would like me better if . . .

I can't imagine letting anyone see me when . . .

The thing I like least about myself is . . .

The way I feel about needing anything from anyone is . . .

The aspect of myself that I take greatest pride in is . . .

I would be most hurt and offended if somebody told me I was . . .

The way I get people to like me is . . .

When I feel bad about myself what I do is . . .

I feel good about myself when . . .

The answers to these questions will tell you the things about yourself that you find most shameful. Your answer to the last question will tell you something about what you do to compensate for those feelings.

From what you've said about yourself, make a list of your negative beliefs. For instance, you may realize that you believe that "I'm bad if I'm angry." Or "I'm bad because I'm sexual," or "I have to work hard to be liked." Try to imagine what it would be like to live your life if you didn't hold those beliefs.

THE GOOD PART OF GOODNESS

We don't feel shame continually or about everything in our lives. We're all affected differently by the injunctions of the Goodness Code. We each have a "target" rule that leaves us feeling bad and more intensely ashamed when we don't measure up. Some of us feel more ashamed if we're not perfectly competent, others if we're not perfectly unselfish.

Equally, all our "good" behavior isn't motivated by a need to overcome female shame. Sometimes we make choices to do good things. We choose to be giving to someone or we enjoy exercising our competence at the things we're good at. We take real pride in a job well done or in an accomplishment that's been the outcome of a lot of good hard work. We can enjoy the benefits of being appreciated for the good things we do. It feels good to be liked and approved of.

When we behave in ways that we ourselves define as good, we have a sense of inner control, of acting in a way that's consistent with our values. We may even enjoy playing the part of a "female" female, of occasionally being ladylike, of having access to behavior that's part of us and determined by us. We may act "good" as a way of fitting in or being part of a group that appeals to us.

Being good for each of us is something different from living by the Code of Goodness. It has to do with living by values that we define for ourselves. It has to do with allowing ourselves to *feel* good. When we're ruled by the five injunctions of the Goodness Code, we lose our capacity to choose. We become driven by the need for approval and by fear that we may be powerless to get it. Our life is taken over by basic female shame, and we become too good for our own good.

5

THE HIGH COST OF GOODNESS

———— ✳ ————

Ann was the only daughter of two hard-working, nondrinking parents. She grew up surrounded by a family who doted on her. But the expectations of her were high. She was reminded of the dictates of the Goodness Code on an almost daily basis. Work hard, look your best. Be sensitive to others. Don't wear your heart on your sleeve. Be honest. Go last. Don't act too smart. Marry well. Live up to your potential. Do something for the world.

Whenever Ann got too emotional, she was called a Sarah Bernhardt. As a young child, if her feelings were too intense, especially if she was angry, she was put in a tub of ice water until she "calmed down." To help overcome her shyness she was given drama lessons. To help ensure her popularity she was taught tennis, dancing, and other important social skills.

Her mother tells her she was a likable, even charming, child who was full of imagination and creative projects. She was never at a loss for friends. By her senior year in high school, she had won two national scholarships, and her school record was so impressive that a special award was created for her for outstanding achievement.

Having been accepted to an Ivy League college, Ann's future seemed assured. With the right schooling, the right social background, and enough allegiance to the Goodness Code to generate approval from friends, family, and the many boys she dated, Ann seemed destined for a bright, successful, and rewarding life.

Except that at her Ivy League college, Ann began to drink. She would have called it social drinking. But before long Ann was drunk almost daily. She'd wake up and find herself in other people's rooms not knowing how she got there. She, who had always been so disciplined, found herself, even when not drunk, staying up nights, sleeping days, missing the classes her parents were paying for.

Ann got involved in one disastrous relationship after another. Other people thought of her as promiscuous. Her grades suffered. By the end of her sophomore year, Ann had attempted suicide and been hospitalized. Only her innate resilience and intelligence got her through her last two years of college, because in spite of the suicide attempt and thousands of dollars spent by her parents on psychiatrists, Ann continued to drink.

After she graduated, Ann took a job with one of the most prestigious companies in the country. She was engaged to be married more than once. Through all of it, she describes herself as feeling "never good enough," less adequate than others, as if she never really "fit."

Her drinking began to cost her jobs, and she found herself waking up in even more unfamiliar rooms, sometimes with strangers who threatened to hurt her if she didn't go along with things they wanted her to do. She smashed up more than one car and somehow escaped being killed. People began to find her obnoxious and rude. She lost friends or simply dropped them herself. She became more and more isolated. She spent a night in prison for her obnoxious behavior, she passed out in a bus terminal, and for a year she lived in an apartment bare of furniture except for a mattress on the floor. She smeared the windows with soap to avoid buying curtains.

Ann had gone, in a few short years, from being a model child, the image of a "good" girl about to become a good woman, to being a desperate failure almost destroyed by alcoholism.

COPING WITH GOODNESS

Ann's story offers a vivid illustration of the ways that the pressure on a woman to be good can get so great that addiction can seem like the only way out. It's a reminder that being too good often leads to going out of control. Hidden in the narrative of Ann's life is the truth about what happens to many women who try too hard to live up to the impossible expectations of the code. Ann's experience tells the tale of goodness gone bad.

As therapists we could see Ann's addiction as a rebellion, though it wasn't a rebellion she was conscious of. "I tried so hard to please that I was strung as tight as a high wire. For that matter, it's more like I was walking a high wire, frantic to keep my balance but also sometimes furious that I had to walk it. Finally the wire just snapped."

Other women who suffer from the high cost of goodness have similar stories. They say that they tried too hard as children to please their parents. They say they never felt attractive or smart enough. Some tell us about the pain of keeping shameful secrets about sexual abuse. Some tell us about being totally unable to express emotion so that all their feelings—sexual ones, nurturing ones, needy ones—began to seem bad and shameful. They talk about the pain of living with addiction in their own families.

Ultimately, no matter what they achieve as adults, they say they never feel good enough, never adequate enough. Like Ann, they try desperately to control people and things around them in order to still their deep fear and feelings of inadequacy. Yet they always end up feeling even worse about themselves, more *out of control,* more shamed, less responsible. For a woman who develops an addiction, it becomes impossible to feel like an effective, worthwhile person.

ADDICTION AS IMBALANCE
CARING TOO LITTLE FOR SELF

What really happened to Ann? How did her life get so off course? What can we learn from her story about the process that can develop that results in women turning to a drug or some other compulsive behavior to help them manage their lives?

In Ann's case, the stage was set for addiction by three factors that deeply affected her developing sense of self:

1. Ann was overly focused on by all the members of her family. Everything was done for her, and most of her decisions were either criticized or made for her. She became underresponsible and therefore felt incompetent to take on the tasks of living and of making decisions for herself.

2. There were enormous expectations placed on Ann to be successful and to be a "good" woman. The expectations were sometimes conflict-

ing ones. She became too pressured by the needs and expectations of her parents—her focus was always on pleasing them and on winning their approval. Every time she lapsed, her parents got highly anxious. She protected them from anxiety by being good.

3. Ann was shamed for having emotional needs. She was valued for what she did and how well she succeeded at being good. She felt as though no one knew who she really was and if they did they wouldn't love her.

Ann managed to live comfortably enough with this state of affairs while she was still at home. She thought she was happy. But when she was on her own at college, a number of things simply broke down for her. New feelings and emotions flooded her, and she had not the first idea how to handle them. She had left the protected environment of her small-town school, where she had clearly stood out as a star, to the competitive environment of an Ivy League college, where she was one star among many.

Feeling frightened and confused, Ann began to drink to numb and cope with these feelings that threatened to overwhelm her. She told herself that it was sophisticated to drink. She aspired to be a writer, and she romanticized drinking with images of F. Scott and Zelda Fitzgerald. With her peers, Ann thought that drinking made her popular and "adult." In fact what she was doing was avoiding her feelings and avoiding making the choices that would direct her life at a very critical point in her development. The drinking pulled her down into a spiral of self-destruction from which she nearly didn't recover.

Ann became physically as well as psychologically addicted to alcohol.[1] Not everyone becomes physically addicted, but women in the grip of any form of addiction or compulsion experience very much the same process that drove Ann to the edge of destroying her life.

In a most basic way, an addictive behavior is a way of avoiding shame. We try to correct our own feelings in a way that ultimately becomes hurtful. Every time we fail to live up to the dictates of the Goodness Code, we come one step closer to needing a "fix" to relieve our sense of failure. For many, the fix may at first be an intensified effort at being good. But whenever we become too responsible, we're in danger of flipping to the opposite extreme and going out of control, sometimes with the help of a drug. The addiction takes on a life of its own. It becomes a disease. We lose control and we deny it. We end up hurting rather than caring for ourselves.

COVERING UP THE SHAME OF WHO YOU ARE

As we've pointed out in chapter 4, all of us carry around a basic shame about being female. But the woman who becomes addicted or who behaves compulsively in an attempt to control, correct, or tranquilize these feelings gets caught in a cycle of shame that locks her into a descending spiral of out-of-control behavior. Her attempt to have power over herself renders her powerless. This kind of cycle can develop for a nonaddicted woman as well, as we'll see later in this chapter.

When a woman is caught in this shame cycle, it's usually obvious to the people around her who care about her, although they may not know what they're seeing. In the beginning phase of the cycle, what they see is their friend or mother, daughter or lover, acting prideful and in control. She may be seeming to handle everything for everybody. She may be involved in an abusive relationship compulsively insisting she will make her partner love her by changing herself.

In this phase, she may act very controlled and controlling. She may take pride in her capacity to handle everything, and typically she'll deny that some things in her life aren't being handled well. She tells herself that she can handle whatever comes her way and that furthermore she must handle it. She fails to see options, and she does little to care for herself.

She has a counterfeit sense of self in this phase. She holds up the image of the "good woman" and tells herself that she is one. She may seem distant, she may seem sorry for herself, she may seem to suffer from a "martyr complex." Attempts to help her or to respond to her self-imposed stress will meet with a "thank you very much, but I don't need anything." She appears the picture of independence except that somehow you don't quite believe it.

Sometimes women break the cycle at this point and get help. This outcome is most likely if a friend or employer or family member recognizes that the woman is really in pain and insists on her getting help. But often, so long as a woman looks like she is functioning for everyone else, her own pain is ignored until her addiction is even further advanced. Then gradually the pieces of her carefully constructed image begin to fly apart. Whatever her addiction of choice, it will become more noticeable now. She will begin to drink more, to eat more, to focus more on the person who is being abusive to her or on the person with whom she seems obsessed. She may start to use tranquilizers, to spend more time at work, to become more unreasonable, overly critical, angry, distressed. She may become deeply depressed. She may seem to create emotional crises that force others to respond. She acts preoccupied and unreachable yet still denies there is anything wrong.

As she reaches the final phase of the cycle, she either goes out of control or goes inward with her stress, expressing it in forms such as physical illness, deeper depression, phobias, or chronic anxiety that sometimes becomes attacks of panic. She may alternately do both. Her addictive or compulsive behavior is at its most extreme. She gets drunk, takes pills, binges or purges. She stops eating, acts out sexually, breaks down in some way.

At this point, she may become actively "not good." She fails to care for her children, she doesn't show up at work, she goes on a binge of spending, she allows herself to be physically abused. She feels over-whelmed by anger, resentment, and self-loathing. She alternately feels that she's the most selfish and loathsome person in her own life and that everyone in her life totally fails her. Her feelings and behavior are out of control, and only a desperate revival of control, denial, and false pride can save her sense of self.

These cycles may happen from day to day, week to week, month to month, or year to year. But the woman caught up in such a pattern is trapped by her battle against her own feelings and against her own internalized self-hatred. Over time, the physiological effect or the prac-tical consequences of the drug or compulsion of choice will drag her to the edge of disaster.

If she seeks help, she has the chance to free herself from the trap of female shame. But to do so, she'll need the support of many other women, addicted and not, who struggle together to overcome the pres-sures in our society that shame us and rob us of the right to define our own lives. More than for most women, it's critical that the addicted woman free herself from the dictates of the Goodness Code because they serve to reinforce the shame that will keep her addicted.

Ann ultimately joined Alcoholics Anonymous after a series of loving confrontations from several of her old friends. When she first got sober, however, she felt so guilty for the ways that her alcoholism had hurt others and so ashamed of the mess her life had become that she tried too hard to be good again. She didn't drink anymore. But she over-worked, set no limits on what she gave to others, and tried with renewed passion to live up to the code. Grateful to AA, she never said no to helping someone else, spoke frequently at meetings, and doubled her expectations of herself. After a year of sobriety, she drank again.

Getting sober a second time was harder. But this time she had the help of a sponsor who told her to "be a little bad" and who ruthlessly challenged her any time she was hard on herself. She also came into therapy and worked to achieve a better balance between her behavior, her feelings, and her beliefs about herself.

COMPULSIONS ARE A CONTAINER FOR RAGE

Like Ann and like the heroine of the musical *Oklahoma*, most of us are "girls who can't say no." [2] As children, we can't say no to the demands of our more powerful parents. As adults, we often fail to say no to the demands of a society that expects that we give ourselves over to the needs and expectations of others. It's no wonder that we then can't say no to a drug or some other dangerous behavior.

Often, as women, the feeling we have the most difficulty with, and the one that a compulsion most contains, is anger—or, more accurately, rage. We feel rage at the impossible expectations imposed on us; rage at not getting our needs met; rage at being shamed, perhaps at being sexually or physically abused; rage at having to be responsible for our parents; rage at being unable to say no. We feel rage at our own guilt, rage at not feeling better about ourselves. We may or may not be aware of our rage or of the depth of it. But, on the bottom line, many of us feel rage at being robbed of our identities, at the requirement that we meet the expectations imposed by others rather than those dictated by our own experience.

Ann's anger found expression in alcoholism. Even as a small child, she must have reacted with rage to the intense emotional pressures of her environment because her parents put her in ice water to dampen it.

Women in recovery groups frequently talk about their rage. One woman was multiply addicted to alcohol and drugs and also suffered from anorexia. Her father had sexually abused her. "I was a very angry woman. I had rages. What I wanted was contact. I went from feeling the rage to feeling numb inside. It was always inappropriate, out-of-control anger. I never really expressed all the rage. Underneath it was this loneliness and need for love and human contact."

Another woman who had been sexually abused spoke of the way that her addiction helped her keep her feelings down. "I was afraid of releasing emotions. I had to be in control, I had to keep this secret. I was afraid I would kill if this rage came out. I knew if I opened my mouth the words would never stop. Alcohol helped me keep the lid on my feelings for years, and then alcohol turned on me, the lid flipped, and I began to go out of control."

For most women, then, an addiction or a compulsion helps to either dampen feelings, to tranquilize them or make them more controllable, or it allows permission to release them.[3] The woman who becomes phobic, for instance, is often avoiding her rage. The feelings lie so buried underneath layers of dependency and loyalty that she's not even conscious of anger, only of the surface feelings of fear. The woman who develops an eating disorder goes to great lengths to avoid feeling her emotions, but always those feelings involve deeply buried anger that must be controlled. The focus on food, on depriving herself or bingeing and then purging herself, represents her attempts to control *herself* rather than express the anger directly toward those she is angry at.

"I didn't feel shame at first because my denial was so ingrained," Ann explained. "Drinking was glamorous, it was the cool thing to do. But then I started feeling real miserable. My shame was so deep, I never even saw it. I developed so many defenses. My drinking was the only way I could cope—I had so much rage."

KEEPING UP WITH THE CODE

If compulsions help women handle their anger, they also help them to stay good. Over and over again women say that drinking or drugs helped them to feel more in line with the image of how they should be, it helped them meet the demands of the code.[4]

"I felt more acceptable to myself when I drank. I became confident and outgoing. When I drank I could be anything in any situation, particularly charming and sparkling. I felt more womanly and attractive when I drank, I had more self-esteem. To be charming you had to feel attractive."

Often addictions help women to do the work of relating in all their various roles. While some women felt deep shame at the ways that drinking led them to fail their children, for instance, other women often talked about needing to drink to help them mother their children at all.

"I drank and took pills to be a better mother—to be able to sit and listen when I couldn't calm down. I was trying to be a good mother."

Another mother talks about the need to be responsible and the conflicting dictates to Be Competent and Make Relationships Work.

"I was overresponsible because I felt such shame about my feelings and emotions. I wasn't 'accomplished' in any intellectual or business sense, so I had to be 'Miss Community' and 'Miss Super-Mother.' It was funny, I had a house and children and I thought I had everything I needed to make me happy. And yet I became very overresponsible in the community, I became a 'yes' person. But the shame and insecurity was always there. One day my son came home from school with a problem, and I had to go to the school to see the principal. Before I could go, I had to have a drink. I had to take a drink to have the courage to go and be a good mother."

A recurrent and powerful theme for addicted women relates to the injunction to Be a Lady, the rule that one should not show feelings or appear to have needs. In the end, the repression of feelings that drugs helped achieve made them feel that they didn't have a right to have feelings, they didn't have the right to be themselves.

"I had to be strong, together. I don't remember shedding a tear. You shouldn't be so emotional, hysterical, we were told. And so I think it's dangerous to show emotion. My father would tell me I had no right to be upset. Emotions weren't permitted, and I was always the one who was most emotional."

Finally this distortion and repression of emotion, and the overresponsibility and shame that are a result, have serious consequences in terms of a woman's sense of self-acceptance. Most addicted women have the feeling that no amount of accomplishment, achievement, love, or approval is enough to overcome some basic sense of worthlessness.

"When somebody says something about what I've done, I take it as a commentary on who I am. I feel embarrassed when I'm praised. If they only knew, they would find out what a fraud I am. I would never take credit for anything."

IMAGES OF "BAD" WOMEN

When a woman tries to face her problem with an addiction,[5] she has to battle our society's negative attitudes toward any woman who goes out of control. If the movies and the media helped portray the standard image of the "good" woman in years past, they also help to portray a standard image of a "bad" woman. The worst kind of woman, of course, is an alcoholic, addicted one. In the movies she is depicted as either crazy or sexually wanton. Perhaps the best-known image is the alcoholic slut brilliantly portrayed by Elizabeth Taylor in the screen version of *Who's Afraid of Virginia Woolf?* Or you may remember Jessica Lange's portrayal of the thirties film star Frances Farmer in the movie *Frances*. Frances was diagnosed as insane. Her alcoholism went undiagnosed and eventually she was lobotomized for her "out-of-control" behavior. Recently, in the movie *The Morning After*, Jane Fonda gave a sensuous performance as a woman alcoholic suspected of murdering a pornography king.

The images we see on the screen reflect the archetypal images we have in our minds of women who become addicted. The archetypes prevent us from seeing the underlying woman-blaming that is society's response to any woman who fails to live up to the dictates of the code, any woman who goes out of control.

COADDICTION AS IMBALANCE
DOING TOO MUCH FOR OTHERS

Some women suffer from addictions themselves, and others are affected by the addiction of someone else. It's become a part of our cultural language recently to refer to the person who relates to an addicted person as a codependent.[6] The addicted person may be a parent, a spouse or lover, or even one's child. The term implies that when you relate to someone else's addiction or dysfunction, your behavior and feelings become dysfunctional too. It suggests that the addicted person is addicted to a drug and the codependent is addicted to the addict.

As we said in chapter 1, "codependent" has quickly become a catchall phrase for the types of behaviors that have traditionally been ascribed to women. What the phrase refers to is the fact that when you become anxious about someone else's behavior, a typical response is to do more for them, make more gestures of help to them, and to get so focused on what they do, say, and think that your own feelings go unacknowledged. The addict's life begins to take on more importance than yours. In an effort to "make things right," you find yourself willing to make excuses for them and to put up with their hurtful behavior. You take most of the responsibility for what goes wrong. In fact, you become willing to take most of the responsibility for everything.

But in effect codependency is really an extreme form of the injunction to Make Relationships Work. It's what women have learned over the centuries is the core of their identity—to give up oneself in return for love and approval. When the person who holds the power of approval is addicted, there's also the deep-seated desire to "save the day," another twist on the injunction to Be Competent. People who live in an addictive environment know clearly that something is very wrong, and they harness whatever resources are at their disposal to try to heal, change, and make things better.

What's confusing about the term codependent is that women have always adapted, accommodated, and focused on others. To now label all forms of this behavior a sickness seems to blame women for doing too much of what they've been taught to do. Rather than labeling these behaviors sick, we need to see them as potentially good behaviors that go to an unbalanced extreme in certain situations and become hurtful rather than helpful to everyone concerned.

If making relationships work is so much a part of a woman's definition of herself, so strong an element of the code, what makes the kind of overfocus that is a response to addiction so damaging and dysfunctional?

CLAUDIA'S BURNED CHICKEN STORY

Since I don't cook, this isn't a story about me. It's about one of the first times in my professional life that I really confronted the reality of a woman's trying too hard to make a relationship work.

After I graduated with my degree in social work, I took a position working in a local school system. It was my job to evaluate the family relationships, the medical history, and the social factors that affected children with learning problems.

In school, we saw children only from the perspective of their functioning in the very structured setting of the classroom. In order to understand more about their lives and their world outside of school, we would try to meet with their parents in their homes. Since I worked during the day, I would routinely meet mostly with mothers. Only rarely was a father available and, when he was, often he spoke "from the sidelines," kind of wandering in and out of the conversation in the midst of his puttering around the house. I soon realized the drawbacks of learning about the children I worked with only from the perspective of their mothers. Often the fathers had critical but silent roles to play in their children's problems.

One of my very first interviews was with the mother of a child who appeared in school to be very frail and very vulnerable. In class Bobby was never a behavior problem—he was often sleepy and unable to pay attention, and he had fairly severe problems learning to read. Bobby had an older brother who had similar problems. The two boys were very close, and they defended each other in the various ups and downs of life with their friends at school. And any attempt to talk with them about their lives outside of school met with evasive answers meant to suggest that everything was "just fine."

I didn't expect to have the conversation that I had with Bobby's mother, Carol, on our first visit together.

Like her boys, Carol was a small person who seemed fragile and physically vulnerable. She had reddish hair and bright blue eyes, and in spite of her seeming frailty, she seemed like a woman who was determined to protect her children. She seemed like a survivor.

We met in the afternoon at the end of her work shift at a local department store. She had made coffee for the two of us—she seemed almost eager to have someone coming to talk to her. Her small bungalow, a converted summer cottage, was neat and orderly. Attempts to improve the cottage were evident, and I found myself wondering whether it was she or her husband who had been the "handyman." I had been a little disturbed by two garbage pails overflowing with beer bottles that I'd noticed by the side of the house on my way in.

Carol and I talked for a while about the boys, their medical histories, their bond with one another, the milestones in their developmental history. When I asked about their relationship with their father I could see Carol get tense. She got up abruptly to pour herself another cup of coffee. When she sat back down, she pointed to the fading marks of a large bruise on the side of her face.

"I probably shouldn't be talking to you about this," she said, "but I do want my boys to get help. This bruise will tell you something about their father—he gave it to me. Not that it happens a lot. And he doesn't really hurt them. It's just he drinks a little too much. He's a hard man to get through to. He doesn't show his feelings much, not to me or to the boys. I try to keep them out of his hair. He can have a temper. I'm never really sure what's going to get him mad.

"It's funny, the night this happened I wouldn't have known that he was mad about anything. Everything was done around here. The boys were in their room, not bothering him any at all. He just came in and started in on me and finally just let go and smacked me. I tried and tried to figure out later what had happened, what was wrong. I finally decided the whole problem must have been that I burned the chicken a little. It's the only thing I can think would have caused him to be that way."

Carol sat at the table shaking her head as if still perplexed about what it was that she could have done to avoid being hit. She talked for a while about the ways she'd tried to make her husband less angry. The angrier he got, the harder she tried. She seemed convinced that it was all her fault. Slowly, as she talked, she started to cry. She was relieved to be talking, but she was also realizing how exhausted she was from trying. I knew that Carol was ready to get help. She thought the problem was burned chicken, but I knew that really it was alcoholism.

GOING BEYOND GOOD

Under normal circumstances, Carol might simply have been a woman who followed the typical dictates of female goodness. She would have been devoted to her children, intent to please her husband. She would probably have worked hard at keeping house. She might always have expected herself to be more responsible for certain aspects of their life together.

However, as her husband's drinking began to have greater power in the life of the family, predictably Carol got frightened. The fears weren't just ones about what was "wrong" with her husband. She also started to question what was "wrong" with her that things were getting so out of control. Like many women who assume that their husbands have affairs because they are undesirable, Carol just assumed she was to blame for her husband's anger. Her female shame was triggered. Her response was to do more and try harder to manage all the relationships in the family. The harder she tried, the more out of control he got. The right answer one day turned out to be the wrong answer the next.

Carol made excuses for her husband's behavior. She thought if he loved her he wouldn't drink so she tried to make herself more desirable to him. The more she fought to understand him, the more violent he became and the more he pushed her away. Instead of protecting herself, she kept trying to understand him. She lost sight of her own rights, and finally he began to hit her when he came home drunk. Her basic female "goodness" had turned into a self-defeating pattern of trying too hard, doing too much, and living with physical abuse.

Women like Carol are often identified as "loving too much." But it's important to see that really Carol and women who become involved in relationships with people who are violent or addicted are simply attempting to solve a problem in a way that expresses what they've been taught to do as women.

Women make relationships work at any cost; they don't leave them. They give unselfishly; they take responsibility. If a man behaves badly, a woman assumes there is something she can do about it. If a man acts unloving, it must be that she has failed to accommodate, serve, sustain, or it must mean that she has failed to control herself. If she doesn't do these things, she is somehow less of a woman. Since a woman sees herself as responsible, if a man acts abusively she has failed. She gets so caught up in her own self-doubt and shame that it never occurs to her that a man is responsible and wrong.

A WOMAN IN SEARCH OF A LOST SELF

Lois first came for therapy for help with anxiety. She was anxious about many things, but as we talked it would be fair to say that her basic fear was the one that she didn't exist.

It was hard, at first, to understand Lois's feelings because she was an intensely attractive and appealing woman who was often pursued by men. She had four children and was married to a wealthy doctor who ran a busy private practice along with his staff appointment at a local hospital. Lois was talented in her own right—she had studied a very technical area of biological science. She sometimes did free-lance writing for professional journals, and occasionally she wrote poetry. Otherwise, she worked at home raising her four children and caring for the enormous house they lived in. In spite of their wealth, her husband wouldn't agree to hire any household help, and Lois didn't challenge him about it.

Lois had friends and a busy social schedule, yet she described herself as often wandering through town feeling lonely, disconnected, and isolated. Her sense of being nonexistent was most intense whenever she went into the large walk-in closet in her bedroom. Standing in the confined space of the closet made her feel disconnected, as if she had left herself somewhere outside the closet door. She kept a radio playing in the closet to make it safe. The sound reminded her that she was there.

Planning her wardrobe was perhaps the only activity in her day that forced Lois to focus on herself. When she had to notice herself, she became panicky. Talking about these feelings made Lois feel ashamed and "crazy." Talking about herself at all was difficult.

Lois described herself as submissive. She catered to her husband's every whim. She revolved herself entirely around his and the children's schedules. Given the demands of his business, he was rarely home and gave her little in the way of emotional contact or support. She felt that she was little more than a function to him—an attractive companion, a sexual partner, a full-time wife and mother. She feared his angry outbursts when she challenged him or tried to step out of her role.

Lois didn't challenge her husband often. She seemed to feel both trapped and safe in a role that allowed her to avoid defining herself.

We began to look back into Lois's family to understand why she felt so lost and why her life had become so dominated by her husband's demands. It wasn't a surprise when Lois, head bent, almost whispering, began to describe a family almost totally dominated by her father's drinking. Not only had he been a severe alcoholic, he had died from his drinking when Lois was a teenager. She had loved her father but hated his drinking. She still grieved that he'd died and, though she didn't yet realize it, she still grieved that he hadn't cared enough about her to be sober.

The story she told was the story women tell again and again. Lois was an oldest daughter, and her mother was forced to leave her and her siblings alone with her father much of the time in order to work. Lois had been in the position of caring for her father as if she were his wife. She poured him his drinks, held his head while he vomited, did his bidding, fed him, and suffered the beatings when she tried to leave the house to be with friends.

Sometimes seeming to ignore the fact that he was drunk and abusive to her, Lois still tended to idealize her father. She saw him as a brilliant and competent man who would have been successful and living, she was sure, if it weren't for the alcohol. Her therapy sessions for months were spent with her attempting to "understand him"—to understand why he drank, why he wasn't really a father to her. While she could acknowledge anger at her mother for not protecting her from her father, she still tried to deny her anger toward her father. Some part of her blamed her mother for the problem.

It was a difficult task to help Lois search for the traces of her lost self in the midst of this intense loyalty to her father. So much of her emotional energy had gone into that relationship with him that it seemed remarkable that she had achieved any goals of her own at all. It seemed that she'd managed to achieve what she had only against a backdrop of terrible struggle—her impulse to stay focused on the demands of a man and to disown her own life was strong. It undermined every attempt she made to be self-defining.

Often Lois couldn't identify even simple, basic likes and dislikes for herself. It was difficult work for her to stay focused on herself long enough to recognize that she liked a certain kind of music or certain color schemes in her house. Not surprisingly, she often looked to her teenage daughter to model for her what a woman might like or feel or want. She had a recurring fantasy of escape, but the fantasy so lacked detail that it failed to describe what Lois imagined would help. In it, she went away to the ocean totally alone to a house that was entirely white. She slept in a bed that looked out over the water. The fantasy pictured her inner life as a void waiting to be filled.

Part of Lois's therapy involved work with fantasy and imagery to help her find and recognize the unfound parts of herself. One day, Lois tried to call up the memory of some real scene from her childhood that she would like to rewrite in fantasy. She saw herself as she had often been, at a cottage at the shore with her father and brothers. Her mother usually refused to go on these vacations, so Lois would be in her familiar position of having to "take care" of her father. In the rewritten scene, Lois's longed-for outcome occurs. Her mother is there and walks with her father down the beach, her father is happy. Lois sees herself going to another part of the beach to join her friends, free for once of worry and responsibility. She sees herself happy and connected to other people. She feels free to be herself.

Lois's solution in real life had not been so freeing. As she felt safer to talk about herself, she revealed that one of her main anxieties was her desire to leave her husband for another man. In fact, she had met a man socially who was responsive and kind to her. She maintained an ongoing fantasy relationship with this man in her mind. Periodically she called and talked with him on the phone. Even though he gave no indication that he was interested in a relationship with her, Lois saw him as a potential perfect mate. She had obsessive romantic fantasies that he would rescue her from her difficult husband. In her mind, he would give her all the caring and attention that she felt was missing in her marriage.

Lois's fantasy was that she would find herself by losing herself in a relationship with another man. She looked for someone to give to her in a way that her parents hadn't. In rewriting the family story from her childhood, she had "found" herself by being able to leave her parents to face each other while she walked away down the beach. But in real life, like many women, Lois was convinced that her identity could be reclaimed only in another relationship. While her fantasy helped her to avoid the pain that she needed to face in her relationship with her husband, and while it told her something about what she longed for in her life, it didn't do the job of freeing her to own herself. Her fantasy didn't show her that her hopes to be cared for by another man would inevitably lead her right back into doing too much and putting herself aside to maintain his love and approval. The walk down the beach was one she needed to take by herself. And it would take months of therapy before she was ready to take that walk.

Even though Ann, Carol, and Lois all have a different involvement with addiction, it isn't hard to see the common themes that run through all of their stories. They each suffered from a self-imposed pressure to do too much. They all felt intense shame. Each was unable to be positively focused on herself. As Ann overresponsibly tried to live up to the demands of her own perfectionism, she went out of control with alcohol. Carol worked harder to try to control herself and her relationships. Lois overworked in her marriage and found relief in the escape of fantasy. Ultimately, she might easily have acted on that fantasy, only to create greater problems for herself.

The woman affected by addiction, her own or someone else's, represents one end of a continuum of imbalance that affects any woman who tries too hard to live by the Code of Goodness. Doing too much for others and too little for self, caring too much for others and too little for self, are destructive patterns for all women. Throwing off the code is a difficult challenge, but, when addiction is a factor, the job becomes even harder. It becomes a shortcut to feeling good that leaves us feeling awful.

We all need to define our own lives, to make choices, to find a balance between focusing on others and focusing on ourselves. Whether we become addicted ourselves or relate to someone else's addiction, the first task we face is to free ourselves from the drug. Then, along with all women, we need to challenge the injunctions of the code, and in the process to wake ourselves from the trance that hides our real feelings, needs, and strengths.

PART TWO

BREAKING FREE

6

GOODNESS THAT LEADS
TO FEELING GOOD

———— ✳ ————

The New Code of Balance

In Part One, we listened to the stories of many women who've paid a high price for being too good. They've lived by the Code of Goodness because they've been unconscious of its power. They didn't realize they had other choices.

We've seen that the Code of Goodness keeps us enslaved by other people's expectations. It makes us responsible for others rather than for ourselves. In the process of trying to live up to the code, we get caught in cycles of shame, and we are molded into patterns of caring that leave us out of balance with ourselves. We learn a great deal about the self that can be competent, responsible, hard-working, and focused on the needs of others. But we learn little about the self who can feel enjoyment, who can be in tune with her own needs and feelings. We don't value who we are, we value only what we do.

But once we're more aware of the rules that we live by, we have the choice to change them. We can replace doing good with feeling good. To accomplish that shift, we need to live by a new Code of Balance. That new code should help us to be in better balance both within ourselves and in relationship to others. It should be based on the assumption that self and relationship have equal importance. A woman's work is not to make relationships work and to sustain others; it's to develop herself as a whole human being who can express a range of behavior, interest, and capacity. A new Code of Balance needs to define ways that women can feel good *in relationship,* not define *how* we must relate.

This new code will avoid telling us how we need to be and what we need to do to satisfy the requirements of others. The new code won't be shame-based. It will convey the belief that as women we are strong, powerful, and important. The new code will assume that we have the power and right to make choices based on the inherent value of our own inner convictions and feelings. The new code won't be rigidly defined or enforced—we each have the right to decide for ourselves what's good.

NEW GUIDELINES FOR GOODNESS

In counterpoint to the old Code of Goodness, we suggest new general principles that might help to change our assumptions about how we need to be to be good. These are principles that work better for us, principles that help us feel more balanced when we apply them. Part of your task is to define what principles will work better for you.

THE CODE OF BALANCE

BE COMFORTABLE: A woman in balance values feeling good more than looking good.

BE DIRECT: A woman in balance is honest about how she feels.

BE RESPONSIVE: A woman in balance empathizes with others.

BE NURTURING: A woman in balance empowers herself and others.

BE FIRM: A woman in balance sets limits.

REPLACING GOODNESS WITH BALANCE

Each of the principles of this new code counteracts a prevailing injunction of the old one. Let's look at the difference between goodness and balance by comparing the underlying principles of each.

• Rather than Be Attractive, a woman freed from the Goodness Code values *comfort*. She likes her body and feels accepting of how she looks. Her standard is to be comfortable in whatever setting she's dressing for. She can dress to please herself in ways that express her own tastes and sense of style. She can take care of her body, enjoy it and nurture it, and she is concerned to be healthy and physically fit. She can let herself have many kinds of sensually enjoyable experiences. She enjoys her sexuality. She values her inner life as much as her appearance and doesn't believe that she's only as good as she looks.

• Rather than being concerned to Be a Lady, a woman freed from the Goodness Code is *direct*. She can be honest about how she feels. She doesn't avoid her needs and feelings; rather she values and expresses them. When she has a problem, she talks about it. She expects to be heard and respected. She lets people know directly when they're violating her rights. She's free to express herself in physical or sexual activity as she chooses. She's controlled by her own internal sense of values rather than outside rules. She feels passionate and alive.

• Rather than being focused on others in a way that is Unselfish and of Service, a woman freed from the Code of Goodness is *responsive*. She can acknowledge other people's needs and feelings without being compelled to take care of them. Instead, she can empathize with and feel compassion for others and express it. She believes that it's important to say no when she truly doesn't want to give, and she recognizes that it's often not in another's best interests to take care of them. She can let other people give to her. She is a whole person with a range of feelings and interests who has needs and wants of her own. She gives because giving is a choice. She doesn't give in a way that ignores herself.

• Rather than feeling that she needs to Make Relationships Work, a woman freed from the Code of Goodness is *nurturing*. She relates to others in ways that support the growth of both her and the other person physically, emotionally, and spiritually. She focuses on enjoying relationships rather than working on them. She relates in ways that are mutually respectful, comforting, and self-enhancing. She assumes that both she and other people have a right to be separate as well as involved with each other. And since she assumes that two people are responsible for making a relationship right, she doesn't feel exclusively to blame when things go wrong.

• Instead of being Competent without Complaint, a woman freed from the Goodness Code is *firm*. She makes choices, sets priorities. She recognizes that she has limits and says no when expectations of her are unreasonable. She asks for help when she needs it, and she expects others to do their share. She chooses the work that most expresses her true talents, values, and needs. She achieves because she's working at something she loves to do, not to be loved, not because someone else expects it, and not because she'll feel bad if she doesn't. She knows that no one can do everything and do it well and that there is always a price to be paid for doing too much. She knows how to relax and have fun—she doesn't have to be perfect and she doesn't have to work to be good.

HOW ONE WOMAN LIVES BY THE NEW CODE

As uncomfortable as we may be with the old Code of Goodness, to think about change may seem overwhelming. We think of being good as who we are. But balance can be learned, and it can be achieved with practice. It may be simpler than it seems. To illustrate what it's like to feel a sense of balance in your life, this is a story about a hypothetical woman named Barbara.

Barbara is married and in her early forties. She and her husband, Tom, have two daughters, Abby and Linda, who are teenagers with the usual assortment of traumas and insecurities, particularly with their boyfriends. Barbara is an executive in a computer software firm. She has a busy and demanding schedule, but she loves her work. She is hypothetical because, unlike most of us, she manages to avoid most of the injunctions of the old Goodness Code. She's about to model three of the principles of the new one.

The Situation: Tom is about to go away on a business trip and the girls will be gone for a long weekend. It's been awhile since Barbara's had a vacation. She's been feeling irritable and a little depressed lately. The pressures at work have been more intense than usual. She decides to take advantage of the fact that Tom and the girls will be gone for a few days. She tells her boss that she won't be at work on Thursday or Friday. She looks forward to having the house to herself, she makes plans for lunch with a long-neglected friend, and she buys herself a good book to read. Four days of solitude stretch before her like a luxurious oasis in the midst of her hectic life. She begins to think she may even get back to work on a watercolor she started on her last vacation. She lets Tom and the girls know that, as of Wednesday night, she's "off duty" and asks that they respect her need for a break by getting themselves ready for their various trips and leaving the house in order when they go.

Enter Tom. It's Tuesday night. As he's getting ready for bed, with the plans for the rest of the week already outlined, he says to Barbara, "Gee, it's my mother's birthday this weekend and I haven't bought her a card or a present yet. I've got a terrible week—I won't be back from Chicago till late Sunday. She'll be hurt that we have no plans with her for the weekend."

To which the hypothetical Barbara responds: "I know you've been really pressured this week. It's frustrating to have so much to do and so little time to do it. Do you think you'll be able to pick something up before you get back? Maybe there'll be a gift shop at the airport. If not, your mother knows you care about her, and I'm sure she'll understand."

As the week proceeds, Barbara takes her time off as planned and is just sinking into a hot tub full of bubble bath with her book on Thursday night when the phone rings. It's Abby. "Mom, I'm in a terrible mess. I've only been here a few hours and already I'm in trouble. First of all, I forgot to bring money so I don't know how I can go out to the movie or roller skating with everybody else. Then the chaperone got mad because I skipped the afternoon workshop and was sitting outside talking to this new guy I just met, and he says if I break any more rules I have to come home. What am I going to do?"

Barbara says, "Abby, I really want to help you with this but you're going to have to give me the phone number and wait around there for about a half hour while I finish my bath."

"But, Mom, I want to go out, everybody's leaving."

"Sorry, honey, but if you want me to help, I need to finish what I'm doing first. What do you want to do?"

Abby decides to wait. Barbara finishes her bath and calls her back. "Now, Abby, what do you think you want to do about all of this?"

"Well, I've already missed one night out with my friends. I can't believe this is happening. I thought since you're not working you could drive up here in the morning with some money." (Abby is at a church retreat center two hours away.)

"Abby, that's a solution that tells me what to do. Tell me what *you're* going to do."

"Mom, I don't *know* what to do." (Abby is whining and getting more demanding.) "You're supposed to help me, what *can* I do?"

"Abby, honey, you're very upset, I know. You're probably embarrassed and frightened to be there without money. But I think you can think this through if you take a minute. You need to ask somebody there to help you out. A suggestion would be to ask your sister to help."

"Linda!" (Abby's shouting.) "*She* wouldn't give me money if her life depended on it. C'mon, Mom, be reasonable. I'll never ask her for anything!"

"Abby, you need to stop shouting if we're going to keep talking. OK?"

"Yes, OK."

"I think if you explained the problem to your sister, she might understand. Otherwise, you might ask a friend or one of the counselors that you know well. Bottom line, if you feel too embarrassed to ask anybody, you'll just have to stay in and skip the evening activities."

"So you won't bring me the money?"

"No, sorry, honey, I won't. This is a weekend I set aside for myself and I'm sticking to my plan. And, by the way, if you break any more rules and have to leave, you'll have to call Gram or Uncle Ted and spend the rest of the weekend there. I'm serious about being alone this weekend."

"I don't understand you, Mom. What's so important about being alone? You act like you hate all of us and just want to get rid of us."

"No, Abby, I don't hate you at all. This is just something that's important for me. I'm going to get off the phone now. I love you. I know you'll get this straightened out one way or the other. I really want you to have a good time. I'll see you Sunday night."

Barbara goes back to reading her book and manages to put Abby's problems out of her mind. She knows that her daughter will resolve things one way or the other. During the course of her time alone, Barbara does some thinking about why she's been feeling so irritable and down lately. She realizes that she's assumed too much of the burden for a new project at work. She resolves to tell her boss that she wants more help. And Abby's call reminds her that the two of them haven't been getting along well lately. She senses that Abby needs something from her and she isn't clear what it is. She decides to talk to Tom about it. And she decides to give Abby a little more attention to see if she can understand better what's happening in her daughter's life.

Barbara starts to feel better and more relaxed. She's glad she's decided on some new solutions for some of the problems facing her. On Sunday morning she calls to wish her mother-in-law a happy birthday and invites her for dinner the next weekend. Tom has sent flowers. Linda has sent a card and called, but Abby forgot. By afternoon, Barbara starts to miss Tom. She decides that she'll take him to dinner that evening without the girls, knowing that he likes dinners out with her alone. She cancels the airport limo so that she can pick him up herself.

THE ALTERNATIVES TO GOODNESS

It must be clear from her story that Barbara is a woman who feels self-assured and in charge of herself. She actively strives to be comfortable and to make herself feel good. She has few of those "voices" in her head that keep her constantly questioning her adequacy. Barbara is direct. She lets everyone know calmly and kindly exactly what she thinks and feels. And her story is one that models most powerfully the three principles of the new Code of Balance that provide clear alternatives to being too good in our relationships with others:

Be Responsive

Be Nurturing of Self and Others

Be Firm

LEARNING TO BE RESPONSIVE

Responsiveness, or responsivity, is a skill that can be practiced only where there is a basic assumption in a relationship that one person is not responsible for the other's feelings, needs, expectations, or tasks. It suggests the capacity to respond to the other person's feelings without reacting to them or referring them back to yourself. It means that you hear what the other person has to say as a statement about them and not about you, and that you make an effort to validate those feelings by reflecting that you understand them. Sometimes, it means responding with similar feelings of your own to let the other person know he or she is understood. Psychologists who are studying new approaches to understanding the ways that women relate to others call this skill empathy.[1] It's a skill that women are good at if they don't feel guilty, ashamed, or responsible for the other person's feelings.

In her story, the first thing that may have struck you was what Barbara didn't do. When Tom began talking about his problem with his mother's birthday, Barbara was not critical or reactive. She didn't say to Tom, "Well, you should have thought about that before you got so busy." Or, "I suppose you think I'm going to run around and buy a gift." She also didn't give Tom advice about how to handle the situation. She didn't get defensive, and she didn't justify her own decision to take a weekend off. She communicated that she assumed that Tom would take care of his mother's birthday himself.

Because she didn't live by the Make Relationships Work or the Be Unselfish injunctions, Barbara was able to be responsive to Tom. She acknowledged how he must feel and let him know that she was willing to talk with him about how he might solve his problem. She tried to be reassuring, though simply acknowledging his feeling would have been enough. She gave him something more because she wanted to. Notice that in being responsive, Barbara was communicating very clearly without having to say it that she in no way assumed that it was up to her to have to take care of Tom's problem, but that she still cared about him and his difficulty.

At this point, Tom might have done one of three things. If secretly he really expected Barbara to take the time to solve his problem, he might have gone on talking about being pressed for time, indirectly communicating that he wanted Barbara to shop for him. Barbara, being truly free of a sense of being responsible, would have picked up a hidden agenda and asked for clarification. "Tom, you seem to be asking me to shop for you. Is that true? If it is, I'd feel better if you just asked me directly." Or, "Tom, did you hope I could help out in some way? Were you hoping that I would make plans with your mother for her birthday?" Notice that Barbara didn't just "jump in" and offer. She can't decide if she's willing to do something for Tom unless he clarifies that he really would like her to do it. And it's up to him to make that clear.

The second possible outcome is for Tom to have said directly to Barbara, "Could you help me out by running to the store for me or by stopping by to see my mother?" In this scenario, Tom communicates that it's not his expectation that Barbara take care of his problem and that he respects her time and schedule. He asks directly for help. Barbara is free to say yes or no. If she says yes, doing for Tom is a choice, not an obligation or an assumed part of her role. It is not a statement to herself that he is more important than she is or that her sense of self is dependent on giving to him. It is a statement that she cares and chooses to help him out. It represents an agreement between two people who care about each other and have mutual needs for help at different times. It assumes that Barbara feels equally free to ask Tom for help when she needs it.

What is most important is that Barbara remains centered in herself, able to make decisions based on her own needs as well as Tom's. She's able to be responsive because she's not being too good. She's able to say no if she needs to. No is a valid response to a direct request. Tom may not like it, but Barbara has been clear about her own limits. He has a right to feel unhappy about it, and Barbara need not justify or defend her position any further. Finally, Tom may simply talk out his dilemma with Barbara and come up with his own solution. If he asks for her suggestions about how to handle his problem, it would be appropriate for her to offer them.

In these interactions between Barbara and Tom, Barbara is responsive and the symptoms of overdoing are absent. Barbara is not vaguely angry at Tom; she doesn't experience pressure or anxiety about not pleasing him; she doesn't get reactive or critical toward Tom because she suspects she "should" do something for Tom but really doesn't want to. She doesn't have "voices" in her head that tell her, "What a selfish and mean person I am for not helping him out. Probably he'll leave me for a woman who'll take better care of him." Or, "It's such a small thing, I should probably go ahead and take care of it just this once." Barbara doesn't have to feel angry or upset with herself *because she believes she's free to say no.* She believes it's acceptable and appropriate to stay focused on herself. She shares a relationship with Tom in which they both have needs and feelings. She doesn't become the caretaker of him at the expense of herself.

Because Barbara's hypothetical, she's able to be consistent. When Abby calls, rather than getting angry at her she's able to acknowledge how it must feel to Abby to have left without her money. She doesn't shame Abby for forgetting or for breaking a rule. She doesn't feel responsible for Abby's problem. In her role as Abby's parent, she tries to guide, advise, suggest, and communicate her confidence that Abby can handle her own problem. She doesn't feel embarrassed to know that Abby's broken the rules—she doesn't view Abby's behavior as a reflection on her—it's Abby's problem. Her feelings stay out of it and so do criticism, reactivity, overresponsibility.

As Barbara thinks about Abby, she senses a problem in their relationship with each other. Rather than blaming Abby for the problem, she decides, as the parent, to try to be more responsive to Abby so that she can understand Abby's feelings better. She takes appropriate responsibility for her job as a parent by deciding to be more responsive to her daughter.

Responsiveness is a skill that women can practice only if they're not feeling a sense of overconcern for the other person's feelings, needs, expectations, or tasks. If you're responsive, you acknowledge the other person's feelings and you convey the message that you understand how it feels to be them. You don't feel angry, critical, reactive, or defensive, and you don't hear what they have to say as a statement about you. If you sense a hidden expectation, you ask for clarification.

Believe it or not, it *feels good* to be responsive to another person. You end up feeling closer to them and closer to yourself. The process of being responsive requires that you be in touch with your own feelings, not reactive to theirs. It's out of your own experience that you respond to theirs. You don't feel the heavy weight of having to be good or to "do something" in response to their feelings. You don't feel ashamed *because of* their feelings. You feel more real to yourself. Since you really can never solve someone else's problem for them anyway, it feels good to be free of that burden and still let them know that you care.

LEARNING TO BE NURTURING OF SELF AND OTHERS

You may be about to object to the idea that nurturing is different from what women are normally expected to do. You would be both right and wrong in your objections. Women are viewed as inherently nurturing, yet it's never assumed that that nurturing should ever be focused on themselves. Moreover, our concepts of nurturing are very narrow and fail to acknowledge the full range of our capacity for caring behavior. We often associate nurturing only with the behavior of mothering.

Webster defines nurturing as "feeding, nourishing, maintaining, fostering. To nurture is to educate, to train with fostering care." Uncharacteristically, he provides a synonym for nurturing along with the definition. It is "to cherish"—to hold and treat as dear.[2]

To be nurturing is another antidote to being too good and too responsible. As a different premise for behavior in a relationship, nurturing can have many expressions. It can mean talking, it can mean listening. It can mean encouraging, supporting, validating feelings. It can mean teaching, helping, guiding. It can mean reassuring, sympathizing, soothing, comforting. It can mean letting someone know that you think they're special and important to you. Sometimes it can mean simply being with a person, being a supportive presence as they cope with a problem that is uniquely theirs. Basically it means communicating caring and concern. It means the act of cherishing and valuing and encouraging the separateness, experience, and growth of the other person.

One can't nurture from an empty well. If you have few resources, you can't give them away. When you nurture from a sense of fullness and choice, you feel renewed and more filled by giving. A deeper sense of connectedness is always renewing. But trying to give from an empty well leads to resentment and an even greater sense of depletion. It's as important to be nurtured as to nurture. As adults, we can learn to participate in mutually nurturing relationships.

Our hypothetical woman, Barbara, was highly skilled at nurturing, and that nurturing began with herself. When Barbara realized that she was feeling bad, her first response was to check out the possible ways that she could do something for herself and give herself time off. She almost instinctively knew that what she needed was some time to herself, to rest, restore her sense of self, and regroup so that she could deal with the challenges in her life more effectively. She knew she needed time away from pressure and responsibility, time away from giving to others, and time to be more in touch with her inner feelings.

Instead of getting angry at other people, calling herself bad for being needy, and making ten excuses why she couldn't possibly take time off, Barbara went about giving herself what she needed. She called a friend and renewed an important connection. She asked for and gave herself nurturing.

As she felt more centered and renewed, Barbara began to feel more nurturing toward Tom. She decided to pick him up at the airport herself and take him to dinner. She understood how drained and pressured he might be feeling, and she wanted to give him some time and attention. She made a similar decision to give Abby more of her time, more of her concern. As Barbara felt more renewed and nurtured, she naturally wanted to foster the well-being of the people she cared about.

Notice that being nurturing didn't mean actually "doing" anything for them, though at another time it might have. It didn't mean taking care of them so much as it meant taking care of the relationship *between* them. Tom and even Abby at age sixteen can do the things they need to get done for themselves. They can and must take care of their own problems. What they get from Barbara is the sense that she cares about how they're doing and with what level of well-being they lead their lives. She cares about their growth and their problems. She communicates that by what she does. What she does not do is try to take care of their lives and problems for them, nor does she try to direct or comment on how they do it for themselves.

One other thing that Barbara didn't do was to seek nurturing for herself from someone who probably couldn't give it to her right at that time. While we have to assume that the hypothetical Tom is also a caring and nurturing person, he was obviously under stress during the week that Barbara decided she wanted time out. Barbara made a positive decision that wouldn't be self-defeating in terms of the way she decided to meet her needs. She sought out a friend, knowing that contact would make her feel good. But if Barbara can never look to Tom for responsiveness and caring attention, then the relationship is out of balance because it's not mutual. If Tom takes no time to nurture his daughters, then Barbara is doing too much.

✳A GUIDE TO BEING NATURALLY NURTURING

If we get out of the trap of our own definitions, we see that all people, even children, have the capacity for nurturing. Yet as a society we don't value nurturing behavior, so it takes low priority in our cultural and emotional lives. It's probably the kind of behavior that's in shortest supply in our perfection-driven and achievement-driven world. Yet we all become diminished without it. Our environment suffers because we forget that even it needs ongoing nourishing. And, ironically, it's the behavior that is most critical to feeling good.

As adults, we suffer from getting and giving too little nurturing because we assume that we're too old to need it. And much of the responsibility for nurturing has been delegated to women because we are the biological bearers of children. Many men are never taught how to be nurturing. They may equally tend to deny a need to be nurtured, yet they indirectly expect it from women. Women may learn to deny their need for nurturing and to focus all their energies on giving it to others.

Nurturing makes us feel good because it comes naturally if we don't do things to block and constrict it. The biggest block to nurturing ourselves and allowing ourselves to be nurtured by others is the conviction that we don't deserve it. The biggest blocks to our nurturing others are to confuse nurturing with being responsible for them and to feel foolish if we let somebody know we care. Here are some dos and don'ts for allowing an openly mutual, nurturing relationship, followed by some random examples of nurturing things to do.

DOS

DO show it when you really care for someone, whether that person is a friend, a family member, a lover, a client, a student, a patient, a workmate, your child. Show it often and as much as you want.

DO follow the impulses that tell you what you need to give to or do for yourself.

DO what you enjoy doing and do as much of it as possible.

DO realize that the level of nurturing in our lives tends to balance out. One person may not give as much back, but some other may give more. Only when you feel that there is no positive or mutual exchange between you is a relationship a problem.

DO believe that you deserve to be happy and cared for and to have what you need.

DO give by letting others give to you.

DO learn to ask for what you need and to accept that at certain times other people may need to say no.

DO give in ways that enhance the growth, well-being, and separateness of others—people who are separate can be more deeply connected.

DO nurture children selflessly, but remember to restore yourself in your relationships with other adults.

DO realize that we live in a naturally nurturing environment and that only people with negative beliefs and uncaring behavior block the process.

DO acknowledge, respect, be clear about the needs of the other person. It's inappropriate to nurture if the other person doesn't need or want it.

DO be most conscientious about nurturing yourself when you feel bad or are under a greater than usual amount of stress.

DO remember that not only people but relationships, talents, projects, environments—anything alive and taking shape—needs nurturing and can be rewarding in return.

DO remember that the more you nurture and are nurtured, the more you'll feel good.

DON'TS

DON'T think about yourself in negative, punishing ways, and don't accept the negative definitions of others.

DON'T confuse nurturing with doing for and taking care of.

DON'T give if it's not a choice, but sometimes give more than you want to.

DON'T block out the awareness that people care about you.

DON'T look for caring from those who can't give it.

DON'T make excuses about why you can't give yourself time or attention —when you need it, do it.

DON'T stop people from giving to you, it doesn't obligate you to give back.

DON'T assume that there is a limit to how much nurturing you should have or should give.

DON'T expect people to give. If they want to give, it will flow naturally.

DON'T expect yourself to give. If you give and don't want to, you'll give trouble and not care.

NURTURING THINGS TO DO

- Bring your lover a cold drink on a hot day or a hot drink on a cold day.
- Send a card to a friend.
- Spend a day outdoors alone or with friends.
- Make your friend dinner for her birthday.
- When your friend calls in a crisis, be there to listen.
- Tell your sister how great you think she is.
- Turn on your favorite music while you cook dinner.
- Let somebody else cook your dinner.
- Buy yourself the new book you've been wanting to read and read it.
- Plan a celebration for your boss's birthday.
- Plan to spend a day alone with each of your kids.
- Take a few days' break from your work and don't think about anything.
- Give or get a massage.
- Remind yourself that you're a wonderful person.
- Ask somebody else to tell you what your five best qualities are.
- Plan a celebration for your own birthday.
- Reassure your friend that things will work out.
- Sit and do nothing and think about whatever comes into your mind.
- Give your lover something you know he or she wants or needs or would enjoy having.

- Talk to people and tell them your thoughts about life.
- Listen to people and really understand what they feel and think.
- Try to comfort someone in pain.
- Paint a painting, tell a story, sing a song.
- Keep a journal of your life.
- Call all of your friends and ask them how they are and really want to know—do the same with everyone in your family.

To be nurturing sometimes requires making hard choices. We have many competing demands on our time. Sometimes in order to nurture ourselves or someone or something else, we need to let some other job go. We have to believe that it's a priority to nurture, a priority to feel good.

This principle applies to our work lives as well as our personal ones. If we continually feel that we're not in a position to be giving at all because our work is too demanding and stressful, and if our work environment is not a nurturing one, then we're out of balance. We need to make adjustments that allow nurturing to be a principle that informs all of our relationships and activities. If we don't, we'll be trapped by goodness and end up feeling depleted and bad.

LEARNING TO BE FIRM

The final antidote to being too good and too responsible is to be firm. To be firm is to draw a boundary—it's to call people's attention to the fact that your separateness and your self are to be respected. It's a statement about what you will and won't accept and what you will and won't do. One can't be nurturing and responsive without being firm, because firmness protects you from giving to others at the expense of yourself. In therapy language, we call firmness "taking a position."

The woman trying hard to be good often fails to be firm. Because she feels and does too much for others, she fails to define what is or isn't acceptable to her. She simply takes on other people's burdens with no thought to her own limits or to what burdens are appropriately theirs. Because she can be easily persuaded to relax her boundaries and give in or do more if it's hinted that she's "bad," she's vulnerable to the abusive behavior of others. When a woman doesn't set limits, people feel free to impose inappropriate expectations on her. She fails to command their respect. In her need to have others see her as good, she fails to define herself.

Let's look at the way that Barbara took positions and the effect they had on her relationships. First, Barbara took a position with her boss—"I'm taking two days off." We don't know the context of her work environment. Many of us might assume that we're not free to be so self-defining when it comes to work. But we routinely assume that we're not free to do the things we need or want to do. Given that Barbara truly believed in her right to take time for herself, it's likely that she made the request to her boss in a way that let him know it was important to her. She must have conveyed that she felt she had a right to the time and that she'd accept the consequences of taking it. Undoubtedly, she communicated that she expected his respectful understanding of her request.

Barbara remained firm by not taking care of Tom's problem with his mother. She had blocked out time for herself. It was important. She stuck to her plan, even though it might have been "nice" of her to shop for Tom or to see her mother-in-law on her birthday. Barbara was unwilling to do those things, even though her decision might have made her unpopular with her husband and his mother. She decided that, in this case, her own needs came first.

And finally, when Abby called, Barbara was consistently but gently firm. What she communicated was, "Abby, I'm willing to help you and listen to you, but I want to finish what I'm doing first. If that's not OK with you, you can make other choices." "Abby, I'm not willing to talk to you if you're shouting." "Abby, I'm willing to help you and listen to your problem, but I'm not willing to solve it for you. It's your problem to solve, and I'm protecting the time I've taken for myself."

By now, a less hypothetical person than Barbara would be exhausted from the strain of being so consistently firm. In order to do a relatively minor thing for herself, Barbara has had to negotiate and set boundaries with almost every important person in her life. This is a testament to the centrality of a woman in both family and work life—it's a demonstration of the level of expectation that is routinely imposed on us without our even realizing it. There is nothing more certain to stir up a reaction than a woman who sets a boundary on giving and remains firm.

But let's look at the positive effects. Barbara reinforced her own respect for herself and in turn communicated that she expected respect from others. She took responsibility for her own needs and expected others to do the same. She was nurturing and responsive, but she knew her limits. When she didn't overwork to help Tom and Abby, they figured out solutions to their problems. Tom had to do his own nurturing of his relationship with his mother, and Abby had to learn that one skill in being independent is knowing how to ask for help.

Barbara didn't have to be rejecting or get angry in order to be firm about her position. When Abby accused her of "hating" everybody because of her decision to be alone, Barbara didn't get defensive. She recognized this as Abby's anger, Abby's problem, having nothing to do with her real feelings. She was able to be clear and reassuring in response. She didn't worry that maybe she did hate everybody, or that her desire for time alone was strange and abnormal. She didn't question herself. She stayed clear about what she wanted and what she was or wasn't willing to do. She was firm about what she would and wouldn't tolerate.

The effect of being firm, marking boundaries, taking positions in a relationship is to help everybody feel good. While there may be negative reactions at first if the behavior represents a change, ultimately a woman feels good because she's advocated for her right to focus on herself. Her self-esteem improves, and she feels strong and responsible rather than powerless and victimized. She also feels better because she gets what she needs. Her needs and the needs of her relationships are in balance.

Children feel good because knowing the rules and knowing the limits makes for a sense of safety and security. Seeing a parent set boundaries helps a child to know that parent more intimately, and it provides models for balance rather than models for "good" behavior. Our intimate partners feel better because although they may not get what they want, they take some pleasure in seeing us happy. They know that the more we are self-defining, the more we can be available to participate fully in a relationship. And they know that if we respect ourselves, we are equally likely to respect their separate needs and feelings.

Remember that Barbara is hypothetical. She's living easily by a new code because she was never trapped by the beliefs of the old one. For most of us, getting to balance and to feeling good will take some practice —it will require the work of change.

7

GOODNESS EQUALS RESPONSIBILITY

———— ✳ ————

Changing the Equation

A good friend of ours called one day to ask if either of us would write a review of her latest book. We had talked about it with her months earlier and without really saying yes, we led her to believe one of us would do it. But by the time she called, both of us were harried and overloaded with work of our own. What do you do when a very generous friend calls and asks a favor at precisely the time you're least able to do it? Do you just say yes and live with the awful pressure? Or do you say no and live with the guilt? What is the good and responsible response?

We both said no and we both suffered. Jo-Ann was too uneasy to end the conversation and asked for reassurance that our friend wasn't angry and still loved her. Claudia knew just the solution: Since she couldn't do the job herself, she'd help to find someone else who could. We were ashamed and guilty, and it only added to our misery that our friend responded by dramatically telling us that she was going to get off the phone and go hang herself in a closet.

We hung up on our "conference call" and met each other somewhat sheepishly in the waiting room between our offices. "What is going on with us," Jo-Ann said. "How could we be writing a book on giving up goodness and still feel so bad?"

Claudia knew that she had violated the Be Unselfish injunction of the Goodness Code; Jo-Ann thought she failed at the Be Competent, do-it-all rule. Having to say no plunged us into a "crisis of goodness." The crisis was a typical one. Either decision—to focus on our friend's need or on our own—had its consequences. If we'd written the review it would have disrupted our own work schedules. We might have been resentful and secretly angry that she'd asked. But saying no left us feeling bad. It made us wonder whether she'd care about us less. It made us vulnerable to being too good in some other way (looking for someone else to do the job) to make up for failing her in this one.

Goodness crises such as these plunge us headlong into a click, or trance-breaking, experience. The conflict between pleasing ourselves and pleasing someone else can be so painful that we're faced in an unavoidable way with the power of the rules of goodness. We had both been firm and said no—an important principle of the new Code of Balance. But we were still plagued by feelings of guilt. We were ashamed that we had to set a limit at all. Somehow our belief was that we should never say no to someone we cared for, someone who was generous with us. That belief kept us feeling bad.

Clearly we hadn't achieved the balance of the hypothetical Barbara in the previous chapter, who could say no easily and without fearing it would damage her relationships. And yet we weren't as driven by the Goodness Code as women like Lois or Ann or Carol in chapter 5. We managed to say no—we just felt bad about it. Like most women, we were caught somewhere in between balance and the extremes of being too good.

As it is for most women, our dilemma was to be able to Be Firm about our limits without feeling bad. Barbara's situation, after all, represented a whole series of crises in which she was challenged to focus on the needs of Tom, Abby, and her mother-in-law, after having made a clear decision to take care of her own. How do we achieve the sense of balance that Barbara had in which we're comfortable walking the tightrope of being good to others versus being good to ourselves, of being responsive to others rather than responsible for their needs?

MAKING THE CHOICE TO CHANGE

Goodness crises like this one challenge us to make the choice to change if we want to feel better about ourselves. Clearly we need to change our beliefs about goodness before our feelings change. But most of us are still behaving in ways that are too good. It's often only when we do the thing we don't really want to do, or when we don't do it and feel bad, that we realize that we're uncomfortable being trapped by the Code of Goodness.

The events that trigger our decision to change this state of affairs can be seemingly minor. Women frequently change as a result of some event that has motivated them to question their goodness patterns.

"I had just broken up with a man I'd been going with for a while. I was alone in my apartment and, for some reason, on this particular night, I found myself really just enjoying being alone. I was cooking Indian food for myself and reading a good book. He called and wanted to talk just as the onions were browning. I felt so strongly that I needed to just be alone and to do what I was doing. I said no and hung up, which was unusual. Somehow I realized that something had shifted for me—that I was really aware for the first time how important it was to me to stay focused on me. That whole relationship had been one where I always dropped everything if he wanted something. I was so desperate for his attention. I decided I wanted to sort out what makes me ignore myself so much."

Another woman knew that something was wrong, but she didn't know what—the crisis was less obvious.

"Susan ended our relationship without really letting me know that that's what she was doing. One day she announced she had met someone else. I just accepted it. I thought, well, this is probably for the best. But for months I walked around being depressed and just feeling this sense of heaviness. Somebody said to me one day, 'Aren't you angry at her? Didn't you ever tell her how you felt?' I've always thought, I can't do that—I can't tell somebody how mad I am, even if it's justified. It was even more complicated because I really still wanted her in my life as a friend. But part of me knew that getting mad was exactly what I needed to do. I started to think about all the times I don't tell people how I really feel."

Both of these women experienced pain or conflict that led to more awareness of the ways that they were being too good. When they say "I realized" or "I started to think about," they're saying that their goodness trance was broken and they realized they needed to find a new way to behave.

A goodness crisis is a crisis of *focus*—it challenges us to decide whether to be too good in the interest of someone else or to act responsibly for ourselves. "Should I talk to him when I really want to be alone?" "Maybe I won't let her know how I'm feeling because it might make her uncomfortable or angry back." The challenge is to change our beliefs about goodness so that we have different principles for directing our behavior. Changing our behavior and changing our beliefs will ultimately change how we feel about ourselves.

KNOWING HOW IT FEELS TO CHANGE

In the beginning, it may feel as painful to give up goodness as it does to be too good. We all need to learn our way through the process of change so that ultimately we can feel good rather than be good. Adopting a new Code of Balance takes time and emotional energy. Barbara's comfort with herself and her belief that it was valid to say no are qualities that we can aspire to—getting there can feel like being on an arduous journey, and some of us may feel tempted to just stay home.

But there is always a resolution and an end point to change, a point where we achieve a new level of comfort with ourselves. In thinking about changes she'd made in the past, one client tells this story:

"There was a time when I made a major change that stands out for me. When Don and I decided to get married, we thought we wanted a small intimate kind of wedding with just our closest friends there. My mother, though, wanted a large, fancy wedding—a gaudy, garish place, a lot of people, a big, flashy ceremony. At first I did the usual thing, I dragged Don around looking at places my mother would like. I told myself that I might as well do what I'd always done and please her. Don and I talked about it for months. I complained to my friends and anybody else who would listen. Finally I thought, no, I'm not going to do this. When I told her she said, 'How can you do this to me? I've waited for this day all of my life, this day only happens once in my life.' I just said quietly, 'Mom, your day already happened. This one is mine.'

"After that it was much easier to stop trying to please her. She never stopped being upset about it, but somehow it just never got to me in the same way again."

As we describe the work of change in this book, we'll be spending the most time helping you with the stages of the process that generally make women most uneasy. Feeling you can handle the rough spots will help you save your energy for the change itself. The process is always easier if you go through it with other people. While you can work on changing goodness patterns on your own, a therapy group, a support group, or a twelve-step program such as Alcoholics Anonymous or Al-Anon might make your work more effective and rewarding.

By now you're probably asking yourself, "What exactly are you asking me to do here anyway and why should I do it? Yes, I feel bad now and then but I have some questions about giving up 'being good.' I'm not so sure I want to be like Barbara. I like being good, and it feels good to be giving." As one woman put it, "If I'm not good, where will the good come from? I'm not willing not to do something if it means it won't get done." Another woman tells us, "Being good has gotten me where I am. Why should I change?"

These kinds of questions are valid. If you're not a person who feels bad often, if you rarely experience the symptoms of a goodness crisis, if feelings of shame rarely overtake you, then you shouldn't change. But the real issue these questions pose is "What exactly, concretely, does it mean to be too good? How will I know it when I'm doing it? How will I feel different if I change?"

To help you with a decision to change, we need to sharpen the definition of goodness, to name it more clearly, and to outline both the benefits of change and the consequences of staying the same.

WOMEN'S RESPONSIBILITY
TOO MUCH OF A GOOD THING

To be too responsible is another name for being too good. We could as easily have named the Goodness Code the Woman's Code of Responsibility. The underlying message of that code is that women are responsible for the well-being, pleasure, happiness, comfort, and success of the others in their lives. Whenever we feel that we're failing to meet this responsibility, a typical response is to try harder and do more. To fail is to feel shame.

What this means in terms of our feelings is that, in the situation with our friend who asked us a favor, for instance, we really felt *responsible for* her well-being. She had a job that needed to be done. We felt both responsible to do the job *and responsible for her feelings about it.* If she was disappointed or unhappy, it became our fault. Instead of being focused on our own feelings, our own limits, and reacting responsively but firmly to her direct request, her problem became our problem and her feelings became our problem. The boundary between her and us got blurred. We had become too good, too responsible.

The Goodness Code tends to create confusion about the difference between caring for and being responsible for. It's not being too good to care. Actually, the nurturing behavior suggested by the Code of Balance is powered by the same energy as responsibility. But when we nurture we stay focused on and centered in ourselves. We are *nurturing of* rather than *responsible for*. When we're too good, we take on the other person's problems, needs, and feelings as our own. And we tend to forget to take equal responsibility for ourselves. As one colleague puts it, "For most women, caring for themselves is a new thought. They never broaden the idea of being responsible to include themselves."

Our responsibility for others is too much of a good thing. When we're being too responsible, we may act as if we care more about another person's feelings than we do about our own. We may protect their feelings, advise them about their feelings, get depressed when they're depressed, anxious when they're anxious, upset when they're upset. We brood about them, get anxious *for* them. We work at making things right *for them*. In the process we forget to focus on ourselves. In fact, we sometimes focus on others as a way of avoiding focusing on ourselves.

When we're too responsible, we get both too involved with the other person's feelings and we become overly concerned with their reactions to us. We make them responsible for making us good. Our worth resides in their approval.

We've seen an example of this form of being too good in Carol's story in chapter 5. Carol assumed that if she just tried hard enough, her husband wouldn't be angry. If she just cooked the chicken right, kept the boys quiet, took care of everything, he would be approving and not angry. She took on his problem with anger as if it were her problem with not being good enough. She took too much responsibility for him and too little for herself. If she were responsible for herself she would have said to her husband, "Your violent behavior and your drinking aren't acceptable to me. You need to get help. If you don't, I'll have to leave because the boys and I aren't safe." But having learned the lessons of goodness so well, Carol would achieve this clarity only after much work at changing her automatic tendency to be too responsible.

Other forms of being too responsible are very concrete. We do jobs for someone that they could and should appropriately do for themselves. Then, while we're busy paying their taxes for them, we forget to pay our own parking tickets. Or we focus on how they pay the taxes, sometimes by commenting on it or by reminding them that it's time to do it. Whether we do it or comment on it, our focus is still on them and on their job.

Jo-Ann tells the story of one client who had an ongoing battle with her son about taking out the garbage. Garbage day would come around and she'd start reminding her son at breakfast that the garbage had to go. "Yeah, OK," he'd say. He'd leave for school without doing it. Luckily, the pickup was late. Her son would get home from school, and the same conversation would go on until the garbage truck could be heard pulling up the road. Her son would race out with the bags, but the driveway would end up lined with orange peels or egg shells. "I would never have believed them if anyone told me that I could spend fully two days a week obsessed about the garbage. My sole concern would be whether he was going to get it done. It would have been easier to just do it myself. Except that really it was his job and not mine, so I learned to just keep quiet about it and eventually he remembered the garbage himself."

Of course, it would have been possible for this mother to take out the garbage herself. But there would have been certain consequences to that choice. Her son would have failed to learn responsibility for himself. She would have been angry and felt like a failure as a mother. The question of who was responsible for what would continue to make their relationship troubled and unbalanced.

We're always free to choose how involved we want to get with other people and their problems. But we need to be aware that our choices always affect our own feelings, the other person's feelings, and the rules of interaction that develop between us.

The injunctions to be good and responsible may appear to be simple, even harmless, rules. But they have many profound and complex consequences. In the sense that they affect women, they have enormous impact on men and children as well. They are injunctions that influence all the important relationships and activities in our lives. They determine how we relate to our friends, lovers, parents, and children. They determine the significance and influence of work in our lives, and they shape our reactions to and involvement with the larger social issues of our time.

RECOGNIZING OVERRESPONSIBILITY

To decide if you're trapped by behaving in a way that's too responsible, these are some signals to look for:

- You protect people's feelings by not saying what's on your mind.
- You have a hard time saying no.
- You assume that you know what's going on in another person's mind and adjust your behavior accordingly.
- You feel guilty or angry if other people are upset.
- You feel that you can't ask for what you need or want.
- You feel guilty when you get angry.
- You feel it's up to you to make people happy by giving them your time or attention.
- You do things for other people that they could or should do for themselves.
- You feel that you should advise, direct, or comment on the way the other person does things.
- In any family, relationship, group, or work activity, you take on more than your fair share of the work.

A NOTE FROM CLAUDIA

When we talk about women's overresponsibility, remember that only one form of being too good actually involves doing too much. A woman may be too good and not lift a finger. The issue is how much she focuses on someone other than herself. I was acutely aware of this tendency in myself during the time we worked on this book.

At about the time we started planning the project, my mother became extremely ill with cancer. I live about five hours away from her and couldn't really be there often to do a great deal to help her. But she was on my mind much of the time. I felt like I carried her around with me mentally, and the weight of it often prevented me from getting on with my own life and work. I felt responsible to do something to make her feel better. I called her often and felt guilty when I didn't. I often felt that I should be doing more to take responsibility for her medical condition, even though she had a very good and involved relationship with her doctors. When she got depressed, I got depressed. I spent many an evening reading medical books on her condition, as if by reading enough I could cure it myself. It was a struggle to keep focused on writing and on the events that needed attention in my own life. Even though I wasn't doing anything in particular for her, I was being too good. None of it really helped her a bit, and when I thought about it, I was really responding more to my own anxiety than to her real needs. My anxiety covered my shame that I wasn't doing more.

Eventually, I realized that no amount of my being focused on her would help my mother to do the job that she alone could do: take responsibility for her own life, her own illness, and her potentially imminent death. I couldn't live for her, and neither could I die for her or keep her alive.

This recognition didn't change my outward behavior significantly, but it did free me from guilt and from taking on the emotional weight of my mother's life. It helped me to realize that we are two separate people who share a relationship—we can't both take on her feelings and problems. This allowed me to talk to her more about what was really going on for her and for me. In the midst of her illness, it became possible for me to talk to her about my life and to have her respond to my problems as much as we talked about hers. It didn't mean that I stopped feeling anxious, sad, and pained at her condition. But it did mean that we talked more about real issues and that I became freer to focus on my own life agenda. My decision to face my feelings and to think differently about how I was behaving helped me to get on with my life. Since I no longer felt so guilty, it helped the two of us to have a more meaningful relationship.

HOW BEING TOO GOOD HURTS
THE RESPONSIBILITY WHEEL

When we live by the injunctions of the Goodness Code, we set up rules in our relationships that are unbalanced, and we often end up doing too much. When we give ourselves the message that we're responsible *for* others, we're telling ourselves that we're of less value than them and we're telling them the same thing. When we're too responsible for others, we end up becoming *underresponsible* for ourselves.

We've already seen the effects of the message that we're of less value in chapters 4 and 5. That message creates shame. And when we feel shame, we end up doing more for others to try to feel better about ourselves. We get caught in a shame cycle and feel worse and worse as we do more and more. We also get angry.

If we're too responsible, like Ann in chapter 5, we tend to go to some other extreme both as a way of dealing with the pressure of goodness and as a way of trying to get back in balance. We may start drinking or eating too much. We may overwork and then go on a spending spree. We may diet rigidly and then eat a hot fudge sundae. Or we may go from being totally focused on our lover to paying no attention to him at all. We may overwork in one area and not take care of our physical health or of small details like getting the car serviced. The price we pay for this "rebellion response" is to feel bad, selfish, or crazy.

To help yourself to better visualize the ways that being too responsible keeps us cycling back and forth from being too good to feeling bad, look at the Responsibility Wheel on page 104.[1]

When we're at the top of this cycle, we're trying too hard to be good for others. In this position, we have the illusion of being in control, we take pride in our ability to be good. But inevitably, because we're ignoring our true feelings and needs, we make a slow progression from being too controlled to going out of control. We become underresponsible for ourselves. We go from feeling a false sense of pride in our goodness to feeling shame and worthlessness. We feel bad and we behave in ways that are hurtful to ourselves.

Feeling such shame, we make a progression back up the wheel, resorting to being too good and too controlled again to try to feel better. Pamela in chapter 4, for instance, did too much for her sister as a way of feeling better about losing her job and bingeing on pie.

The antidote to being at one extreme or the other is to be neither too responsible nor underresponsible. It's to stay in the middle zone of the wheel—balance. In this zone we feel neither shame nor false pride. We are neither too focused on others nor underfocused on ourselves. We feel a sense of self-worth and, rather than being too responsible and good, we live by the new code. We have relationships that are mutually respectful and nurturing. We are appropriately responsible for ourselves.

We stay in the zone of balance primarily by getting help and support from others. Women who become addicted use the twelve-step programs as a context for learning to think and behave differently. But all of us need to depend on others for feedback and support to stay balanced. Others often see us better than we see ourselves, and the caring, acceptance, and concern of others can help to counteract the negative messages of the Goodness Code. We can all benefit from being part of an informal support network or even a therapy group as we attempt to maintain balance in our lives.

The wheel helps to demonstrate that the work that we need to do as women is to reassess who is responsible for what so that our functioning

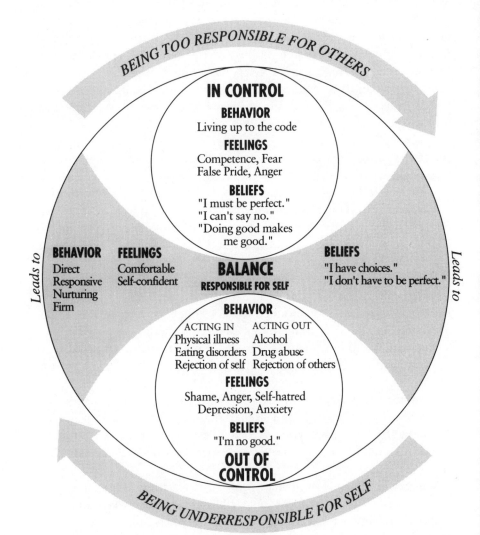

for others doesn't leave us out of balance with ourselves. If we find that we're angry, not meeting our own needs, and that we have to get out of control to relieve the pressures of being too good, that means that we're being too good for our own good.

Most important is that the way we define what is and is not our responsibility shapes our inner feelings on a day-to-day basis. If we are too responsible, we deprive ourselves of the balance and fullness of spirit that is critical to the ongoing development of our lives. We become fatigued, have no energy for or interest in our own inner life, and we lose a sense of joy, play, and passion. In our efforts to be perfect for others, we feel deprived and empty for ourselves.

TOO GOOD TO BE TRUE
THE MESSAGE OF WOMEN'S ANGER

Clearly, for a woman the consequences of being too good are often negative ones. But perhaps the most important of those consequences to think about is anger. As you'll note on the wheel, we often feel anger if we're being too good as well as anger when our own needs aren't met. As author and psychologist Harriet Goldhor Lerner says, "Anger is a signal and one worth listening to."[2] If one continually overdoes for others and never meets her own needs, inevitably she begins to develop a deep reservoir of rage. We often tell the people who come to us for therapy that in the heart of every overresponsible person is someone who deeply wants to be taken care of herself. The person who never feels cared for is an angry person.

"This weekend I gave my daughter a party," one woman told us. "I spent weeks planning it and I really put myself out for her. After it was over I started being depressed and just sad. I realized nobody would ever do that for me—nobody ever did. It was like I wanted somebody to give me what I was giving to her. I think I'm very angry at my mother for not being there in this way for me."

Ultimately anger always emerges in some way. It's either held in or it's acted out, sometimes, as in Ann's case, in the form of an addiction. More typically it's in the form of some smaller rebellion, some small way of going out of control, some small way of being less than responsible for ourselves.

As we see on the wheel, if anger is held in a woman may develop physical symptoms of stress such as headaches, chronic fatigue, irritability, stomach problems, or heart palpitations. (These stress symptoms are not to be confused with actual organic problems that often go undiagnosed in women because it's assumed by doctors that all women's problems are "emotional.") In the worst-case scenario, a woman becomes depressed and suffers chronic feelings of being worthless and powerless to affect her own happiness.

Our society tells women that rage and anger are unacceptable. We are supposed to overfunction and like it. Often we fear that our anger will be overwhelming and that if we express it, we'll "go crazy." We often fear that others can't "take it."

But when a woman denies her rage, she loses access to anger that would allow her to take a firm position about what she will and won't do. She turns her rage against herself rather than be firm with others. By failing to get angry directly, she protects those around her from the necessity of looking at their inappropriate expectations. A woman is sometimes so good, so emotionally overresponsible, that she is likely to define herself as bad rather than force an issue that will make others uncomfortable. Many women learn to be assertive only to end up feeling guilty and uncomfortable anyway. They may manage to change behavior, but they remain frozen in the belief that they don't deserve to get what they need and that they're bad for asking.

HOW TOO MUCH GOODNESS HURTS RELATIONSHIPS

When two people are in a relationship together and rules about goodness are unclear, they tend to adopt two rigid roles: the role of the overdoer and the role of the underdoer. If one person is too responsible, the other person becomes underresponsible. Just as doing too much has consequences for the overdoer, doing too little has certain emotional consequences for the other person as well. Achieving a balance where both people function in a way that's appropriately responsible and emotionally satisfying is quite a neat trick.

We've looked at some of the damage that being too good can cause for a woman herself, but what are the potential harmful effects for her partner or others in her family?

Here are some equations that describe problems that can evolve in the balance of a relationship if one person is too good and does too much. Our relationships usually reflect widely varied ranges of imbalance—no one behaves in extremes in all the areas outlined all of the time in every relationship. And no one sets out deliberately to maintain this kind of imbalance. Men often overdo in some of these areas as much as women.

WHAT HAPPENS WHEN ONE PERSON DOES MORE AND THE OTHER DOES LESS

- If one person is too adequate or too good, the other person becomes, or feels, inadequate and bad.
- If one person is always the competent one, the other person remains incompetent.
- If one person does all the work, the other person never learns how it's done and never gets the satisfaction of doing it.
- If one person is always emotionally available, the other person never learns to be alone or handle feelings alone.
- If one person automatically meets every need, the other person never learns to ask and comes to think that it's a right to have every need met.
- If one person always knows what's best, the other person never gets to decide.
- If one person always thinks of everything, the other person never stops to think.
- If one person always takes care of the other's happiness, the other person begins to think that only his happiness is important.
- If one person always "picks up the pieces," the other person never has to face the consequences of his own behavior and choices.
- If one person is always focused on the other, really only one person exists—there is no relationship.

The point of these equations is to suggest that *overresponsibility in one person always leads to underresponsibility in the other person. Being too good for your own good means being so overresponsible that the other people in your life take less and less responsibility for themselves.*

The bitter side of doing too much in some of the ways that the equations suggest is that the person you care for so much may end up feeling controlled, devalued, incompetent, and angry. His or her sense of self suffers just as much as yours.

And yet the person you focus on may communicate very ambivalent messages about your efforts. After all, who doesn't like to be given to and taken care of? How many of us women wouldn't enjoy having a wife or a personal secretary to take care of many of our responsibilities? If a person has been the object of a great deal of overfocus in the family that he came from, he may simply assume that he's entitled to more of the same without recognizing that one side of his personality is being constricted by learning not to take responsibility for himself.

People, adults and children, who become underresponsible because they are too much the focus of attention and overdoing feel some of the following feelings:

Guilt, frustration, inadequacy

A sense of being special yet of having no real power or control

Fear of losing the caretaker

Fear of trying anything on their own

Anger because they feel so dependent

A lack of confidence in their own abilities

As you may have noticed, some of these reactions to being too focused on are quite similar to the feelings of a woman who is too good. The common theme is that if you focus on someone else to excess, you become underresponsible for yourself, and if you are too much the focus of someone else's attention, you become underresponsible for yourself. Neither person in this equation thinks about what he or she feels, or acts on what he or she wants. The interaction becomes hopelessly muddled and both people end up feeling bad.

A fairly innocuous example of this muddle is the kind of interaction that we have all experienced around deciding what to do on a Saturday night.

She says, "What would you like to do tonight?" (Focused on him.)

He says, "I don't care, whatever you want." (Leaves the responsibility of deciding to her.)

She says (thinking he would like this), "Well, let's go to that war movie you mentioned awhile ago."

He says, "OK, whatever you want."

Outcome: They go to the movie. She hates it. He's distant and quiet the whole night. When they get home, she says to him, "Is anything wrong?" He says, "I could just as easily have stayed home and watched TV." She says, "Well, why didn't you say so?" He says, "I thought you wanted to go to the movies." Both had a miserable night and feel bad.

In this scenario, she is overresponsible, too good. She anticipates what she thinks he wants and tries to meet his need. He fails to take any responsibility for the evening, assuming that he has to please her. Subtly, he blames her because now he's missed his favorite TV program. Neither one is clear with themselves or one another about what they really want. Both end up angry, disappointed, and frustrated.

Let's look at how this scene might have worked out differently.

She says, "I've been thinking about what I'd like to do tonight. I really feel like getting out of the house. I thought I'd like to go see that new movie in town. Would that be OK with you?"

He says, "Well, I'd rather stay home and watch TV. I'm tired and I don't feel like going out."

She says, "I know we usually spend Saturday nights together, but I guess we have different needs tonight, and I really feel like I have to get out. Would it be upsetting to you if I go out myself or call a friend?"

He says, "Yeah, I don't like spending Saturday night alone."

She says, "I know, it'll feel bad to me to go out without you too. But to tell you the truth, I feel like I really need to do this, so I'm going to go ahead and go out anyway. I'll be home early and we can have the rest of the night together, and you're still welcome to change your mind and join me."

In this scene, she is responsible for her own needs, which happen to differ from her partner's. She's clear about what she needs, is direct about it, responds to and acknowledges his feelings about it, but nevertheless decides it's important to focus on herself in this particular situation. She is responsible for herself, not him.

He's left with a choice. He can focus on his own need to stay home or he can decide that needing to be home is less pressing than wanting her company. He can join her at the movie. On another night, she might decide her need is less pressing and choose to do what's important to him. The important difference between the two scenes is that in the second she's clear about her wants rather than assuming she needs to take care of his. Since she's so clear, he doesn't feel he needs to please her by going along. He can be clear as well. Both make choices about what they're willing and not willing to do.

ESCAPING THE TRAP OF RESPONSIBILITY
WHAT'S APPROPRIATE

The frustrating "responsibility game" that gets played out in most of our relationships speaks to the general lack of clarity in our society about the rules of responsibility. What does appropriate responsibility look like? Who is supposed to take care of what or whom?

If we're to define new rules that help us achieve balance in our relationships, we have to think differently about goodness. We propose this new rule:

> BE RESPONSIBLE FOR YOURSELF AND
> LET OTHERS TAKE RESPONSIBILITY FOR THEMSELVES

Another way of stating this would be to say:
Never do something for somebody else that they're capable of doing for themselves

Unless they ask you directly
Unless you honestly choose to
And so long as your doing it won't result in a negative consequence for them or you

This new rule is a revolutionary departure from the cloudy, unclear responsibility game that is played out in most relationships. It's a suggestion that can awaken women from the trance that has made us overly responsible for the physical and emotional needs of others and under-responsible for our own. Concretely, it means that we are not automatically in charge of everyone else's

feelings	difficulties at work
problems	jobs that they can't finish
needs	tasks they forgot to do
tasks	things they can't find
meals	negative situations
clothing	emotional pain
homework	important decisions
headaches	illnesses

THE BENEFITS OF GIVING UP GOODNESS

Because women have been trained to equate goodness and caring with being overly responsible, the suggestion that they give up a focus on others often plunges them into a great deal of confusion and pain. "If I'm not taking care of someone or something, who am I? If I can't do things for someone, how do they know I care? Isn't it unfeminine, unmotherly, selfish, not to take care of others?" In the words of one client: "Being good, competent, and a caretaker is who I am. Do I have to be less of who I am to be healthy?"

In fact, because of our socialization, we have a highly developed sensitivity to the emotional concerns and needs of those we relate to. We have a highly developed skill for bonding and nurturing. These qualities are strengths and resources for our entire culture—ones that need to be celebrated and enjoyed. They are qualities that need to be cultivated more in all of us.

But being uniquely equipped to do something is not the same as being required to do it for someone else's benefit. And because women *can* move comfortably within the emotional domain of life, they are not automatically responsible to inhabit and populate that domain for everyone else. For women, being emotionally skilled becomes confused with being responsible. The two are not the same.

What the client who questioned, "Do I have to give up who I am to be healthy?" was really questioning was: "How do I let people know I care? If I don't do for or take care of or focus on them, how will they know that I'm concerned about their welfare—that I love them? If I don't take care of them, of what use would I be? Why would they care about me?"

The new Code of Balance provides us with the alternatives to being too good. It suggests ways for being in relationship without losing the sense that our own needs and feelings are as important as the other person's. Barbara, by being responsive, nurturing, and firm, had achieved strong and balanced relationships with the people in her life. She also took care of herself. She had no doubt that saying no makes sense. She didn't bargain over who would do what—she made decisions and choices based on a sense of her own value. She's the kind of person who would probably think, "Well, if Tom gets mad or stops loving me because I won't go shopping for him, I guess he's got a problem. I'm a pretty nice person to have around."

Barbara's beliefs about herself were free of shaming messages. She thought things like:

- I'm not responsible for them. Tom and Abby need to handle things themselves.
- My needs are important.
- It's positive to do things that I enjoy.
- I'm good *and I enjoy* nurturing Tom and being responsive to my children.
- It's important for me not to get overwhelmed.
- I'm responsible for my own needs.
- It's appropriate to expect others to respect my needs and to do their share.

The most important benefit of giving up goodness is the growing sense you'll develop that you're cared about for who you are and not for what you do. As you learn to be direct, responsive, and nurturing rather than too good, you'll feel closer to the people in your life. They in turn will be less angry at you and more confident in their own capacity to handle their own lives. They'll feel freer to make their own choices and decisions.

As you begin to value your own feelings and needs more, you'll feel less shame, less guilt, less anger. As you give up the burdens of being too good and too focused on others, you'll be freer to focus on your own internal life. You'll become more creative, more relaxed, and you'll have more fun. You'll feel more balanced, you'll feel good. As you focus more on yourself, you'll want to take a look at the important areas of your life where you can begin to take better care of yourself.

Most importantly, you'll protect your right not to be devalued, treated disrespectfully, or abused. In any situation that holds the potential to be devaluing, whether it be in a relationship, a family, or a work situation, you'll advocate for and demand respect for yourself.

A NEW FOCUS FOR GOODNESS

If you make the decision to change, you'll be making different choices about some of the responsibilities in your life. Meeting your own needs in the following areas is important to feeling good. A new focus for goodness assumes that you're automatically responsible for:

- Enjoyable social relationships and friendships.
- Intimacy with those you choose to be close to
- Enjoyable (for you) sexual contact
- A satisfying relationship with your child(ren)
- A satisfying relationship with your parents and siblings
- Money to live on
- Solitude and time to yourself
- Fulfilling work
- Creative expression
- Physical well-being
- Fun and recreation
- Spiritual meaning
- Getting help with any of the above

Giving up goodness for others doesn't necessarily mean that we are taking responsibility for ourselves. As you become more responsible for yourself, you'll be able to answer yes to the following items. Check them and notice which ones you need to work on.

AUTONOMY READINESS: HOW TO TELL THAT YOU CAN BE RESPONSIBLE FOR YOURSELF

__I am or am capable of being fully self-supporting economically.

__I can manage the family finances and allocate our financial resources as appropriate.

__I am fully informed as to my own or the family's tax situation. If we use an accountant, I am part of those meetings.

__I can take care of or I can hire appropriate people to take care of all routine maintenance on my home and car.

__I can travel comfortably by myself, making reservations as appropriate and arranging transportation to airports, train or bus terminals.

__I can spend at least a weekend away from home by myself without having a friend along.

__I can attend a workshop or convention on my own and make conversation with people when I get there.

__I can and do plan and cook a good meal for myself when no one else is at home to cook for.

__I schedule and follow through on my own medical and dental care.

__I can make decisions about my next career step, seeking advice if necessary.

__I am in touch with some interests I would like to pursue. I have made at least an initial phone call to see about pursuing those interests. I can follow through on them as time permits.

__If there's a movie I want to see and no one is available to go with me, I can comfortably go to the movie by myself.

__Similarly, if I want to have a meal out, I can enjoy doing it alone if there's no one to be with.

__I know what activities and things make me feel better when I'm down, and I take responsibility for seeing that I do them.

__When I have an impulse to relax and stop working so hard, I can give myself permission to give in to it without feeling guilty.

__When I don't feel well, I can give myself a day off from work without excessive remorse.

__When I've become reactive, angry, or out of control in any way, I take responsibility for acknowledging my contribution to the problem with anyone I may have hurt. If I'm out of control with alcohol, a drug, or food, I take responsibility for participating in a twelve-step recovery program or some other form of treatment.

__If I suffer from depression or anxiety and seem unable to get over it, I take responsibility for getting professional therapeutic help.

__If I'm unhappy in my relationship, I share my concerns with my partner and express my willingness to look at and change my part of our interaction. I expect similar participation from him or her.

__If my life seems to need meaning, I take charge of exploring spiritual answers to life's questions through reading and attendance at spiritual gatherings. Or, I become involved with some form of political or social action.

__If I'm lonely, I take responsibility for calling people and becoming part of a community.

__If I'm hurt by a friend, I call that friend and explore the issues between us by being honest.

—I am emotionally honest with myself and with others.

—At work, I take responsibility for expecting and requiring that I am fairly compensated financially.

—Whenever I start to blame someone else or circumstances, I look to myself to see what contribution I've made to the problem I'm experiencing.

—I protect my physical well-being and, when I'm suffering from stress, I give myself time off and am otherwise good to myself.

—In sexual interactions I let my partner know what pleases me. In general, I don't have sex only to please someone else.

—Whenever I feel unfairly treated, I assert myself. For example, if a doctor rushes me through my examination and doesn't answer my questions, I say something.

—If I feel that someone has a hidden expectation of me, I take responsibility for asking them to clarify it rather than just feeling resentful.

—If others behave abusively toward me, I take appropriate steps to stop the abuse, and I leave the relationship, if necessary.

If you make the choice to give up goodness, you'll want to be more clear about what injunctions of the Goodness Code most dominate your thinking and your behavior in relationships. The next step in the process of change is to look back to our families to track the way our ideas about goodness and our good behavior patterns were formed and reinforced. It's important to understand how goodness rules developed because, as the old adage suggests, "Those who fail to learn from the mistakes of the past are doomed to repeat them."

8

FROM THE PAST INTO THE PRESENT

---- ✳ ----

Unraveling the Rules of Goodness

A goodness crisis tells the tale of the everyday influence of goodness injunctions in our lives. We struggle with conflicts about responsibility on a day-to-day basis. But to search for the roots of those conflicts, the original sources of our hypnotic trance, we need to look to our families. We need to look across the generations to our parents and their parents, and then to the new families that we create to tell us how the potion was mixed, how it was administered, and what mythical forces keep it alive. We carry our pasts with us into the present. The goodness code and its rules about responsibility may form the fabric of women's socialization, but our past and current relationships weave their thread in our individual lives.

TWO STORIES ABOUT GOODNESS
CLAUDIA GROWS UP AND JO-ANN SEARCHES FOR PEARLS IN OYSTERS

CLAUDIA

It's probably not surprising that some of the most vivid memories of my childhood are set in the kitchen. I think that probably it's in the kitchen, that symbolic place of feeding, caretaking, and nurturing, that the stage is set for the careers of all good women. We are either firmly rooted to it or trying to get out of it.

If your family is an Italian one like mine, kitchens take on even greater importance. There seems to be some unwritten rule that all family communication must take place in one. If one family member is in the kitchen, everyone else needs to be there too, including an odd assortment of neighbors, friends, aunts, uncles, and the family pet.

This particular kitchen memory happened when I was about nineteen years old. My mother and sister were in the background somewhere, but the scene took place between me and my father. I was home from college on a semester break. For some reason I was standing in front of the oven. My father, in rare authoritarian form, stood leaning against a counter, his arms crossed, shaking his head at me. "I wonder when you're going to grow up," was the statement that hit me, wounded me to the core. I thought I was quite grown up.

"What do you mean, Dad?" I asked, being careful to be sweet and unchallenging.

"Well," he said, "Joe Smith has a daughter about your age. She stays home. She helps him out, goes to the bank for him. She doesn't spend her time with her nose in books—she's more mature than you. I wish I could say I had a daughter who was grown up."

Truthfully, I can't remember how I responded to my father. Ultimately, my response took years to develop. But I do know that a powerful message remained indelibly fixed in my mind:

I am bad. I am not a good daughter. I am not "truly" a woman. In order to get my father's (a male's) approval and love, I need to want to do things for him, take care of him.

The problem was, I liked reading books. I didn't want to spend my time going to the bank for my father. This was a dilemma. At nineteen I was already a "bad" woman, and I hadn't even done anything wrong.

Of course, despite that conversation with my father I did go back to school and I kept reading books. But the message stayed with me, and over time it had a powerful effect on how I felt about myself. For many years I was to struggle with the conflict between wanting to do what I wanted for myself and the knowledge that I needed to focus on others if I was to be thought of as a "good" woman.

As in all families, the lessons taught in mine about being a woman were often contradictory and always complex. My mother had her own part to play in teaching me what it meant to be good. I struggled hard to please her because, unlike my father, she held up for me a vision of what I could become, and I thought she would love me if I achieved it.

In another vivid kitchen memory, I am sitting with my mother at the breakfast table on a Sunday morning. She is reading the society page of the local paper, and I am reading the *New York Times Book Review*. By now I have graduated from college and am planning to go on to graduate school. I keep thinking she must be pleased about this. Her constant message to me over the years has been, "Do something with yourself." This imperative had always been delivered to me as she, the housewife, endlessly cleaned the stove and wiped the kitchen counters. It had been our ritual after-dinner conversation during the years of my growing up. Sometimes as she was talking, she would cry with frustration and tell me she was upset because there was something she felt she wanted in her life, but she didn't know what it was.

My mother had seen to it that I had the best education that my family could afford and that our house had been stocked with as many books as my father's income would allow. This support of me had cost her dearly. My father had resented it.

So I was more than confused by this morning's breakfast conversation.

"Well, I see here that two more of your high school classmates are getting married. I wonder what's the matter with you." This from the woman who had told me repeatedly during my adolescence that there would be "time for boys" after I had finished my education.

My mother had changed the rules on me. What I did to be a good daughter would now not work to make me a good woman. Having encouraged me to have a life different from hers, my mother had become uneasy and now communicated clearly that it would be good if I did the safe and secure thing: get married. The other part of the problem was that I now had *her* dream and she was only too aware that my achieving it still left her empty. For my part, all that I could see was that trying hard to be the good daughter that my mother wanted had gotten me in trouble again. As you can probably guess, I was married before I finished graduate school.

JO-ANN

A number of years ago I worked as a family therapist on a community outreach team for the mental health center of a large medical school. CBS produced a documentary of our unit, featuring me doing family therapy for about a third of the program. Whether because of good therapy or good film editing, the segment made my work look brilliant.

My parents lived in a rural area with little access to New York City television, so I arranged to have a copy of the film shown to them during their Christmas visit. I thought it was a particularly nice present for my mother, who always told me I was her "star." She watched the program, and I will never forget her words when it was over. Her first comment was, "Is *that* what you wore?"

This story captures her basic belief about female achievement: It is won only at the price of dressing to please. Her own not inconsiderable achievement in becoming the first woman principal in one of the best school districts in her state she always attributed to "knowing how to get along with people" and dressing properly. To me, being good meant "being competent." To her, it meant "looking good." How sad, and how clear, that in minimizing her own achievement she had also to diminish mine.

My father's beliefs about women had less to do with achievement than with competition. I learned his beliefs on this subject in the endless hours that he and I battled it out over the chess board and the ping-pong table. Having been blessed with an only daughter and having lost his own father when he was fourteen, he may have sought to re-create a father-son rivalry that had been prematurely ended. But, in fact, I was a female so I heard his message to me as a lesson about how to be a good woman.

There were two messages that often conflicted with one another. The strongest, most overriding message was, "Do your best and play to win." He was fiercely competitive and gave no handicaps to his younger opponent. That I was fiercely competitive as well was attested to by a contract from my childhood that I happened to come across a few years ago. The contract, written when I was eight years old, reads: "If I do not beat Dad fair and square at chess within one year of this date, I vow to spend the rest of my life looking for pearls in oysters." I signed it! Never mind that some might say that that is exactly what I've done, because I never won the chess game. Nor did I win at ping-pong with him although I played tournament level table tennis in college. Not ever, not once. My level of frustration would grow so high that I would become infuriated. Then he would invoke the rule about good sportsmanship. And he would become enraged himself if I was upset about losing. When I think about it, it really was an archetypal male message to a female. Lose but with good grace. Don't embarrass me, the male, by disliking my dominance. Smile and keep playing the game.

The messages in these stories are all too clear. Once again, they demonstrate the ways that the injunctions to be good for women always conflict, and they demonstrate the power of family rules about goodness. Claudia's father saw women as caretakers, assuming that their appropriate focus was to be on relationships. But her mother, unhappy in that role, encouraged her to achieve, be competent, but not in a way that would ever leave out relationships.

Jo-Ann's mother did achieve but was convinced that a woman's achievement was dependent on her ability to Be Attractive—you are only as successful as your appearance. Jo-Ann's father encouraged her to achieve, be competent, compete, but to Be a Lady at the same time, always in control of her emotions. These were almost totally contradictory injunctions. His was a requirement that Jo-Ann be aggressively "male," a winner, and submissively "female," a good sport, at the same time.

While it's tempting to assume that we develop our sense of ourselves primarily in relationships with our mothers, it's clear to us that our father's beliefs and messages to us were equally powerful in transmitting the rules about how to be good women.

It's also true that these messages we heard were affected by many different anxieties that had been transmitted down the generations in our families. Our parents were not villains. In exploring the patterns in her family, Claudia learned that women who were intellectual often never married and seemed to be cut off from close contact with other family members. Her father feared loss. Claudia was the first of his children to go to college, and this change raised his fears of separation. "Care for me" really meant, "Don't go away."

Jo-Ann's parents had been married during the Depression. They tried to instill strength and competitiveness in her so that she'd be better prepared to face life's potential losses. But at the same time they felt it was important for her to be traditionally "feminine."

Some of our family messages were shaped by a generalized sense of "how women are" that our parents absorbed from the culture around them. But clearly other messages developed to satisfy needs and expectations that our parents had in response to their own family experiences. In other words, the legacy of rules handed down from our grandparents, as well as the many difficult life events our parents faced, were critical in shaping the dreams and expectations they had for us.

STORIES THAT HELP DEFINE GOODNESS

We tell these stories about ourselves from the perspective of many years of exploration of the family patterns that shaped us. They are stories that we tell about ourselves. But more important are the stories that our families tell us *about* ourselves and about the significant events of family life.[1] Just as certain images of women's roles are transmitted in the media through books, movies, television shows, and commercial interruptions, all families tell favorite stories that convey just as powerfully the rules we are meant to live by. Some of these stories become family "myths" that lend a special significance or meaning to certain people or events. They have the power to put us or keep us in trance.

There is, for instance, the "myth" of Jo-Ann as the family "star," a major theme developed in several family stories that all point to her specialness. Jo-Ann wasn't born until eight years after her parents married. She was premature but a "perfect baby." And she was born during the hurricane of 1938. It's said that as her father drove her mother to the hospital, at the height of the hurricane, he could see trees being uprooted by winds whenever he glanced in his rear-view mirror. Her father also supposedly gave up his bad Bohemian temper on the day of her birth, allegedly renouncing anger and trying for perfection from the day she was born. And, at Jo-Ann's christening, when the priest kept the family waiting outside the church in the cold, so the story goes, Jo-Ann's mother and father were so angry that the baby was kept waiting that they left the Catholic Church.

Mythological family stories like these confer a magical specialness, but they create a burden, an overstated responsibility as well. If the baby Jo-Ann was so powerful as to be such a force for change, it's easy to see how she might later accept the Be Competent without Complaint injunction as her destiny. After all, someone so powerful and so special should be able always to do it all, without limitation and without feeling overwhelmed. In the myth, Jo-Ann was a "stormy" person who had the power to make other people change. What her cumulative family stories didn't convey was any sense that she had the power or permission to live her own life.

Often the underlying effect of a family myth is to warn us about what happens to women who don't live up to the Goodness Code. "If you're not a good woman, you'll end up unmarried, writing unpublishable poetry, with only seventeen cats for company like Great-Aunt Meredith."

Think about who the mythic characters were in your family drama. Were they men or women or both? The circumstances surrounding a birth or a death often provide the stuff of myth. Was your brother born just as two white birds flew by? Who was made to seem larger than life by the stories told about them? Perhaps your family has a "black sheep" or an eccentric uncle, a "rebel" or a "sensitive, artistic type" who becomes the subject of much family mythology.

What was the mythology about? Good deeds or bad? Great adventure that came to a bad end, or good choices that determined your family's fortune? What were the roles of women and men in your family mythology? Did women spring from the head of men, like Athena from the head of Zeus? Did one sex corrupt the other, like Eve and Adam?

Maybe you've been told that your great-grandmother Silsby tried to run away from home at seventeen but only had enough money to get to the railroad depot in Kansas City, where she was rescued from hanging around with the bums in the railroad yard by Great-Grandfather Harry, who just happened by. What would the message about women be?

Myths implicitly idealize certain personality traits and demand conformity to a "story" of who we are. They constrain us from writing a story of our own. Culturally, larger myths of motherhood, femininity, and "goodness" prevail. Our task in our families is to differentiate who we really are from the "story" that tells us who to be.

THE TIES THAT BIND

Stories and myths convey indirect and metaphorical messages about goodness. Family rituals carry the messages further.[2] Celebrations of holidays and other special events often become statements about who is responsible for what. In most cases they function to reinforce a woman's position as the sustainer of family relationships. Chances are it was always Great-Grandmother's job to cook the holiday meal, to clean it up, and to plan the whole affair from the beginning. It was probably Great-Grandfather Harry's job to string the lights on the Christmas tree. The breakdown of roles and functions at ritual times tells us a great deal about family expectations of men and women. We get further reinforcement for being good by fulfilling these expectations when we go on to form new families of our own.

While the rituals of the families that we come from may tell us who is responsible for *what,* there is nothing so powerful as the magnetic pull of emotional loyalties in those families in shaping our sense of who is responsible for *whom.* By loyalty, we're referring to a "special tie" to someone in our family of origin.

This loyalty dilemma that occurs for most, if not all, of us at some point in our family relationships is called an emotional "triangle."[3] It means that something about the way we relate to one person in a family affects our relationship with someone else. The closer we move to one person, the more the other is left out. The more we take care of or focus on one relationship, the less we participate in another.

We learn the lessons of emotional triangles in our childhood families. But whenever three or more people relate to one another in any context, the potential for a triangle exists. When we feel ourselves being drawn to a special or more intense focus on one person that makes us uncomfortable or in conflict with another, we are part of an emotional triangle.

As an example of a childhood loyalty that gets carried on into adulthood, let's say your brother has proposed selling the family's summer house in Vermont. Your first reaction might be to call your father to see how he feels about the proposal. You're concerned because you know that it was his father's house and he gets depressed every time the subject comes up. You know whose side you're on in the dispute. You might even feel special because you're the one who understands your father best and you're the one who looks out for his interests.

But the problem is, your tie to your father often gets in the way of your relationship with your brother. Your brother may get angry that you support your father and not him, that you talk to your father about him. If you want to spend some time with your brother, taking him out alone for his birthday, for instance, you might feel a little funny leaving your father out. Special loyalties also convey special responsibilities.

LOYALTIES START YOUNG

Loyalty triangles aren't problematic if they're not very intense. It's normal to be more attached to or more fond of some family members or some relationships than others. A triangle becomes problematic only when it becomes so rigid that relating to one person strongly affects the way we relate to someone else.

Some of the most intense forms of triangles begin in families between parents and young children. If they develop in an extreme way, these triangles can be damaging because they distort our sense of what is good and they call on us to be overly responsible for another at the expense of defining ourselves. A triangle defines what it means to be "good" because loyalty is yet another word for goodness.

Triangles often occur between parents and children when a "ledger of justice" needs balancing. In other words, if either one of our parents was deprived of some important developmental need in childhood, and if they don't feel that need is met by their marital relationship, our parent may look to us or to our siblings to make up for the missing emotional contact. In effect, our parent says, "You be my missing mother or my missing father." This parent develops a close bond with us that leaves the other parent and perhaps our other siblings on the outside of the relationship. Eventually, all the relationships between other family members become unbalanced as a result.

Loyalty triangles are ways of asking a child to take too much responsibility, to be too good. Having too close a tie with one family member puts pressure on us that prevents our relating easily to all the other important people in our lives. A triangle creates a bond that constricts us rather than enhancing our sense that we're free to be engaged with many other people and activities. For instance, divorce between our parents may heighten the loyalty expected of us. Certainly, it heightens our conflicts about which parent to be good to.

Recently, we've seen the enormous growth of the movements recognizing the special needs of children from alcoholic or other types of dysfunctional families. These movements reflect an awareness of the damage that can occur when family loyalties become distorted. Those distortions result in children not having their developmental needs met. Children aren't allowed to be children because they're asked to be loyal to or responsible for their adult parent in inappropriate ways. As therapist Lorie Dwinell describes it, the parent's prevailing attitude toward the child is, "Oh, good, you're here, now you can take care of me."[4]

Dysfunctional families put these pressures on children to an extreme degree. But it's important to remember that the woman's Code of Goodness predisposes all women to becoming both too good and overly loyal to parents at an early age. As women, the types of triangles we find ourselves in take on special meaning because of the dictates of goodness that surround women's roles in general. We are looked to, even as young children, to be nurturing caretakers. Perhaps because of our common bond of womanhood, most of us feel an intense, if unacknowledged, loyalty to our mothers. The loyalty pull may result in a relationship that's full of conflict, or it may result in one in which we feel a deep sense of obligation to care for our mother's feelings.

Lois's relationship with her alcoholic father, described in chapter 5, is a good example of a loyalty triangle that was extremely dysfunctional. Lois had been put in the position of caring for her father, and as an adult she felt that she "didn't exist" separately from her relationship with a man. As a child she came to feel intensely responsible for her father. Her mother was on the outside of this relationship. Because Lois had to have her father's interests dominate, she was deprived of a relationship with her mother. She was left to feel that her mother was to blame for her father's problems. Those problems between her parents were never handled by the two of them. Lois became a surrogate wife whose presence in the triangle helped them to avoid each other. Because her mother had to struggle with many other problems, Lois was never really parented by either her mother or her father. The triangle kept all the family relationships off balance, and Lois went into her adult life feeling that she had to behave in the same loyal way to the man she married.

It's from triangular loyalty interactions that we learn many of the lessons of being too good and responsible in our families. We become our parent's parent, focusing on one relationship rather than receiving the support and nurturing that might be available from separate relationships with all our family members. We don't learn that our needs can be met because our role, though it may be subtle, is to meet the other person's need. We don't learn to handle our own feelings because we're focused on theirs. And eventually we learn not to ask for what we need, even assuming that we could identify it. The problem with trying to take care of a parent when we're a child is that we truly don't have the resources to do it. We are bound to fail at the job, feel shame, and respond by trying harder to be good.

If, as children, we learn to be a part of loyalty triangles in our family, we'll set up similar rules in our adult relationships. An ongoing loyalty triangle with one parent may even get in the way of an eventual relationship with a husband or partner. We may find ourselves unable to be fully involved emotionally with our new partner because our loyalty to our parent demands that we please them first. Unproductive patterns of goodness will keep developing down the generations.

As an adult, our goal is to stay out of loyalty triangles, to have separate person-to-person relationships with each of the important people in our lives. Our relationship with one person shouldn't affect or have bearing on our relationship with another. For this to happen, we need to learn to give up goodness, to give up those loyal behaviors and feelings that keep us tied to the expectations of the other person rather than focused on our own goals. Some of the most important work we can do in the interest of giving up goodness is to shift these loyalty relationships in the families that we came from.

ASSESSING YOUR LOYALTIES

One of the most common forms of loyalty triangles that occurs in families is one in which a daughter has an intense bond with her mother and a father is on the outside. For example, you may have had the experience of calling home, saying hello to your father, who answers the phone, and having him say, before you've said three words to him, "Just a minute, I'll get your mother." He simply assumes, along with everyone else, that he is in the outside position.

As a way of assessing how intense this triangle may be in your family, try the following exercise. If you find that the exercise feels too threatening, it's probably an indicator that this triangle is a strong one for you. Try the exercise in fantasy instead. Even thinking about making this shift will give you an idea of the power of emotional loyalties.

✳TRIANGLE EXERCISE

Imagine that you call home and your father answers. When he says, "Just a minute, I'll get your mother," try in response, "No, Dad, don't get Mother. I called to talk with you." Have a conversation with him in which you don't mention your mother. Then hang up.

✳STEPS TOWARD BREAKING TRIANGLES

You may find the following suggestions about assessing and taking small steps toward breaking triangles difficult and anxiety-producing. Most people can make these moves only with the help of a family therapist who can "coach"[5] them through the process. But beginning to understand some of the forms triangles take can help you to recognize their power as well as some of the goodness patterns that may be affecting you. Try making the suggested changes only if you feel courageous and ready to do so.

You may be part of an emotional triangle with a parent, family member, or other significant person in your life if:

• You find you are consciously on one person's side in their argument with someone else. Try talking to the other person to understand their side as well. Try not to take sides if it's important to you to have a separate relationship with both people.

• You know a lot about one side of your family and almost nothing about the other. Try finding out more about the "forgotten" part of your family.

• You are the recipient of secret information from one family member about another or are the keeper of that person's family secret. Try not agreeing to hold secrets.

• You feel tense whenever you and two other people in conflict with one another are together. For instance, it's hard to be in the same room with your partner and your mother. Try not to take care of one to the exclusion of the other. Relate similarly to both. Let them work out their problems with each other. Get out of the middle.

• You feel blocked from having a relationship with one person in your family because it would affect your relationship with another. For instance, if your mother is mad at your aunt, you feel you can't call your aunt because your mother would be upset with you. Try talking with your mother about this and try calling your aunt. Your relationship with your aunt is separate from yours with your mother.

• You realize that you talk with somebody else about the problem you have with your partner and you don't talk about it with him. This means that you try to work out the issue by leaving your partner out. Try discussing your feelings directly with your partner, preferably before or at least as well as getting advice from others.

• You're unhappy with your partner and you find yourself having a secret affair with someone else. This is a kind of disloyalty triangle. Try working out your issues with your partner openly and then make decisions about how you want to relate on an intimate basis with other people. Try not to keep secrets—they maintain triangles and triangles work to everyone's harm.

ON DOWN THE GENERATIONS

Our ways of being loyal and good in relationships in our family get carried with us into our current relationships. In chapter 2, Mary's nursery school report described her, at age four, as already a perfect "lady."

"I've always known I was a 'good girl.' I think I was trying to be good mainly for my mother. She always seemed to take such delight whenever I was particularly polite and nice. My father worked long hours so he was never there much. It didn't really seem to matter whether I pleased him. It was my mother who was the center of my world."

Clearly, Mary was part of an emotional triangle in which she was loyal to her mother while her father remained in a distant position. She learned certain rules about how to be good in a relationship from being a part of this triangle. Describing how she expressed her goodness as an adult, Mary said that she had a major problem with "peanut buttering." Her husband likes smooth peanut butter and she likes chunky style. Of course, she always buys smooth. The couple have developed the phrase "peanut buttering" to tag behavior of hers that's too good for him at her expense, behavior that expresses her need to gain approval by still being the good little girl she had already learned to be by age four.

An even more difficult dilemma comes up for Mary whenever there's a conflict between an expectation from her mother and one from her husband. The old loyalty tie to her mother still exerts its powerful influence. Mary finds it difficult to say no to either her mother or her husband; when their needs conflict, it's hard for her to shift her loyalty to her husband, where it rightfully now belongs. And in an attempt to please both her mother and her husband, Mary often ignores her own needs.

Like Mary, if we've been too good as children, we carry overly loyal behavior patterns with us as we move into relationships with husbands, lovers, and others, sometimes with disastrous results. If we've been in the position of "parenting" a parent, we also often carry the sad legacy of having had our needs neglected. Those feelings can burden our new relationships with unbalanced rules and expectations. We may keep on being too good. But often a hidden anger emerges toward our partner. We may unconsciously expect our current relationships to meet the needs our childhood ones didn't, at the same time that we try loyally to meet every need of our current partner or spouse. Confusion and conflict may be the result.

HOW RULES DEVELOP IN CURRENT RELATIONSHIPS

From our families we inherit a legacy of rituals, rules, and beliefs that form the basis for our behavior in the present. The dictates of the Goodness Code are reinforced in us in a way that's unique to our particular family style. We learn what behaviors of ours are rewarded by approval and which aren't, and we learn what loyalty patterns work to make us feel loved. The myths of our childhood shape our adulthood in deep and unconscious ways.

While not every relational rule we inherit from our families is a mistake, those that reinforce our tendency to be too good limit our choices and opportunities as adults. The rules reflect hypnotic legacies from the past, and they often reflect and reinforce the Goodness Code.

Allegiance to the rules of loyalty and goodness is behavior that gets played out in relationship to others. It's behavior that results in a mutually created set of rules, interactions, and expectations that evolve *between* two or more people. We call these mutually reinforcing interactional patterns a relationship *system*.

To think of a relationship as a system describes the ways that the behavior of one person always affects and is affected by the behavior of another. One person behaves in ways that either encourage or discourage the other's actions. The ultimate effect of this back-and-forth process is to create "rules" that define how people involved with one another are permitted to interact.

For example, if the first time you and your new friend meet for lunch she keeps you waiting twenty minutes with no good reason, you have a choice about how to handle your reaction. And your choice will help to create the rules of your relationship. She may or may not offer an explanation of her lateness. You may or may not let her know that you're upset at being kept waiting. If she offers no explanation and you say nothing about your annoyance, you've begun to create the rule together that it's acceptable for her to keep you waiting. The rule makes a subtle statement that she's more important than you and that you agree to that premise by not challenging it. Gradually that rule might creep into many other interactions in your relationship.

Most of us have little awareness of how we've created the rules in our relationships. We're not aware of the ways that we're automatically affected by the Goodness Code and by the reactions of the people we relate to. It's hard for us to see that a relationship may feel difficult and conflicted because of a series of small behaviors and choices that have created rules that don't really work.

In the situation above, for instance, you might feel that it was being "good" or polite not to make an issue out of lateness early in a new friendship. You might have learned that women in your family generally didn't challenge other people's behavior and always accommodated to other people's schedules. You might tell yourself that you could give your friend another chance. When another chance resulted in some similar offense, you might begin to assume that something was wrong with your own expectations.

Unconsciously affected by the injunctions of goodness, you'd set up a pattern of rules in your friendship that were unbalanced. In response to that imbalance, eventually you'd feel angry, disappointed, and distant from your friend. Ultimately you might feel that "cutting off," becoming emotionally distant or even ending the relationship, was your only solution to resolving the problem.

The negative effects of being too good are most apparent and most painful in our relationships with other people. So it's the rules of our relationships that most need to change if we're to overcome being too good. Once we've begun to understand the legacies and emotional loyalties that we've inherited from our families, we can better pinpoint the ways that we're too responsible for others. And we can begin to look at the problematic goodness rules that we've established in our current relationships.

9

ELLEN AND BRAD

——— ✳ ———

Shifting the Balance

Ellen felt the knot in her stomach tighten the minute she found out she'd been hired as a photographer for the Mexican fieldwork trip. Actually, the knot had been there for a couple of weeks since she'd learned that she was in the running for the job. She had decided not to tell her lover, Brad, until she knew for sure whether she'd be hired. But she was nervous for the entire time anticipating his reaction. She knew he sensed that something was wrong because he'd been complaining that she wasn't talking to him and that she was less affectionate. They had a couple of fights. She had reacted one time because he acted suspicious and questioned her about a phone call. The other incident was what they called a "kitchen sink" fight. In other words, it was about everything and nothing.

The day she went home to tell Brad she got the job marked a special event for the two of them. It was the anniversary of their moving in together. They had made a ritual of celebrating with a romantic dinner.

Ellen walked in late from the university. Brad had been preparing the dinner.

"Hungry?" Brad calls from the kitchen.

"Smells wonderful," says Ellen.

"Remember what day this is?" asks Brad.

"It's the day I got hired to go to Mexico as a photographer," says Ellen.

"You what?" Brad leaves the kitchen and comes into the living room.

"Mexico. I'm going to Mexico for five weeks . . . Don't get that look."

"What look? What are you talking about? Mexico for five weeks?"

Brad's jaw tightens in a way that Ellen knows all too well. She braces herself. "Don't start."

"When were you going to tell me? When is it anyhow?"

"In three months—July first."

"July first! That's when we planned to go backpacking!" Brad was furious.

"No, we didn't plan. *You* planned. I don't remember ever being asked about it. You just assumed and made the plans for the two of us, as usual."

"Wait a minute, hold on, Ellen. You like backpacking."

"That's right. Tell me what I feel. Tell me what I like." Ellen, already tense when she walked in the door, was getting more and more angry.

Brad was dumbfounded. "You didn't want to go? What am I? A mind reader? I was supposed to guess?"

"I did tell you. But you didn't listen. There's no use telling you."

"So you're going to go off to Mexico just like that. That's great. What am I supposed to do, feed the cat and walk the dog while you're gone? Oh, and maybe pay the bills too?"

"I'm getting paid for the job," said Ellen coldly.

"That's supposed to make it OK? Look, it's not that I mind, it's just that you're springing it on me."

"I just found out today. Sorry. How much notice do I have to give? Don't tell me you don't mind. You mind my doing anything you can't control."

"Ellen, stop it! What the hell is this about?"

"If you cared about me, Brad, you'd be happy that this is the biggest dig in North America and I'm going to be the photographer."

Brad tries to control his upset. "OK, so tell me about it. I do care about you. I'm sorry I didn't ask. Tell me about it."

"I don't feel like talking about it."

"Listen, I'm sorry. It's just that it feels like you don't care about me, about us."

Ellen leaves the room. Brad follows her. She turns on the television. He turns it off. The fight escalates into a screaming match. Finally, Ellen goes into the guest room. Exhausted from fighting, she cries herself to sleep. In the morning she calls for an emergency therapy session to talk about leaving Brad.

SORTING OUT THE RULES

Ellen had been working in therapy for several months to be able to shift her focus away from Brad and more to her own goals and interests. But the confrontation about Mexico came up before she fully understood the impact that a change like this would have on their relationship.

"I thought I loved Brad," she said. "But I've gotten to feel so smothered I can barely breathe."

Brad called for a therapy session too. The fight had been as upsetting to him. He said he was glad that Ellen was pursuing her interest in archaeology and that she was involved in a graduate course to study it. But the prospect of a month's separation really upset him.

"Besides," Brad said, "I've looked forward to our backpacking trip together in the Tetons for months."

It was clear that he was bitterly disappointed and didn't want Ellen to take the job.

Ellen, on the other hand, felt that Brad was undermining her efforts to be more involved with her own interests. Their fight had brought a lot of issues to the surface. Ellen hadn't even realized she had feelings about many things, like the backpacking trip, that had suddenly become major conflicts.

Ellen and Brad had reached an impasse. The rules they had established between them were making this change painful and difficult.

"I never do things separately from him," Ellen said. "I don't know why he has to get so bent out of shape about this. He could even fly down for a weekend. That is, that would have been OK with me until we had the fight. Now I'll be damned if I want him horning in. When he had his passion for theater and got a play produced I went to every rehearsal. It was OK for him to have separate interests, and I supported it. But it doesn't seem to work the other way. I hate it that he's giving me such a hard time about this. I don't know how I could be with somebody who cares so little about my life. Everything is him." Then she started to cry. "But I hate to hurt him."

As Ellen talked, it was clear that she and Brad had created some unspoken rules in their relationship. One rule was about togetherness versus separateness. Briefly stated, Ellen believed that "Brad gets to decide how much separateness we have." The way the rule was unconsciously written, Ellen interpreted it to mean that separateness for Brad was acceptable and that she should support his interests by not making an issue of hers. He could be separate but she couldn't, or at least not in a way that made him uncomfortable. She had never really talked with him about her assumption. The trip to Mexico challenged a rule that had never been directly discussed or agreed to.

The separateness rule had evolved, as rules do, in the course of many small decisions made over time in their relationship. The stage was set by their mutual ideas about what "togetherness" meant. Brad and Ellen spent most weekends and vacations together, shared mutual friends, enjoyed each other's interests, and felt the same or almost the same way on major emotional issues. If Brad was angry at Ellen's brother, he expected Ellen to be angry with her brother. If one of them was tired at eleven o'clock, the other went to bed at eleven o'clock too.

"Brad was so much fun to be with in the beginning that I didn't care that much about being with other people. But there was this one friend of mine, Jill, who I've known since high school. She's been divorced twice, and Brad has never really trusted or liked her. She and I would usually make an evening of it in New York once every month or two. We'd have dinner, go to a show, and talk till very late. I remember the first time I came home later than midnight. Brad was literally pacing the floor. He told me he had been worried. But then he got furious. He accused me of meeting another man. I really blew up. I took off the earrings I was wearing that he had given me on the anniversary of our first date and threw them at him. I held the phone out to him and told him to call Jill to verify where I had been. How dare he accuse me of cheating on him? I am one of the most honest people I've ever known. I hate lies. I had never gotten so angry with him. Then he said he was wrong. He couldn't apologize enough. He had tears in his eyes. I knew that he had gotten so upset because of his mother leaving his father. I calmed down and we made up. I guess I felt pretty stupid for having lost control. One of the earrings broke and I felt terrible about that. But I also didn't stay out so late anymore when I saw Jill."

Not staying out so late anymore with Jill was one of Ellen's first tactical errors in creating an unworkable rule about separateness. Because she empathized with Brad's fear, she began, almost unconsciously, to take care of it at her expense. It seemed to develop naturally that she went out and stayed out less. It simply didn't occur to her that there were compromises possible in which Brad could be anxious *and* she could still do the things that were important to her. The separateness rule was reinforced each time she stayed home or didn't do what she really wanted to do.

Brad and Ellen had a second rule that was hidden within and reinforced by the first. It too was created by many small decisions that were made early in the relationship.

"I remember the first vacation we took," Ellen said. "Brad has always liked rugged vacations, and we went to Canada camping. I knew camping was his passion. So when it poured rain for sixteen days I cheerfully took hikes in the rain, sat for hours in a cold lean-to waiting to see caribou, learned the name of every mountain wildflower, and thought it was romantic. But then I suggested we spend the last weekend in a fabulous hotel in Quebec City. After the camping ordeal, I wanted a little luxury. Brad went along with it but complained the whole time. He said the hotel was overpriced and the French food was overrated. He criticized the entertainment. I ended up apologizing for wanting to go to the hotel."

Clearly Ellen and Brad were establishing rules for their relationship in that first vacation. There was an expectation that Ellen would do everything Brad suggested and enjoy it. Brad could criticize Ellen's choices, and Ellen would feel responsible for his discomfort. By not being straightforward about the kind of vacation she might have preferred and by not letting Brad know that she didn't like his criticism, Ellen was inadvertently co-creating a rule that said, "Brad's needs are more important than Ellen's and mutual respect or consideration is not required."

Without a new understanding of goodness to help her, it would have been hard for Ellen to do anything else. She felt she had to be unselfish and not challenge Brad on his desire to camp, even though it was pouring rain and she was physically uncomfortable. She thought it was good not to get angry when he criticized her weekend plan. But allowing the rule to define their interaction made it impossible for them to negotiate a solution as two separate people with differing needs and wants.

In her next therapy sessions, Ellen talked about some of the events that made her feel that she couldn't have separate interests if they made Brad uncomfortable. She began to see more clearly that what looked like a choice to give up parts of herself had really resulted from a series of small, almost unconscious, decisions.

"Before I met Brad I was interested in photography," Ellen said. "I spent hours in the darkroom and hours going on photographic jaunts. In the beginning Brad would come with me on these expeditions, but he would get bored. It *was* boring I suppose. He might have to just hang around while I took a long time setting up each shot. And then, of course, the dark room took a lot of time. He worked very long hours at his job. So when the weekend came I just really felt that I owed it to him to spend more time with him. Gradually I stopped taking pictures and started spending more time with him at the theater. Anyhow I was interested in theater too. He'd often ask me to read a part when he had a staged reading of a new play in his workshop. I enjoyed it.

"I realized I was giving up more and more of myself, and in my mind I blamed him. Sometimes I'd try to talk to him about it. But often I'd just act annoyed. I'd accuse him of being self-involved and arrogant. He would ask me for examples. I always had a hard time giving him examples. He said that I wasn't interested in the creative side of him, that he needed my support. I knew that his family always compared him to his brother, who was the football hero type. They kind of made fun of Brad's playwriting. His parents had divorced. His father took custody of the two boys, and I know Brad felt very abandoned by his mother. So I guess I thought I was being selfish or that I needed to be especially sensitive to him or something. I just know that I got more and more drawn in to being there for him and letting my own life go."

Ellen's expressions of annoyance were her way of trying to break the relationship rules. But because she didn't really know what the matter was, she wasn't able to use her anger effectively. When Brad asked her for examples, she backed down. When he said he needed her support, she felt it was selfish of her not to give it to him. The fact that his mother had left him inspired her empathy and caretaking. But that sensitivity to feelings that seems to come naturally to women got Ellen in trouble. *Instead of using her sensitivity to understand Brad, she used it to make excuses for his behavior and to justify her own goodness.*

Ellen's story reveals her commitment to several goodness rules. She assumed that it was her job to make relationships work by being unselfish. Being unselfish meant that if Brad wanted to go camping and she wanted to go to a hotel, she should go camping. If he wanted to go the theater and she wanted to take pictures, she should go to the theater. But the more insidious rule was a rule about emotional responsibility. She was to be a lady and control her own needs so that her needs would never upset Brad, make him anxious or insecure, or compete directly with his. If he was nervous about her spending the evening with Jill, she quickly established the rule that she wouldn't see Jill too often.

What we've seen evolving in Ellen and Brad's story is a relationship system—the process of two people developing, over time, sets of rules and behaviors that determine how they can be with one another. The behaviors became reciprocal. The more Ellen gave in to Brad's feelings and failed to express her own, the more Brad expected Ellen to take care of him. Together they began to create negative and relationship-defeating patterns.

Both Ellen and Brad brought certain assumptions about themselves and about acceptable rules into the new relationship. Looking back at Ellen's family, we had learned that Ellen's mother always accommodated her father and never challenged any of his behavior. She always waited dinner for him and didn't expect him to call if he was going to be late. Ellen watched as her mother stopped going to the opera because her father didn't like opera.

In Ellen's family, men's needs always came first. Ellen had seen her mother caught in a loyalty triangle with her father. Ellen's mother never challenged her father on his behavior, even when he was inappropriately hard on Ellen. She never had separate friends or even voted for a different political party. Her mother had learned that being good to the person one was close to meant never focusing on another interest or relationship. Ellen had learned this loyalty lesson well because she was repeating her mother's pattern and being loyal to Brad at her own expense.

Brad had become a focus of attention in his family because of his parents' divorce and the secret of his mother's alcoholism. Because they were eager to compensate for the losses of the divorce, his father and stepmother focused on him continually. He learned that whatever he did was important, with the exception of his playwriting, and he came to expect that other people would accommodate his every need. He was rarely expected to be aware of the feelings of the other people in his household. While people focused on what he *did,* there was little responsiveness to his feelings. He secretly hoped that one day he'd find this kind of emotional attentiveness in a lover.

When Ellen first came for her emergency session, she was thinking in extremes: Either Brad changes or I leave. She had made previous ineffective attempts to change the rules by getting angry. While her anger may have made her *feel* more separate and more powerful, it didn't really shift anything. Ellen raged, Brad apologized, and Ellen backed down, only to go right back to being too good.

REVIEWING RELATIONSHIP SYSTEMS

Remember that at least two people always create the rules of a relationship. Responsibility is like a seesaw. When one person sits heavily on her side, the other goes up in the air. If the one person is too "heavy," too responsible, and doesn't push back toward the other person, the seesaw never rebalances itself.

Ideally, the seesaw of human relationships goes back and forth, up and down. First one person is up, then the other. First one person is too responsible, then the other. It's when the motion gets stuck in one position that we get into trouble.

Although Ellen was sitting too heavily on her end of the seesaw by taking responsibility for Brad's feelings, in other areas of the relationship Brad sat too heavily on his end. When Brad eventually joined Ellen in therapy, it became clear that he was too good in other ways. He and Ellen rarely had sex unless he initiated it. He tended to worry much more than her about paying the bills. The more Ellen gave up making decisions for herself, the more Brad felt he had to make decisions for the two of them.

It isn't fair or accurate to say that Ellen caused Brad's lack of respect for her separateness. But Brad's sense that he was entitled to her attention was heightened by Ellen's tendency to be too good.

ELLEN MAKES THE DECISION TO CHANGE

The togetherness rule and the assumption that supported it, "Brad's needs and feelings are more important than mine," were an outgrowth of Ellen's belief in the Goodness Code, as well as her loyalty to the many rules of the family that she came from that reinforced it. But as the relationship progressed under the old rules, Ellen felt less and less respect for herself. She felt trapped and depressed by a burden she couldn't name. The burden was goodness, and she was beginning to realize that she wanted to give it up.

"You know, I really have to make this trip. I had started to realize that I really have to make a change with Brad. Going to Mexico is part of that. Trying to be so loving to Brad, always giving in to him and never putting myself on the line to do what I want has made me feel terrible about myself. It was like I did too much for Brad as a way of trying to get him to love me. But it turns out that I'm not loving or valuing myself. I feel almost ashamed about that. But I realize nobody can give me the kind of love I was trying to get from him by being accommodating. Making this decision is kind of a statement to myself: 'I'm important, my life is important.' It doesn't mean I don't love Brad.

It would be nice if I could just *think* that I'm important and really believe it, but I know that I have to *do* things differently. I guess I'm saying that going to Mexico is a symbol of my wanting to care more about myself."

Changing one behavior, going to Mexico, was about to unleash a whole shift in the way Ellen and Brad related to each other. Ellen's decision to go to Mexico was her first real attempt at changing the rules of the relationship, her first solid effort at giving up the burden of goodness. Not only was it important *that* Ellen make a shift, it was important *how* she made it. The question for her was how to make the change effectively without having to end the relationship.

CHANGING RELATIONSHIP RULES EFFECTIVELY

Unfortunately, when we haven't learned how to negotiate a change in the rules of our relationships, we can get caught in fights like Ellen and Brad's. By the morning after their fight, each of them felt miserable and neither of them really knew how it happened. Brad felt abandoned. He was sure Ellen no longer loved him. Ellen went to school unsure of whether she should turn the job down, frightened at the intensity of her own anger, and feeling that she was the unloving, selfish woman Brad had accused her of being. She kept replaying the scene in her head, and she couldn't figure out where it had gone so wrong. She knew, despite their fighting, that Brad loved her. She wasn't able to feel good about the prospect of change.

Ellen was trying to change one of the most powerful rules in her relationship with Brad, and her move was really quite a radical one. She was as frightened about it as Brad was. Since the togetherness rule protected both of them from anxiety and from many other uncomfortable feelings, it wasn't unusual that the two of them should act as if they were waging guerrilla warfare. Ellen had come out fighting and Brad was protecting himself.

TAKING A CALM POSITION

The first trouble spot in their unproductive change sequence was Ellen's decision not to tell Brad about the possibility of the job right away. Brad's mother had been alcoholic, and he didn't find it easy to trust people. By withholding information that Ellen knew might upset him, she actually fostered his mistrust. Sitting on the secret had also made Ellen so uptight for two weeks that by the time she told him about the trip, Brad was already feeling uneasy about their relationship. When Ellen did tell Brad, she blurted out the news on what was supposed to be an anniversary celebration. An already upsetting announcement became even more upsetting because of its timing.

Ellen knew that Brad didn't like her to do things separately from him. And so she knew he would be upset. She got defensive in advance about his reactions because she wasn't sure whether or not she was responsible for them.

Ellen's process of change had really started in a smaller way with her decision to resume her interest in photography. She had been able to take small steps. But on a major issue like this trip, it would ordinarily have been her pattern to protect Brad by not even applying for the job. In the past, she wouldn't have considered going away for so long. Knowing she had to and very much wanted to go, she was in crisis. She was choosing not to protect Brad's feelings by staying home. But she still *felt* bad that he'd be uncomfortable. Because she still felt responsible, she got angry. She took a step toward change, but she did it reactively rather than calmly.

If Ellen had been prepared for Brad's reaction without feeling responsible for it, she might have been *responsive* to his feelings but still remained *firm*. A change in behavior represents a change in your *position* on a rule in your relationship. A position is a clear statement of what *you are going to do,* rather than an expression of *how you feel* or what you want the other person to do. Ellen needed to remain calm and to allow Brad to have his feelings. Naturally he wouldn't like a change in the rules, at least not at first. Ellen needed to respond to his feelings without trying to change them. She needed to acknowledge that her position represented a change. And then she needed to repeat her position.

After her emergency therapy session, Ellen was able to go back and express her new position to Brad differently. This was the way the new interaction evolved:

"Brad, I'm really sorry about our fight. I've been thinking about the whole issue of Mexico very carefully. It's a wonderful opportunity to combine the photography with my passion for archaeology. I feel that I really want to take the job."

"That's just great. Like I said, leave me alone with the cat and the dog and the bills, just forget about me. You must have known for weeks you were going to do this. I suppose this is why you've been acting so cold."

"I understand why you're upset. I didn't tell you sooner because I knew you'd be disappointed about the camping trip, and I avoided mentioning the job until it was a sure thing. I think I did withdraw a little from you because I was uptight about your reaction. I can understand why you feel hurt. But this isn't about leaving you. It's about my wanting to take an opportunity. You've encouraged me and been my biggest support."

"Terrific. So if you care so much about hurting me, don't hurt me. Turn it down." Brad is still infuriated.

"I've decided to take the job, Brad, and you and I will work out a different vacation. Right now we're both upset. Part of that is because I'm proposing we do things differently. It's a little frightening to me too to be on my own for five weeks. But I'm not going to fight about it. In fact, right now I'm going to stop discussing it, but I'll talk to you about it again at dinner."

Ellen remained calm in this new scenario. She responded to Brad's hurt feelings, and she understood his anxiety. She was direct, responsive, and firm.

ANTICIPATING THE REACTIONS TO CHANGE

Changes in a relationship system almost always provoke negative reactions at first, even if the other person ultimately agrees with and likes the change. Brad's anger at Ellen's bid for separateness was his initial response. Change is frightening and anger is often our first reaction to fear.

You may be asking yourself why, when Ellen was calm and responsive, Brad was still angry. Another roadblock to change is the belief that if we "do it right" the other person won't react badly. This is absolutely not true. Again, *any change provokes an initial reaction*. The trick is to understand that the reaction is natural, *and that it's important not to react to the reaction.*

Our tendency to react to others' reactions is the biggest roadblock to changing the rules of a relationship. In the process of adjusting to change, people often express their anxiety or anger in the form of an emotional outburst. Once they get past this reaction, they usually respond with a position of their own. At this point change becomes interactional, and a process of negotiating new rules can begin. But unless you can calmly restate or sustain your position in this process rather than reacting emotionally yourself, the success of your change is threatened.

It was important for Ellen to remember that she was trying to change herself rather than trying to change Brad. Her change represented her own decision to pursue an important personal goal. Having recognized that her part of maintaining the old rule was to let Brad make all of the decisions so she could remain loyal to the old Goodness Code, she had decided to take charge of her own life. Maintaining her own position without attempting to force a particular reaction from Brad allowed him to become more clear about his own feelings. Within two weeks, Brad responded with his own position:

"I've been thinking about Mexico. I guess I was just frightened because we've always done things together. Actually I think it's a great opportunity, and I'm glad you haven't let me talk you out of it. But I am going to miss you. Five weeks is a long time, particularly for us."

Ellen says, "Me too. I'll miss you, I mean. How can we make it easier? Do you think you could fly down for a long weekend so I could share some of it with you?"

"I don't know whether I want to do that," Brad says. "Truthfully, I've been realizing that I'd really like to spend some time with my brother. I'm thinking that he and I might take a canoe trip together while you're gone. Then in the fall you and I could take a shorter vacation together. How does that sound?"

HOW RELATIONSHIPS BENEFIT WHEN THE RULES CHANGE

Ellen felt a complex range of emotions about her change. She realized that she'd lived by the rules that had shaped her relationship with Brad because she thought she had to be good in order to be loved. She also loved Brad and genuinely wanted to be caring toward him. But as a woman, she'd internalized the message that caring means giving up self and that one has value only if one lives up to the Goodness Code. She had felt a lot of what we've called basic female shame. That shame was reinforced by family messages—Ellen saw that women had to be loyal in order to be loved.

Ellen's decisions to change grew from her basic discomfort with the way things were. It was only as she actually decided to *do* something different that she started to be more aware of the "price" she'd paid for her goodness. So her first response to change was to feel a good deal of grief and shame about the fact that she hadn't changed sooner. She saw in very vivid detail the ways that she'd failed to value herself. It put her in touch with the many ways other people had failed to value her as well. She felt grief, and then anger, and she was to spend many weeks in therapy exploring those feelings and beginning to let go of them. Brad worked in therapy on understanding better the ways that having an alcoholic parent had made him very fearful of being emotionally abandoned.

Ellen's trip to Mexico made her feel that she'd just released herself from prison—the prison of goodness, the prison of sacrificing herself to another in the attempt to feel valuable and cared for. On that trip she met people who respected her talent, who valued her work. She felt that her skills as a photographer improved dramatically. She loved being part of the archaeological project. She met people who were to become important friends to her. She gained a renewed respect for her own capacity to be in charge of herself—to face her fears and anxieties about being separate and to make decisions for herself. She had made a breakthrough—she felt free of the Goodness Code, and she felt free to be herself.

As for Brad, he and his brother spent time together talking about much that they'd never shared before. Brad came back from his canoe trip with a deeper understanding of how his parents' traumatic divorce and his mother's alcoholism had affected both him and his brother. He saw more clearly why he reacted as he often did to Ellen's separate interests and activities. He felt closer to his brother than he ever had, and he realized how much he needed that kind of contact in his life. And he realized he couldn't get it all from Ellen.

Yet when Ellen got back, their relationship improved dramatically. She said she'd never felt closer to him, and he felt the same. Changing the rules had major benefits for both of them. Ellen felt good about herself. She began doing more of the work she wanted to do. Brad began pursuing closer relationships with his brother and his male friends, and he no longer pulled for so much togetherness from Ellen. When they were together, they had much to share, much excitement about the other's interests and experiences. They had shifted the balance, and goodness was no longer such an issue.

10

APPLYING THE PRINCIPLES
OF CHANGE

———— ✳ ————

Breaking free from the burdens of responsibility is a challenging process, and the skills to do it effectively can be learned. We can best sustain the motivation to change when we understand certain principles. The most important of those principles is that any personal shift affects both the way we feel about ourselves and the way others react to us. So that one part of change is to behave differently and the other is to anticipate and handle the reactions.

We've watched Ellen negotiate major changes in her beliefs about goodness, in her behavior, and in the rules of her relationship with Brad. We saw that her first attempts at change were unplanned and therefore ineffective. But when she learned to apply different tools and principles, her change resulted in better feelings about herself and an improved relationship with Brad.

Ellen went through a number of steps that are common to any process of change:

She faced a "goodness crisis"—she experienced a conflict between her own needs and the rules that had been established between her and Brad.

She realized that she felt burdened and upset about being "too good" and made a decision to change.

She explored the ways that her family rules and legacies had affected her sense of loyalty to Brad.

She made a decision that would involve changing behavior as well as her emotional responsibility for Brad.

She learned to take a position calmly without reacting to Brad's reactions.

AN IMPORTANT NOTE ABOUT OTHERS' REACTIONS TO CHANGE

Usually a change in the rules of a relationship means breaking the injunctions of the Goodness Code. In some rare instances, people around you may be so relieved that you're joining the human race instead of being "too good" that they'll applaud you for it and eagerly assume the mantle of responsibility that you've let drop from your shoulders. Brad, for example, might eventually be relieved if Ellen is less focused on his feelings.

But because all change is uncomfortable at first, even when it's positive, it's most typical that others' first reactions are negative ones. Those negative reactions may take two forms, direct and indirect. People may say negative things about you or behave with hostility. They may become angry and challenging. Indirect negative reactions usually involve an increase in the other person's tendency to be less than responsible. The person you've stopped focusing on may step up abusive drinking or eating, or express more intense emotional symptoms such as depression or anxiety. The reaction may be as simple as Adam's forgetting to put the filter in the pot before making coffee, as described in chapter 1. This "oversight" was an indirect reaction to change.

Reaction statements are always a variation on the themes "You're bad"—"You're crazy"—"You don't love me." The key to sustained and effective change is to anticipate these reactions and remain calm in the face of them. As you're planning your change, predict for yourself which people are likely to react in which way. Have friends or a therapist on hand to help you to live with reactions without reacting to them and have them reassure you that you're not bad for giving up goodness.

Having a planned strategy for making a change and handling reactions is critical. The following steps apply whether the change you decide to make will affect your spouse, your lover, a friend, an employer, your parent, or your child.

1. Tell the person calmly about the change you're planning to make.

2. Choose a time when other issues or events won't get you off track or give the change more significance than it has.

3. Responsively and kindly acknowledge that the change feels hard —for both of you.

4. Don't react to the reaction.

5. Firmly but kindly restate your position.

6. If there's too much anger, postpone the conversation for another time.

7. Get support to help validate your right to make the change.

8. Stick to your position.

9. Give the person time to adjust to the change.

These strategies draw on the Code of Balance and assume your capacity to be direct, responsive, and firm. They result in your taking responsibility for your part in the relationship, not for your partner's feelings or for making the relationship work. Making the relationship work is the job of both of you. Yours is to feel good about your decision to make a change.

GIVING UP GOOD BEHAVIORS

The changes that most of us choose to make are rarely as major or as dramatic as Ellen's going to Mexico, though they may be equally important and symbolize as much. The important thing to remember is Ellen's recognition that feeling better about herself would mean *doing something different*. Although Ellen's change was a major step, even minor shifts in giving up small overresponsible behaviors always produce a realignment of the emotional rules of a relationship. Applying this principle means that small changes in behavior may ultimately be just as effective as large ones.

The rules of goodness get expressed in many different ways in many different situations. We may give up *doing* things for people that we don't really need to do or we may give up *focusing on their feelings*. One small change often accomplishes both.

For instance, Ellen liked to be on time, and Brad was always late.

Ellen would always wait for Brad. They ended up getting to most events after the event had already started. She'd feel embarrassed and angry. On the way to wherever they were going she'd complain and yell about it. Brad would get angry back.

When they started coming to joint therapy sessions, they'd arrange to meet at home and drive there together. They were always late and, since the therapist had given up goodness, the sessions weren't allowed to go overtime. Finally, Ellen took a simple position: "Brad, *I* don't want to be late anymore. I'll meet you at Jo-Ann's office. If you don't get there, we'll start the session without you. If you get there too late, we'll just go on without you."

In very short order, Brad started arriving for sessions on time. The change was simple. Ellen stopped focusing on Brad and simply did what she needed to do for herself. Changing a small behavior in this one area eliminated the need for anger, complaining, and negative scenes between the two of them. Brad was left with the choice to be more responsible for himself or not.

In choosing to make changes in the *behaviors* that represent being too good, try the following exercises:

- Pick something that you do repeatedly. For example, if you always have to find his car keys for him, that would be a better behavior to target giving up than shopping for Christmas presents for his mother. That's behavior that's an issue only once a year.

- Pick something that you're truly tired of doing and that is clearly not your job. It's better to pick a behavior that involves only the other person rather than focusing at first on something that affects the two of you. Finding his car keys is clearly his responsibility. Paying your mortgage payment on time, even if it's his job to write the checks and pay the bills, affects you directly. It's better to save changing your interaction around the mortgage payment until you've experimented with lesser degrees of change.

- Pick something that equally irritates the other person. For instance, Ellen and Brad always got irritated with one another about his chronic lateness. Brad felt controlled whenever Ellen complained. He resisted changing, and she focused more on changing him than herself. Look for an issue that ends in this kind of repetitive cycle of frustration and irritation.

- Once you've isolated one or two key behaviors, practice giving them up consistently for at least a month. Act confused and unaware of what you're doing when the other person starts to question you. "Oh, I guess I forgot." Or, "Gee, I don't know why I haven't been doing that. I guess there were other things on my mind." Be certain not to remind the other person to do what you're not doing unless he or she needs that information because the task is one you've come to be expected to take care of. Don't comment on your change.

- When you feel solidly confident that you can maintain the change, pick other behaviors that are overresponsible to focus on and begin to talk with your partner about the ways that you want the rules of your relationship to change.

CHANGING YOUR FOCUS ON OTHER PEOPLE'S FEELINGS

Ellen protected Brad's feelings by rarely doing anything for herself that would make him anxious. Being too focused on someone else's feelings can also involve asking about their emotions constantly, trying to fix their feelings, trying to solve their problems, or being overly concerned to protect them from pain or the consequences of their own behavior.

We also often protect other people from *our* emotions. Ellen, for instance, never let Brad know that she was considering the job in Mexico because she was afraid of his reaction. As good women, we rightly sense that our feelings and needs, if honestly expressed, may make other people uncomfortable. Since we think of it as our job to be unselfish, of service, and a lady, and never to hurt or inconvenience anyone, we work at sparing people the truth. We fail to be direct.

This work at being too good may take the form of faking orgasm in our sexual relationships, not reporting that we're angry about something, keeping a family secret about our lesbianism or the fact that we were violated by incest. More mildly, but just as dangerously, it may take the simple form of saying yes when we want to say no.

Once you identify the relationship that you want to change, it's important to target one key behavior to change. All large change starts small. It's more important to take one partial aspect of your overfunctioning and change it than to try to change everything about the way you do things all at once.

As a first step toward giving up your emotional focus on someone else, ask yourself whose problem you feel concern about. Where is your focus of attention? Is it on a partner, a child, a lover, a friend, an aging parent? Do you, for instance, tend to worry more about your husband's problems at work than he does? Do you get upset when your boss doesn't turn reports in on time? Do you feel concerned to advise your best friend about handling her current love affair even when she doesn't ask? Maybe you focus constantly on all these people, and your tendency to be too good emotionally is global and pervades every area of your life. If that's the case, it's likely that you aren't always aware of what your own problems and concerns may be. It's also likely that you often ignore emotional needs of your own in order to focus more on someone else's. You probably agree to stay late at work and type the boss's reports, for instance, rather than getting out in time to go to the exercise class that you enjoy.

KEEPING YOUR FOCUS CLEAR

When we focus too much on another person's feelings or needs, we sacrifice clarity about our own for the sake of being good. When we're not clear about our own positions, feelings, and needs, we often become caught up in the kinds of interactions that we saw happening between Ellen and Brad—interactions that become conflicted, confused, and angry. We do things that we don't really want to do. Or we don't do things that we would like to do. We lose track of the self who can be responsive, nurturing, and firm. And as we've seen by Barbara's example (chapter 6) and by Ellen's eventual resolution to the fight with Brad, responsivity, firmness, and nurturing behavior are the antidotes to being too good.

Ellen faced, and eventually resolved, a "goodness crisis." The crisis had to do with her overfocus on Brad's emotional needs. When we're caught in a downward spiral of confused and negative interaction like the one she experienced, it's helpful to have a phrase or catchword to help us focus. As Ellen relates to Brad in the future, when she feels a crisis of focus coming up, or when Brad gets reactive to a decision she's made, she's learned to ask herself the four questions for staying clear: *"What's the issue? What's my position? Whose problem is it? What, if anything, needs to be done about this by me?"*

You can always tell when a goodness crisis is about to happen in a relationship. Ellen could tell by the knot she felt in her stomach for two weeks. You notice yourself become tense. You feel vaguely irritated. Your partner or your child or your friend says something to you or about you and, as much as you try to deny it, you begin to feel angry or defensive.

These physiological reactions give you the warning that your own needs or feelings are in conflict with someone else's. The tightening and the tension in your body tell you that the need to be good may conflict with what you honestly want. Taking the time to question, *"What's the issue? What's my position? Who has the problem? What, if anything, do I need to do?"* gives you the clarity that you need to keep the focus on yourself. Maintaining that focus can abort a negative interaction in which you try too hard to be good only to end up feeling bad. And it can abort any tendency to give up on change.

✳GENERAL STRATEGIES FOR STAYING CLEAR

- When someone brings up a problem, ask them what their thinking is about their options rather than offering a solution. In fact, ruthlessly monitor yourself and give no advice unless directly asked. Do not help unless directly asked.
- Any time you feel annoyed in an interaction with someone, ask yourself, "What feeling of theirs am I taking care of?" and "What emotion of my own aren't I expressing?"
- When you feel yourself reacting to someone else's problem with overresponsible behavior or with anger, anxiety, frustration, or depression, shift the focus back to yourself by using the four questions for staying clear.

PRACTICING THE ALTERNATIVES TO EMOTIONAL OVERFOCUS

The new Code of Balance provides us with the alternatives to being too good. Practice these exercises in being responsive, nurturing, and firm as a way of developing your skill at handling goodness crises and as a way of understanding what it means to give up your emotional focus on another person.

✳GUIDELINES FOR BEING RESPONSIVE

When you talk to a friend or family member about a problem of theirs, you may find yourself working hard to "do something" about it. This often happens when we're particularly anxious. For example, your father may have been talking about what he's going to do if your mother's illness gets to the point that he can't keep her at home. Or your husband may have been talking about leaving the corporate structure and changing careers. Or your friend may have been talking, seemingly endlessly, about her marital problems. Instead of offering help or solutions, practice saying either, "That must feel very painful for you" or "What do you think your options are?" At each point in the conversation that you feel tempted to help, make a similar statement.

✳GUIDELINES FOR BEING NURTURING OF SELF AND OTHERS

1. Directly identify one emotional need of your own each day. For example, you might want to talk about something that's bothering you. Ask someone to meet that need directly. "Could you spend twenty minutes talking with me about my problem with my mother?" "Could you read a paper that I've been working on and give me comments?" "Could you come with me to a doctor's appointment—I'm really anxious about it?" If you're met with a negative response, try someone else. Just because you ask doesn't mean that it's possible or even convenient for someone else to meet your need. Practice getting your needs met from a variety of people.

2. Set aside one hour in a day and try to give yourself exactly what you want. Start reading the book you've been saving for vacation, listen to music, make a long distance phone call to a friend and don't worry about the cost, treat yourself to a massage.

3. Take time to think about what a friend or family member would really like. Not what you would like them to have but what they'd like. Give it to them. Being nurturing is meeting someone's real needs. It may be as simple as asking about their day and really listening.

✳GUIDELINES FOR BEING FIRM

1. Practice stating one feeling of yours directly to the person you're having the feeling about. For example, if it annoys you to be interrupted when you're working or involved with a task, practice saying, "It annoys me that you interrupt me so much. I'll be happy to talk to you when I'm finished with what I'm doing."

2. Think of a situation in which you're vaguely uncomfortable about the expectations someone else has of you. Talk with that person and ask them directly what they want or expect. Tell them directly what you can do, what you can't do, what you're willing to do, what you're not willing to do.

3. The next time you're talking with someone who tends to keep you on the phone too long, practice firmness. When you're ready to end the conversation, tell the person, "I'm going to say goodbye now"—without hesitation or avoidance. Communicate not "I *need* to go," but rather "I *am going to* go."

4. Practice saying phrases such as, "That's not acceptable; that's not the issue; that isn't my choice; I want to do something different; we have different opinions on this; I'm willing to compromise; I understand your dilemma but I'm not willing to do what you ask; that behavior's not acceptable to me."

5. When talking with someone who makes you feel guilty or emotionally overresponsible, practice saying, "I'm sorry you feel that way; I can hear that you feel upset with me; I feel sad that I can't do what you would like me to."

HANDLING YOUR OWN REACTIONS TO CHANGE

However extreme they may be, other people's reactions to change generally fall within the normal range of predictable responses to a shift in the rules of a relationship. (The exception is any kind of abusive behavior, which should never be tolerated.) But other people aren't the only ones to react to your change. You react. You react not only to others' reactions, you react to a sense that you're giving up control. Change may stir up your own anxiety.

When the behavior you decide to change has to do with caretaking and with concrete tasks, your dominant anxiety will be some version of "But it won't get done and done right." You worry that the budget won't get submitted on time at work or that your partner really doesn't understand the correct way to clean a bathroom. You're certain that if you let your partner dress the kids for school they'll appear in mismatched stripes or plaids or in yesterday's dirty clothes. Sometimes you're right.

For changes in this area to be viable and sustained, it's important to accept that it's not the end of the world if somebody makes a mistake or doesn't do things precisely the way you would. Change in this dimension requires flexibility. You need to be able to let the other person do things their own way in keeping with their own standards. And it requires the patience to allow others the time to become competent in areas that you've been handling expertly for a long time. If you find that you are likely to be too uncomfortable with another person's way of handling a task, chances are you should change in some other area and not complain about working too hard in this one.

EMPTINESS AS A SIGN OF CHANGE

Once you've managed to consistently change any behavior that represents being too good in the interests of others, you may feel a sense of emptiness and confusion for a time. When you've lived your entire life in unquestioning obedience to the dictates of the Goodness Code and you've been used to focusing on the emotions of the other people in your life rather than your own, giving up goodness feels at first like giving up your identity. You may feel as if you no longer know quite who you are.

You may also feel confusion, anxiety about what to do with yourself, trouble concentrating, or a lot of sadness. It's not really depression that you're feeling so much as it is a sense of aimlessness, a loss of purpose. Sometimes you don't know what to do with yourself. You may question your relationships, wonder if you really love people you think you love, wonder whether you really like your friends, wonder whether any of your relationships are mutual and healthy ones, or whether they were all just based on your overdoing.

You may feel unclear about what your real values are. In fact, you may feel that, since you're no longer so good, you'd like to go to the other extreme. You may experience a terrific desire to go out of control, become irresponsible, not go to work, leave the house a mess, let the kids and the cats starve. You may secretly believe that a selfish monster lives in the heart of you. You may want, if in a committed relationship, to betray your trust, have wild affairs, run away from home. You may overindulge in food, alcohol, other drugs, sex, spending.

In this phase of the change process, you begin to question all the beliefs that have directed your behavior. Yet you may be in the uncomfortable position of not having accepted a new set of beliefs from which to lead your life. You may feel that you're facing a void. And if your response is to go out of control and become as underresponsible as you were overresponsible, unfortunately you delay the day of reckoning with that void.

JO-ANN STRUGGLES WITH EMPTINESS

Recently I moved to a new town and had some time to myself when I wasn't working yet with clients. I decided to go to the nearby college library to get myself a library card—something I had not had time to do in the past twenty years of working hard at my career. Seduced by the stacks, and taken back in time thirty years to my enjoyable days in college when I often went to the library for the pure pleasure of exploring books and ideas, I picked up a journal that had no relevance whatever to some work that I had been doing on a new topic for a speech. I read an article on a famous woman writer. I leafed through an anthropology book. I imagined myself being an undergraduate student again and felt flooded with joy. I was doing nothing much, certainly not working, and suddenly I was having all kinds of pleasurable feelings and fantasies. I was enjoying myself.

Then I thought that I should really get home. I started to feel very anxious. The dog was in the car—maybe she was cold. Probably, I told myself, I could xerox the articles and read them later. I made myself sit there, aware of the inner dialogue between my two voices—the voice that knew my rising overresponsibility didn't even have a focus or an object and was ridiculous, and the voice that told me I was somehow "bad" for enjoying myself and wasting time with no redeeming purpose. Having chosen to do nothing of importance, I was beginning to feel things that were confusing. I was facing an unfamiliar impulse in myself.

By now, my enjoyment was disrupted. I was back in my trance of responsibility, so I put my articles away and went home. The dog was fine and didn't say a word. Neither did any of the people at home. Nobody had really needed my attention but myself. Maybe that's what was so disconcerting.

✳EXERCISE: FACING THE VOID

One of the things you may be recognizing about yourself is that you tend to keep a lot of chatter going in your mind and a lot of activity in your life so that the feelings of emptiness don't overwhelm you. Your overwork in the interest of others may even have been your way of avoiding the emptiness that we all experience at times, whether or not in response to change. Here is an exercise that will help you to go willingly toward the emptiness rather than running away from it. The purpose of the exercise is to give you a shortcut to experiencing some of the typical feelings that go along with giving up goodness.

To give yourself a firsthand experience of what happens if you stop doing and stop focusing on everybody *out there,* plan at least two hours or an afternoon or a day in which you arrange to be alone with no distractions. Keep everyone else out of the house, take the phone off the hook, and don't even allow yourself to read a book or a magazine. Just *be.* Take a walk or be outdoors if you wish, but don't exercise or engage in any otherwise gainful activity. Allow whatever thoughts come into your head to float in and float out. Be purposeless, aimless, a wanderer. And observe what happens.

Most women react to this "homework" assignment with the response, "I don't have time for that" or "I could never give myself permission to waste so much time." This response says that their inner "shoulds," the injunctions of the Goodness Code, dictate that who they are is what they do—that good women don't take time to do nothing. If they take the time to do the exercise, a wide range of feelings usually emerges. Included among the feelings might be an intense restlessness or anxiety; even, for some, a sense of losing touch with reality—of desperately needing to be back in touch with someone or something else; guilt; worry about all the things that aren't getting done; wondering if Janie got on the right school bus or if she remembered her homework. Suddenly a woman finds herself coming face to face with the "void." Invariably, when a woman begins to actually enjoy time doing nothing, she immediately labels herself "bad" in some way, or lazy, or selfish.

Many women can't tolerate this exercise for longer than a half hour. It is a telling comment on how little women believe in the right to their own feelings and their own time. It's a comment on the fear most women feel without the behavioral props of overdoing to tell them who they are. If most were able to take this time for themselves regularly, some very positive things would happen. Most would begin to identify changes they wanted to make in their lives. They would begin to feel happier and less shameful about themselves. They would learn to enjoy their own company—to have fun. They might begin to make some of their own dreams happen as they took the time to let their thoughts, fantasies, and feelings out to see the light of day.

One of the most difficult reactions to change that we face as women is to sit with emptiness and anxiety long enough to recognize some of the impulses for enjoyment that emerge when we give up our overwork. There is nothing that makes a good woman feel worse than realizing that she'd rather play than work, do something for herself rather than something for someone else. If we can avoid the tendency to run from emptiness, we stand to gain a greater awareness not only of our uncomfortable feelings but of the positive impulses for enjoyment and self-expression that get buried by overresponsibility for others. One of the most positive outcomes of change should be an increase in our capacity to be self-nurturing. Facing emptiness gives us a chance to redefine our values and embrace this newer premise about goodness.

IF I DON'T RELATE, WHO WILL?

Emptiness is only one reaction to giving up good behavior. The attempt to give up your *emotional* focus on another person may leave you feeling anxiety about being alone with your own feelings. If you've always been the one to work harder at being sensitive in a relationship, another potential reaction to be faced is sadness at the recognition that much of the apparent emotional contact you have with your partner, parent, or friend is initiated and maintained by you.

Sometimes we think of relationships as emotionally close ones only to realize that we are the ones who draw the other person out in conversation, solve their problems, plan activities both of us will enjoy, worry about their feelings. We realize with some sadness that we never get asked about us.

Yet when we do all the work of the relationship, the other person doesn't have to. If we've made a habit of always talking about our feelings without being asked, it may be the case that other people have gotten out of the habit of asking because they know we'll tell them anyway. If we make all the plans, the other person gets used to going along. If we always keep the conversation going, the other person doesn't feel the need to express his own feelings or opinions.

Working too hard at the emotional dimension of a relationship can help us avoid feeling afraid that we're not really important to the other person, afraid that we're not caring about them enough, or afraid that we're not socially adequate ourselves. When we start to give up our overfocus on someone else, we feel set adrift without any rules to guide us. We may feel frightened by our own feelings since everybody else's seem more familiar.

JO-ANN GIVES UP

I've found that, particularly when it comes to emotional overwork, if I can only wait out the change there are sometimes surprising results. One night a few years ago, I went with my friend Jerry to a very emotionally charged foreign film about a group of Nazi men on a submarine. The film had a strong emotional impact on me.

I had always thought of Jerry as a very close friend, but I was aware that he never seemed to share his feelings enough for me. I was often critical of him because of it. I decided to try the assignment I had been giving to clients. I made up my mind that I wouldn't volunteer any of my impressions of the film until he did.

After the movie, close to forty-five minutes passed with little conversation between us. During that forty-five minutes I thought the following. "He is emotionally dead. I have made up this whole idea of a close relationship in my imagination. What a fool I've made of myself sharing my feelings all these years." I began to feel profoundly sad and angry.

As I was grieving for what seemed our illusory relationship, Jerry began to talk. For the first time since I'd known him he talked about the fact that his parents were Holocaust survivors and that the rest of his family had died in German concentration camps. He talked about his difficulty feeling empathy for the Nazi protagonist in the film. He shared his pain. I realized that my reactions to the film were superficial in comparison to the depth of his feelings. I wondered how many times in the past I had deprived both Jerry and me of the chance for real intimacy by always rushing in to take emotional charge of the situation and the interaction between us.

The way to apply the lesson Jo-Ann learned from this incident is to follow a simple rule. *When you think you're doing all the emotional work in a relationship, keep quiet and wait to see what happens next.* Note your own reactions as you wait. They are clues to feelings that your overwork may have helped you avoid.

COMMON BLOCKS TO CHANGE

For change to be effective, a woman needs to be conscious of two potential blocks to her motivation to give up goodness. The first is internal. It has to do with the false pride that we mentioned in chapter 4. By now it's clear that we often overfunction to overcome a sense of shame. We begin to take a kind of false pride in our overfunctioning and that pride protects us from many uncomfortable feelings.

Change can be blocked by pride. If our images of ourselves are too bound up with goodness, we'll have difficulty withstanding other people's reactions to our change, and we'll have trouble feeling emptiness. The first time someone tells us we're selfish, our pride in being a giving person may block us from staying focused on ourselves. We'll become more invested in proving we're still good than in maintaining the change. The first time we fail to live up to our own image of ourselves as competent, feelings of vulnerability and insecurity may push us away from our emptiness back to working compulsively.

For some of us, doing too much for others may have been a major source of self-esteem, and it may have given us some power in our family or our primary relationship. It's not likely that we'll be able to give up overdoing easily until we've found other ways to feel good about ourselves. This is especially true since other people have a way of taking over our old responsibilities in a way that suggests that they can "do it better." Our partner now not only cooks, but he or she becomes an instant "gourmet." While we feel at our wits' end after a week alone with the kids, our partner tells us it was "a breeze" when we walk in the door after a business trip. If we're not careful, we can end up feeling bad for giving up goodness. We can see messages of our inadequacy everywhere.

At times like this, it's particularly important to keep the focus on yourself. The point of change is for you to be in better balance, not to win a competency competition with the others in your life. It would be useful for you to review the autonomy readiness inventory at the end of chapter 7 at this point. Each item that you can respond yes to will help your self-esteem. The better able you are to take charge of you, the less dependent you'll be on doing for others to feel good about yourself.

The second block to change is interactional. It involves our tendency to forget that all change is a process that occurs over time and that change in a relationship takes place over time. For instance, if our first attempts to make a direct request for our partner to respond to our needs meet with rejection, we may simply assume that the relationship is unworkable. Instead of recognizing that real change may involve many attempts at sustaining shifts in the rules of a relationship over time, we may simply assume that something about our choice of a partner was bad. Either we give up on change or we leave the relationship only to have the same experience with the next person.

Sometimes we give up on change when we aren't financially able to support ourselves. Whether or not we choose to work outside the home, we will always be and feel most secure when we feel confident that we have marketable skills. We should also know what our financial assets would be if our marriage or partnership were to dissolve. A critical step in our readiness for autonomy is financial readiness. We need not necessarily have a job but we should, at least, have a plan that includes a way to support ourselves. Otherwise, if the other person's reaction to our change is to say, "When you pay the bills around here, then you can do what you want," we'll be rightly tempted to give up our change.

REVIEWING THE PROCESS OF CHANGE

In the last four chapters, we've talked about the typical stages that occur as part of any process of change. Briefly, here's a review of them:

1. Goodness begins to get you down. You feel generally depressed or in conflict. You know something needs to change, but you're not sure what.

2. You experience a "goodness crisis."

3. You begin, with the help and input of others, to realize that you've been too good for your own good and that you've set up rules in your relationships that maintain this problem.

4. You explore the sources of your ideas about goodness. You look at the family mythology and rules that form the basis for your definitions of goodness.

5. You make a small change. You either give up an overresponsible behavior or you stop being too focused on someone's feelings. You do

something that is important for yourself. You take a position calmly and stick to it.

6. You respond effectively to the reactions to change.

Change involves the principles of the Code of Balance. You replace overresponsible behavior with being comfortable with yourself, direct about your feelings, responsive to other people's feelings, nurturing of yourself and your relationships, firm about what you will and won't do.

Practicing the new code involves:

Keeping the focus on yourself.

Taking clear and calm positions.

Not reacting to other people's reactions.

Moving through emptiness to enjoyment and pleasure.

ONE FINAL NOTE ABOUT CHANGE

Embracing the process of change requires courage, patience, and a willingness to sit still with a range of uncomfortable feelings. It also takes time. Our patterns of being too good have a long history. Acquiring new behavior and beliefs often means that we make one small change only to have to repeat it again many times. Giving up goodness is one of the most difficult changes a woman can make. We owe it to ourselves to give it the time to work.

PART THREE

THE POWER
OF CHOICE

11

DEEPER DILEMMAS

———— ✳ ————

Women and Men,
Women and Women,
Women and Work

The Goodness Code is at work behind the scenes in all our relationships. But we often hold particular beliefs that sustain goodness differently in certain categories of relationship. For example, some of us have beliefs about the nature of men that prohibit change. We read the story of Brad and Ellen and we say, "But Brad was an unusual man. Most men wouldn't put up with Ellen's going to Mexico."

However, as therapists, we know that change is possible. We see change happen every day, especially as women begin to make small shifts in the rules of their relationships. Men may not change as fast as we would like. But they do change and more balanced relationships are achievable.

We might also think that we shouldn't have to give up goodness in our friendships or in intimate relationships with women. We may automatically assume that two women together relate on an equal footing and don't play out goodness rules together in the same ways. And in our work lives we often feel that our only choice is to "do it all" without getting help and without looking overwhelmed. Here too change is needed and is possible once we understand our assumptions and are willing to rewrite the rules.

Every relationship is vulnerable to becoming unbalanced in very specific ways. In this chapter, we'll examine the particular dilemmas of goodness in our interactions with men, with women, and with work.

JO-ANN GOES TO THE BEAUTY PARLOR

One day I decided to go to the same beauty parlor that Claudia uses. I noticed it was equipped with the fifties bubble hair dryers that replaced the "handy Hannah" hair dryers of the forties. The beauty parlor also has blow dryers now, but they've decided to keep the bubbles too as a memento of the past.

I went in for a haircut and asked Mona if she'd like to be interviewed. I've titled the responses I got "The Marxist Theory of Marriage—From Each According to Her Ability, to Each According to *His* Need."

Mona said, "Are these questions for the book?"

"You're too smart," I said. "Yes."

Maureen, the owner, yelled over. "You're writing a book. What's it on?"

"I'm writing a section on women and men," I said.

"Interview Maureen," said Mona. "She has something to say on everything."

"It's a good day for an interview—Wednesday," said Maureen. "Wednesday is the day I know everything. Ask me a question."

Jo-Ann: "OK. Who's stronger? A man or a woman?"

Maureen: "A woman. That's easy. A woman is mentally stronger because of childbirth. If men had to give birth, you wouldn't need birth control."

Mona: "A woman should do more than a man. She makes the man strong. She's made stronger to begin with."

Another customer jumped in, an older woman whose hair was being set in tight pin curls. "The man has to make the woman first," she said.

Mona whispered to me, "She means something different."

"I know."

The older woman's hair stylist jumped in. "A woman has to give in to a man."

Maureen got heated. "What! I know women who don't do anything and their men treat them like they're queens. I don't believe in doing too much for a man."

Mona added, "If you give a lot, you get a lot."

By now the discussion was very lively and loud, with several other customers joining in.

"You're in the dark ages, Mona," said Maureen. "It's a different world. It can't be anymore that the man is the provider and the woman does everything else."

"No, no," said Mona. "The woman is made stronger. She gives because she has more ability to give. Ever see a man alone? He's lost. That's the way men are. You see a woman alone and she can handle it."

By now, they were all fascinated and I could hardly get a word in edgewise. "Ask me the next question," said Maureen.

"Who's more of a baby when they're sick?"

They all agreed. "That's easy. Men."

Mona said, "Well, that's because women are more used to taking care of sickness, right?"

Maureen, almost shouting now, said, "Mona, you're behind the times."

Mona waved her scissors animatedly in Maureen's direction. "You're wrong. Men worry more because they have more responsibility. You have to make them think they're the breadwinner. That's just the way men are."

The discussion was going full force as I left. In fact, they barely noticed my retreat.

The attitudes in this story aren't as dated as they seem. Women often talk about their feeling that they're stronger than men.

One friend says, "Listen, women have to be strong because men are totally and completely incompetent—you can't count on them for anything. Women all talk around the coffee table about the secret that men are extremely fragile. You can't tell them anything because they're too sensitive to hear it, and, if they could hear it, they couldn't take it; they would shrivel up and die. There's a story in my family about my Aunt Sally's birth. She was born in India, and the doctor was drunk and couldn't get through the jungle for a day and a half (men are unreliable). So Grandfather assisted at the birth, and it was a difficult birth and he couldn't do it right so later on in life Aunt Sally went mad (men are incompetent)."

Our friend laughed as she told us this story. She doesn't really believe that men are incompetent, but she says the impact of the old family myth sometimes sneaks up on her. "Like I left our summer cabin three days ahead of Sam because I had to get back to work and I thought to myself, 'Oh, no. He forgot to put spaghetti on the shopping list and I didn't write it on for him. He won't have any pasta.' Of course, I wouldn't have openly reminded him because that would have made him feel incompetent. It's just so automatic."

Most of our behavior as men and women is automatic. You may

protest that the women's movement has given all of us more flexibility. And it's true that since the women's movement began, more women have joined the work force and more men spend some of their time in child care. But not only are these changes more superficial than substantial; the truth is that what may seem like greater role flexibility may actually be more role strain. What appears to be true is that both women and men are freer to add new behavior to their existing roles, but they're not truly free to let go of any of the old behaviors that define them as adequate men and women. What looks like flexibility is really an increase in pressure for both men and women to be and do more.

THE MAN'S CODE OF STRENGTH

The patterns of goodness that develop between men and women are patterns in a dance choreographed by the society we live in. As they are for women, male rules are reinforced by family myths and messages. In order to understand more fully how the rules between men and women become unbalanced, we need to pay attention to the ways that men are taught to be too good.[1]

Men live by their own code—we call it the Code of Strength. As is the case for women, the code is made up of dictates that require very stereotyped behavior and that reflect very unrealistic and conflicting expectations.

THE CODE OF STRENGTH

BE A WINNER. A man always competes to win. He climbs to the top of the corporation. He plays competitive sports. He never loses a fight.

BE AN EXPLORER. A man who obeys this rule is characterized by adventure, daring do, and recklessness. He doesn't pay heed to the environment he explores. It's important that he not be bound too close to hearth and home.

BE A WARRIOR/PROTECTOR. A man knows that being a man means to hide his feelings unless they are aggressive ones. He particularly doesn't show fear. He's a man in battle. He never cries or shows his vulnerability. He protects women and children first.

BE THE MASTER. A man must know everything, from the route to take to get to a new destination to how to fix anything broken. A man never asks for advice. He dispenses advice.

BE THE PROVIDER. Making a "good living" is a duty that a man never questions. In fact, from the time he's born he knows that his role is to earn the living for himself and for the woman he marries and the children he raises.

BE A LOVER AND STUD. A man never admits that he needs romance. He is assumed to be sexually turned on at all times, in all places, and by any suitable female object. He is always able to perform.

BE A SENSITIVE, NONSEXIST COMPANION. A man must be sensitive to the feelings of women and others in his life. He must be open and emotionally vulnerable, and know how to nurture and be caring in relationships.

Just as the injunctions of the woman's Code of Goodness are contradictory, obeying one aspect of this code often means a man will inevitably fall short in another. These expectations of men set utterly impossible standards. Today's man is supposed to be a sensitive companion, devote at least half of his time to caring for the children, do household tasks with equal competence if not equal enthusiasm, but still aggressively advance up the corporate ladder. Somehow he is supposed to be equal but still be perfectly competent, taller, and earn more. And while he is sharing his feelings he had better make sure that they're feelings that we women are comfortable hearing. Certain feelings make us think of him as a baby.

It's not clear that men try with as great intensity as women to live up to their code, particularly to its more modern injunctions. But it's probably true that when a man tries and fails, like a woman, he equally feels a sense of shame and inadequacy.

The male and female codes form the foundation for the rules of most male-female relationships. The rules tend to be mutually reinforcing. When men and women rigidly adhere to their respective codes they each become overly responsible for some areas in their lives and less than responsible for others. A relationship may get extremely unbalanced and the emotional climate will become tense. Let's look at the story of one man and his wife who followed their codes too strictly and had problems as a result.

THE GOOD PROVIDER AND HIS UNSELFISH LADY

Judy came for therapy every June with the same complaint. "It's June, and Max would rather play golf than work. He's talking about early retirement again, and he's acting angry at me most of the time."

"Are you thinking about going back to work?"

"Work?" said Judy. "Max doesn't want me to work. Every time I start looking for a job he complains that I won't be able to play golf with him."

Judy had lived her life in blind obedience to the Be Unselfish injunction in every area of her relationship with Max. Max was a recovering alcoholic, and Judy was so relieved that he was sober that she didn't want to rock the boat. He had been in AA for four years, and she was an active member of Al-Anon. But she was still responsible for all the details of running their household. When the cat had to go to the vet, she made the appointment and took the cat. When the roofer had to be scheduled to repair a leak, she scheduled it and was home to let him in. If Max left his golf shorts in a dirty heap on the bedroom floor, she picked them up and laundered them. Sometimes she was tempted to put starch in his golf shorts, but she never complained.

She also felt responsible to advise Max on his relationships with others, particularly his daughter from his first marriage. She managed Max's investment properties for no pay although her graduate degree could have given her entree to much more rewarding work. When their sex life deteriorated, she felt she needed to make herself more desirable whether sex was satisfying for her or not. In fact, it often wasn't satisfying, and she hid the truth about that from Max lest she "hurt him." She felt that Max's alcoholism had damaged his self-esteem enough.

Max joined Judy in the therapy sessions. "I want to retire," he said. "But Judy won't hear of it. She wants to keep living the way we've always lived. Me, I'd like to play a little golf. I'm fifty-eight. I think I've earned the right. And now Judy's complaining that I'm too cheap to take her to Europe."

Max, a financially successful stock broker, fully accepted the injunction to be a good provider. His family had so reinforced that rule for him that Max never questioned it. The rule meant that his wife should never have to work. And when Max finally recovered from his alcoholism, he worked doubly hard to make up for it.

Now Max wanted to cut back on work, and this was the problem in the marriage as he saw it. Although Judy had other income from a family inheritance, she had always kept that income as her "mad" money. During Max's drinking she also kept it in reserve in case she needed to leave him. Max paid all the bills.

Judy had also gone back to school for a highly marketable graduate degree during her marriage to Max, but she really didn't want to get a job.

The fact that Max assumed it was his job to pay all the bills left Judy assuming that she needed to take no financial responsibility. By the same token, the fact that Judy was so good at taking care of relationships meant that Max never developed much competence at handling his own relationships with his children, sister, and parents. He never questioned that Judy should take care of him in the ways she did, because that was what his mother had done for his father.

The result of this fixed state of affairs was a kind of low-level anger on both Max's and Judy's parts that erupted from time to time when specific issues regarding major expenditures arose or when golf season rolled around. Their sexual and emotional relationship had been compromised by Max's alcoholism and was further compromised by imbalance in the rules of their relationship.

Max periodically felt exploited and unappreciated. He knew Judy took a lot of responsibility, but he didn't feel particularly nurtured. Sometimes he felt he was still on "probation" for his alcoholism. Judy felt depressed and deprived. She was glad Max was sober, but he spent most of his free time at AA meetings or playing golf and wasn't very responsive to her. Judy would accuse Max of being cheap, and Max would accuse Judy of being selfish. Since Max took particular pride in being a good provider and Judy took particular pride in being unselfish, they could very quickly get into a fight.

Max and Judy both worked on themselves in AA and Al-Anon. But in therapy they began to work to change the rules of their relationship. It was clear that those changes wouldn't be as far-reaching as the ones Brad and Ellen had made. Judy and Max were products of a much more traditional era. But small changes can often make large differences in how people feel about themselves and their marriages.

Therapy helped to label Max's and Judy's problem as one of unquestioning obedience to their respective codes rather than a problem *within* either one of them. Judy saw that Max got angry because he felt ashamed if he said directly that he didn't want to work as hard anymore. Max saw that Judy hadn't worked outside the home in so many years that she was really frightened that she couldn't do it, and that it was important to her self-esteem to try.

Judy had studied library science and, with Max's support, within a few months she found a part-time job as a librarian. She also contributed some of her investment income to the house funds. Max took a semiretirement and, on his extra days off, he not only played golf but did some of the cooking and laundry. Judy then had some free time for herself, and she also had time to play golf with Max. Yet it wasn't Judy's part-time job or Max's laundry detail that made such a difference in how they felt about themselves and each other. It was Judy's willingness to work and Max's willingness to do the laundry that made both of them feel nurtured. Their mutual willingness to change helped reduce the resentment that had built over the years. And they got excited enough about the changes to really enjoy the process of therapy.

Judy learned that she didn't need to be so good at making relationships work. She stopped trying to handle the problems between Max and his daughter by firmly stating that she would no longer be the go-between. Instead she concentrated on being responsive to Max when he talked about his daughter. Rather than offering Max advice, she'd say to him, "I know how upset you must be that she isn't doing well in college, but I'm sure you'll find the right way to handle it." With Judy's support, Max did handle it, and he let Judy know how much he appreciated her responsiveness.

Max learned that Judy needed him more as a companion than as a provider. Together they took on the challenge of finding different ways of spending time together that were equally enjoyable and nurturing for both of them.

The story of Judy and Max is primarily a story about who *does* what in a relationship. The dynamics between men and women get even more complicated when we look at who *feels* what.

PROBLEMS AND PARADOXES

The rules of goodness dictate that men are to be adventuresome explorers, providers, warriors, competitors, masters, and sensitive but dynamic lovers. Women are to be attractive, unselfishly giving, competent, and uncomplaining. Men are to hide soft emotions. Women are to hide powerful and intense emotions. Even if the codes of Goodness and Strength were desirable ideals, they're not attainable ones. No man is always masterful, protective, adventuresome. No woman is always a lady, competent, unselfish.

But men and women tend to reinforce these stereotypes in one another. The more ladylike a woman is in hiding anger, the more a warrior the man is apt to be in hiding tears.

We see examples of this emotional reinforcing every day. We do it without thinking—the injunctions of our respective codes have become so ingrained that we perpetuate them almost out of habit. A man comments on his wife's weight. "It's too bad, you have such a pretty face," he may say. He reinforces the Be Attractive rule. He says, "I can't talk to you when you're hysterical." He reinforces the Be a Lady injunction.

"What a good little man you are," we may say to our young son as he blinks back the tears at the dentist's office. Be a Warrior. "Why didn't you say something to your boss? Stand up to him." Be Strong. As a highly successful woman physician said to us, "I must admit, liberated though I say I am, when Bill's feelings get in the way of his standing up to his boss, I think, 'Why can't you just be a man about it?' "

THE WARRIOR MAKES TUNAFISH

Chuck was a commercial real estate salesman who certainly followed the male code. He was aggressive and in his male "manner" he would have put Clint Eastwood to shame. When asked how he felt about his work, his reaction was surprising. "Well, every day I put on my male suit and go out into that cutthroat world. It's always 'On stage, next show's at seven.' "

One day, home from work, Chuck took his young son to the beach and then came back and made tunafish for the two of them for lunch. His time with his son was so gratifying that it made him aware of how much he wished he could give up his "male suit." "I guess the male suit," he said, "is just the armor I have to put on to hide any of my feelings about wanting to spend more time with my kid instead of fighting the battles at work. I can't allow myself any soft feelings like that."

Many men, if asked, will describe the pressures they feel in the face of being required to provide and perform. Those feelings often include a sense of fear and inadequacy, a sense of burden and overwork, and a sense of sadness at how much time they need to spend away from their children. But they also operate by a rule that says they shouldn't share those feelings with others, particularly not with their wives.

Could the tunafish maker have shared the story with his buddies? "Are you kidding? As a joke maybe."

The problem for us as women is that often we forget that men have the tunafish-making side to them, the nurturing soft side. We assume that they're bad at expressing feelings and that that's just the way men are. So we don't expect them to learn. We're like Mona in the beauty salon. We do it for them.

Women are taught to *display* dependence and vulnerability while also learning to be emotionally independent. We are taught to be unselfish in our nurturing of others' needs without being needy ourselves. Many women never rely on a man to meet their deepest emotional needs. That's sad, because many men are very capable of being responsive and nurturing if we give them a chance.

The paradox is that we are all socialized to display one set of feelings, but we actually experience another. Women are taught to display weakness but in the process learn strength, and men are taught to display only strength and in the process become dependent. The woman then denies her strength and the man denies his vulnerability. Is it any wonder that emotionally honest communication breaks down between men and women?

THE PARADOX OF THE LADY AND THE WARRIOR

We can summarize the "hidden" or emotional rules for goodness between men and women by saying that men are "good" when they hide their more vulnerable or "feminine" feelings and women are "good" when they hide their more powerful or "masculine" feelings. The paradox in these rules is that men are tender and women are strong, but we tell ourselves lies about that to reinforce our obedience to the codes. Those lies create imbalance in male-female relationships and prevent us from knowing each other's true feelings.

In order to get communication back on track, in therapy we often use assignments that give clients a playful way to talk about the difficulties they're having. Asking them to wear costumes that reflect hidden parts of themselves, or to bring in jokes about male/female relationships, or to share video clips of their favorite film couples are ways of talking about problems men and women have with one another, but in a humorous way.

Jeff and Alison gave one of the best commentaries on men and women's paradoxical and contradictory expectations of one another. They were asked to come to the therapy session wearing masks or costumes that would symbolically represent their analysis of current gender relationships. Jeff came in wearing a mask depicting a large, soft-eyed puppy. He said, "One of the problems that I have with Alison, that I think men have with women today, is that on the one hand women expect men to be faithful, and affectionate, and cuddly like puppy dogs." Here he whipped off the puppy mask and replaced it with an extremely aggressive-looking pirate. He continued, "But they also want us to be bold and daring and adventurous. To reconcile the two is not always easy. In fact, it's very difficult."

Alison came in wearing a black body suit and stocking cap. The front of her face was a mirror. "I just think that the man really wants to see a reflection of himself, and women give off that reflection rather than being who they are. Instead of true energy, it's very distorted energy in relationships, just a lot of reflection."

When a woman, in an effort to reinforce his maleness, gives a man feedback that he must be strong when in fact he's feeling tender, problems result. When a man feels he needs to wear a pirate mask because he perceives that a woman can't really handle the vulnerable puppy dog, problems result. The problems are what Alison called "distorted energy" and what we would call distorted reality in relationships. And, to be good, many of us women—and men as well—think we need to maintain this distorted reality.

Alison's mirror was a metaphor for the double bind she felt. Should she be herself or should she reflect to Jeff the image she thought he wanted to see? Jeff's masks symbolized his conflict. Should he show Alison the tough pirate, or could he share his vulnerable puppy dog? The use of metaphor helped Jeff and Alison create a safe shortcut for discussing what they wanted from one another.

Alison can now say to Jeff, "Do you want a reflection or do you want my opinion?" Jeff can ask, "Who do I need to be tonight? Pirate or pup?"

We don't really do men any favors when we act as mirrors, reflecting only the image they need to see of themselves. That reflection is a form of emotional overresponsibility that robs men of a chance to express their deeper feelings and deprives them as well of knowing us. And if we play the mirror reflecting outward, we lose sight of the person behind the mirror—ourselves.

EVALUATING YOUR EMOTIONAL RESPONSES TO MEN

The emotional rules of any relationship are more subtle than the rules about who does what. Some of us subscribe to the general rule that we are, like Alison, to be mirrors to men, always reflecting what they need to see. If we feel that men have fragile egos, it will be likely that we:

- Pretend to be more dependent than we actually feel
- Avoid competing with any man we're likely to beat
- Protect the men in our lives from dealing directly with the kids or other family members

- Laugh at a man's jokes whether or not we think they're funny
- Rarely give a man feedback on how we'd like him to be different when we make love
- Are the one to talk about emotional subjects
- Give a man too much praise for taking routine household responsibility
- Are careful not to ever disagree with a man in public
- Feel disloyal if we're more successful than a man
- Avoid saying what we really feel on the assumption that he won't listen or understand
- Fail to give him feedback about the ways his behavior affects us
- Fail to demand attention to and respect for our feelings
- Assume that he has no deep or intense feelings and don't expect him to express them

To achieve a different balance in our relationships, it is critical that we develop clear ideas about the rules that *we* choose for our relationships. Once we've made those decisions, we need to communicate them clearly and calmly, giving ourselves and the men we relate to the opportunity to evolve compromises and adjustments as they think about the rules that work for them. Most importantly, we need neither to protect men's feelings nor, as suggested in the "small talk" article Jenn denounced in chapter 3, assume that we must teach them about feelings.

Following the Be Direct injunction of the Code of Balance is the best assurance that we have that we'll do our own part to evolve satisfying and emotionally open relationships with the men in our lives. All behavior is reciprocal. If our own commitment is to emotional honesty and openness, eventually the other person has to respond in kind.

WOMEN AND WOMEN

Just as our belief that "that's the way men are" leaves us expecting that men can't be equally responsible emotional partners, we're apt to hold some equally false beliefs in our relationships with women. We often assume that when we relate to other women, we don't have to negotiate rules or make expectations explicit. We assume that every woman-to-woman relationship starts, by definition, from an egalitarian place, or that all women are equally emotionally responsible for relationships.

Lesbian relationships are particularly vulnerable to too much goodness. Since both partners have been raised to be good women, they often suffer from the myth that all women think and feel alike. It's assumed that conflict shouldn't come up and that, if it does, it should be avoided. Some disagreement is essential in any relationship so that individuals can clarify where they stand on important issues. But in a lesbian relationship, disagreement may go underground until it finally explodes in a damaging way.

Two women may outdo one another at being unselfish, giving, and more focused on the relationship than on their individual goals. And the lack of social sanction for lesbian relationships contributes to a tendency for two women to have difficulty with the "balance of goodness." If we are lesbian women and feel we need to hide our identity from the shaming judgments of the world around us, then our relationship becomes the only safe place to be in a nonaccepting world. Any relationship would suffer damage from this kind of intense pressure to be the only "safe house" in a woman's life.

Lesbian couplehood is shrouded in invisibility—it's unrecognized, unacknowledged, and disrespected. We may see images of good women and bad, alcoholic women in the media, but look for a positive image of a lesbian and you'll see no woman. The validity of their lives and relationships denied, lesbians have few models as they define their relationship rules. Challenged by the difficult task of creating new rules and rituals for themselves as they go along, lesbian women often have much to teach all women about freeing themselves from the old Code of Goodness and creating relationships that reflect a more workable balance.

MARY AND JOAN

Mary and Joan had lived together for three years. Their relationship seemed like a battlefield. They were each so angry at one another so much of the time that they often wondered what had drawn them together. Neither one was sure what the problem was. Mary said, "I feel like I do nothing but work in this relationship, and I get criticized for it besides. I work inside, I work outside, and I have a job that is very pressured besides. There's not much positive emotional contact. I feel like I just don't want to do it anymore. When Joan and I met, things were so intense and emotional. I thought we'd have this wonderful, caring relationship. But now she seems so self-involved and all I do is work. Something isn't right."

Joan said, "I feel depressed and like Mary is always on me, always complaining about something."

Since Mary's complaint was that she had to "do" too much in the relationship, the couple's first task was to make an exhaustive list of responsibilities and to check who did what. The list was to include emotional jobs such as initiating sex and functional jobs like paying the bills.

Here is Mary's list.

- Pay the bills.
- Clean the house.
- Do the food shopping.
- Do the laundry.
- Make vet's appointments for dog and cat.
- Remember, buy and send cards and presents to family and friends.
- Earn the major share of the household money.
- Decorate the house.
- Physically maintain the outside of the house.
- Plan the menus.
- Take full charge of all entertaining.
- Make dentist and doctor appointments for both of us.
- Take cars to be serviced.
- Clean and organize closets.

Here is Joan's list:

- Come up with ideas for vacations.
- Give emotional support.
- Initiate recreation for the two of us.
- Cook (sometimes).
- Help with cleaning the house.
- Arrange for yard work to be done.
- Take care of the animals.

When the two of them saw each other's lists it wasn't hard to figure out why Mary was angry. She and Joan had never explicitly established rules in their relationship about who was responsible for what. They had made many assumptions about what represented "good" behavior.

Joan was an artist. Early on, Mary had rationalized that Joan was too "right brain" and creative to handle the mundane details of living. Her evidence was that whenever Joan walked into a room, things seemed to fly in all directions and Joan seemed to have no sense of how to bring about order again. Mary soon got used to "keeping the house" because she felt that she was the only one competent to do it.

Joan claimed that she did know how to take care of most of those details of living. She certainly took care of them before she met Mary. But after they started living together it became clear to Joan that not only was Mary more organized (there was some truth to the myth that Mary was more "left brain"), but that she was more competent at organizing a household. She also felt that Mary believed her standards were of a higher moral order. If Joan cleaned up the kitchen after a meal, Mary would come along after her and wipe the kitchen counters again. Mary would tell Joan that she didn't do the job right.

Joan said, "No matter what I did, I never did it to her standards."

Mary said, "My standards are just ordinary decent standards."

Joan said, "I hated it that the house always had to be cleaned before we could go canoeing. Who cared?"

Mary said, "She just takes it for granted that I'll do it all."

As Mary and Joan reviewed the ways their relationship had developed, they realized that they had never specifically agreed to any guidelines. Early in their relationship, Joan had temporarily had a job that involved a two-hour commute. Mary had just naturally pitched in and done more than her share. Joan was very appreciative of her help. But when Joan changed jobs after six months, a balance had already been established and Mary just kept doing more.

But by the time she came to therapy she was feeling taken for granted. Once she thought about it, she said, "I guess I don't know if Joan still loves me for who I am or only for what I do. Sometimes I just feel like a set of functions."

When Joan thought about it, she said, "I think part of my depression has been the feeling that I never do it right. Somewhere along the line I just gave up trying. It seemed easier."

Focusing on the very specific details that pinpointed who did what had given them a structure for talking about the rules and assumptions that defined their relationship. Ultimately the emotional issues that those rules expressed came more to the surface.

Joan said, "I guess I've always thought that my work was important, more important than other things, and if someone else would be responsible for those things that was fine with me. I guess I just assumed that if somebody loved me they would take care of some things. I grew up in a family where I wasn't expected to do anything. But I think I'm being unfair to Mary. I guess I've got to pull my weight more."

Mary felt overwhelmed, and Joan felt inadequate. Both were angry. Mary was angry because she thought she was choosing a relationship that would be emotionally nurturing, and instead she found herself working hard with little emotional gratification. Joan felt angry that the rules established by her family would no longer work for her as an adult —she would need to take care of parts of her life besides her work whether she felt adequate at them or not.

Mary said, "I'm just not going to take care of things anymore. I'll insist that we sit and decide jointly who's going to do what. And I'll have to learn to live with the messy kitchen counters. I don't like being the house drone anymore. That's not what I thought this relationship was going to be about." Mary said she realized that if she wanted more emotional contact, she'd need to give up some of her focus on the "details" and be a little less a perfectionist. Joan said she realized she'd have to take more responsibility for her own and the joint household "details."

As their relationship became more balanced around these concrete details, many of their emotional differences became more workable as well. In this relationship "who did what" became a statement about whose emotional needs got met, who was more important. Mary and Joan began to work toward a relationship that was more mutually satisfying for both of them.

A few months after therapy ended, Joan called, chuckling. "I just want to tell you that Mary leaves the kitchen a mess now. It's driving me crazy. I figure I asked for it, and I thought you'd get a laugh."

WOMEN AS FRIENDS

Many women think of their friendships as the most important relationships in their lives. Friendships are often our most fulfilling and reliable sources of emotional support, validation, and love. When asked "What helps?" in terms of being overwhelmed and feeling pressured, Janet's (chapter 1) immediate response was, "My friends." Another woman says, "My friendships with women are the primary relationships in my life, even when I'm with a man."

Yet, as important as these relationships are to most of us, they're often the first to suffer when the pressures of work or a demanding family life become too compelling. A recent article in a national newspaper described a group of women who are chief executive officers of national corporations. These women are forming a monthly support group among themselves because of their recognition that the major price they've paid for their success is to have given up all their female friendships. They've realized that they need the emotional support of other women if they're to keep functioning effectively in the male-dominated business world.

We are quick to deprive ourselves of this source of nurturing for ourselves. Our women friends often feel emotionally abandoned when our focus shifts to a relationship with a man and/or family. They often feel competitive with our single-minded devotion to our work. Finding a balance in which we can allow our women friends to remain the important sources of nurturing that they are is difficult but essential to our well-being.

Often we abandon friendships because the rules of goodness are hard to establish. We sometimes assume we have to give more than we can or want to, and sometimes our friends want more from us than we can give. Often we're afraid to ask for as much as we want. Saying no with friends can be even more painful than it is with husbands, lovers, and children. We want to be generous with our friends. We want them to be generous with us.

If the rules of goodness are a problem with a friend, there's likely to be no easy give and take in the relationship. You may find that you always go along with your friend's plans, and that you always tend to fit your schedule or interests to hers. You have a hard time giving feedback or saying what you really think or feel. You may sense that your friend has a lot of expectations of you and you're afraid of what will happen if you say no. For instance, when your friend calls, you find that you can't get off the phone even if something else important needs attention. Instead of saying "I'd really like to but I can't talk right now," you have someone else answer the phone and say you're not there, or you stay on the phone feeling resentful that she doesn't understand that you're busy. You may be equally afraid to make demands that your friend focus on your interests or plans at times. You worry often about hurting her feelings. Sometimes you feel you give more or do more than her either emotionally or concretely, but you're not able to say that to her.

The most difficult situation for you to handle may come up when your friend wants more of a relationship with you than you do with her. In the interests of not "hurting her feelings," you give ambivalent and confusing messages about how much a priority the relationship is to you. You spend more energy trying to avoid being honest than you would if you simply said, "I'm sorry but I want a less involved relationship than you."

Many friendships evolve easily. The relationship often achieves a level of mutual comfort without the need for a great deal of work at it. But, as any relationship deepens, if we're to achieve a more satisfying level of intimacy, we need to talk about the "rules," the mutual expectations we have of one another, the depth of involvement we want with one another. It's as important not to operate from a position of being "too good" in friendship as it is in any other important relationship. Overdoing, along with hidden assumptions and rules about emotional caretaking, may end up undermining the very relationships that we most look to as sources of nurturing, validation, and support.

WORKING TOO HARD AT WORK

During the time that we were writing our first book, each of us had the experience of being told angrily by our best friends, "You're addicted to work. Your life is out of balance." More disturbingly, they began to spend more leisure time with newer friends. When we tried to talk about the pressures of the lecture circuit we were on, they said, "Well, you chose it. You like the limelight. You wouldn't give it up, would you?" Each of us thought, "They don't understand." We loved what we were doing. And sometimes we felt as if we didn't have the choice to set limits.

Our friends were hurt that we had withdrawn some of our emotional energy, not to mention our time, from our relationships with them. They got tired of our ongoing complaints about a lack of time and energy. They got tired of having somewhat one-sided relationships with us. Their response was to tell us we were "bad" for working hard. We began to feel we were paying too high a price for our involvement with work. Our relationships suffered too much.

We did love what we were doing; it seemed necessary and important. But our lives *were* unbalanced at that point and the conversations with our friends highlighted the imbalance. Ultimately each of us made major changes and decisions that put work back into a different perspective. We said no to certain commitments. We changed our "economic" lifestyles. We worked at building back into our lives the time for our friends that we used to have.

But in the process we realized how driven all women are by certain beliefs about work. And we realized the many ways that the "rules" of the workplace for women create ongoing conflicts and stress.

Work is an important source of satisfaction for many of us. We frankly would not relinquish the joy that comes from mastery, the excitement of fitting our talents to the task, the stimulation of the larger world, or the financial independence that we've achieved. And some of us get a kick out of the power games we've learned to play. A client who was dean of a nursing school said laughingly, "I learned how to subtly rub my wrist in a meeting so they'd notice that not only physicians wear Rolexes."

But no matter how much a woman loves her work, most women feel that good personal relationships are critical to living a balanced life. So most of us try to balance work *and* relationships, whether those relationships include marriage and children, friendship, or a weekend lover. This struggle for balance between work and relationships often results in a woman's feeling like a failure at both.

Tina was a client who was executive vice-president of a large firm. She had extensive background in her field and was only a dissertation away from her doctorate. But the focus of her therapy was her three failed marriages. The more she achieved, the more she felt inadequate at making relationships work. The more her relationships failed, the more she discounted her achievements at work. "I get the recognition for competence out there in the world. But inside I think, 'If they only knew my personal life and what a shambles it is.' I know that I'm a fraud."

Tina's feelings aren't unusual. Discomfort and a sense of inadequacy about relationships continues to be a primary concern for women. In spite of the fact that it's become a major part of most women's lives, our clients rarely talk about work as an important issue in their therapy sessions. If they do, it's usually to resolve a relationship problem that they're encountering in the office. More often they talk about their shame that they can't seem to balance work and relationships more successfully.

Single women who may have very clear career goals but an equally strong desire for children begin to worry at a certain point that the biological clock is running out. They worry that work will prevent them from having fulfilling relationships. They worry that if they appear too "together" it will seem that they don't need anyone. Other single women wonder whether something is wrong with them if they don't want a primary relationship.

And, in fact, advancing a career usually does mean working long hours, bringing work home, and giving work the emotional energy we might otherwise reserve for focusing on relationships with family or friends.

One of the most difficult conflicts between making relationships work and being competent at work occurs when a woman works and is also a mother. Providing adequate child care continues to be seen as the major responsibility of the mother in almost all cases. If we are mothers who work outside the home, we may tell the school to call our husband if our child has a problem. We might even give our husband's phone number to the school nurse or the babysitter. But we typically don't feel good about it when he's the one to get the call. We're more likely to feel vaguely inadequate, as though we've somehow shirked our job. And what if we're a single mother who has no one else's number to give?

The major rule many of us establish for our work lives is to assume that we can be both perfectly present in our relationships and work perfectly competently without ever being uncomfortable and in conflict. We feel chronically bad as a result. We tell ourselves that we *should* be perfect jugglers, and then feel even worse when reality tells us we're not. What we don't do is question our own expectations of ourselves. We can't accept that it's simply not possible to focus both on relationships and on work and to do both perfectly. We need to let our focus move back and forth from one to the other in a way that can let one thing go when the other needs to be more the priority. Sometimes we need to make changes in our work life if our true priority is relationships.

CONFLICTING RULES AT WORK

The rules of the Goodness Code create conflict between our private and our public obligations, but they also create conflict within the context of the workplace itself. Often we're forced to obey two conflicting sets of rules that dictate how to be a "good" woman at work.

On the one hand, being "good" interpersonally means being cooperative, sensitive, and not hurting others. It means being a good team player. It means in some sense being a "lady."

On the other hand, being focused on the task to be accomplished often requires that we be insensitive to our own feelings or those of other people. Since models for success in the paid workplace are primarily defined by males, we may instinctively emphasize more male traits, like aggression or competitiveness. But these are considered negative traits in a female. So the behavior required to meet the demands of one aspect of the work setting automatically renders us bad in the context of the other.

The woman who is a welder in a shipyard and the woman in the corporate environment both need to be seen as strong enough to do the job without looking like a man. But they also can't afford to look like too much of a woman. Being too competitive and aggressive at work or needing too much emotional support at work can equally make us feel bad.

Nora, retired now, but formerly the only woman on the president's executive committee of her university, said, "I did play some games. I can tell you still where I sat in every meeting room. I walked in, sat in the power spot, leaned forward with my elbows on the table, and removed my glasses emphatically. They all waited for my solution. But I still let them know I was a lady. I'd cough gently at some of their jokes to let them know the jokes were too gross for me."

Nora didn't feel bad that she had to balance the male's understanding of the power game with looking so female that she winced at dirty jokes. She considered it a kind of challenge and kept her sense of humor about it. But many of us would feel bad. Jean said, "I hated the power games. It made me feel like I had to use the more male parts of myself. God, I despised it. But once in the game, I was in the game to win. So I'd use tears too, if I had to. I left the corporate world because I hated those games. Now I work independently as a consultant, and I can choose clients with whom I don't need to play those games."

Sometimes we need to prove to ourselves that we're being valued for our professional accomplishments and not for our femininity, so we work doubletime to ensure that our competence will be recognized.

A friend in a middle management job in a large corporation took an afternoon off for some medical tests. Her boss called her late that afternoon and asked how she was.

"I was pleasantly surprised and touched that he appeared to be concerned about me," she told us. "In fact, I was so surprised that I told him I felt better than I did."

"Good," he said. "We're having a real problem with the secretary on that project you've been working on. Would you mind awfully coming back in for an hour to help us straighten it out?"

"Can you believe that I didn't even realize the inappropriateness of his request until after I had agreed to go back to work for the afternoon? I feel disgusted with myself as I admit it. But I felt in a bind. If I had been 'too sick' to go back, he might have discounted my management ability."

ATTEMPTS TO ACHIEVE THE IMPOSSIBLE

As we've seen in chapter 3, career women today operate by a rule that says competence means having it all without looking overwhelmed. We often feel we must juggle a multiplicity of choices and balance many different roles.[2] In the process we have to cope with our alleged fear of success[3] and fight the effects of stress, among them eating disorders, addiction, and a compulsion toward perfection.[4] In the eighties and nineties, the illusion has been created that, despite the inequities that still exist in the paid workplace, women really can have it all if only we're good enough to manage it all correctly. We almost never look at the reality that these expectations of ourselves may be impossible unless we have a ready-made support crew of many to stand behind us. But by trying we convey the message that it is or should be possible, and we reinforce our own as well as other people's expectations of us to keep juggling.

We definitely think that women can have satisfying careers and relationships too. But we think a certain amount of conflict is inevitable if we don't question the premise that we can do it all. And we don't think you have to "do it all" to have a full life. We do think you have to make choices and set priorities that are consistent with your own needs.

What's more, in work as in any other area of our lives, if we demonstrate that we can handle more responsibility, we'll be given even more to handle. Our competence is generally validated by our being asked to do more.

If we find ourselves saying, "I just can't find time to fit that course in stress management into my schedule," the problem isn't one of managing stress. It's a problem of too much stress. It's a result of being too good for our own good.

LOOKING AT THE LARGER IMBALANCE

Our beliefs about juggling work and relationships are probably the major sources of stress in our lives. Of necessity, many of us have jumped into a model of work that's very male-defined. Not only do we aspire to do the same work that men have traditionally done, we aspire to do it in the way that men do it—a way that can be driven, perfectionist, and mechanistic. While we may tend to the immediate emotional concerns of the people around us at work, we often don't see that the larger structure of the work world itself, as well as the environment that we work in, is dehumanizing and unresponsive generally to people's emotional needs.

The beliefs we hold as a society are a major source of difficulty when it comes to the rules of the workplace. Our culture's ways of thinking only in economic terms about work haven't yet responded to the reality that unless this society fundamentally changes the way it works, families and individuals won't survive because they won't have time. There will no longer be an issue of a man working while a wife chooses to stay home. Economic necessity as well as realistic financial responsibility will dictate that everyone work. As that happens, sooner or later, the rigid rules of the workplace must give over to a concern about the quality of our emotional lives. Two adult people in a family or relationship can't both work eight or more hours a day, five to seven days a week, in a pressured, demanding, dehumanized environment, and still raise healthy, happy children or even remain healthy and happy themselves.

There is simply more to do than can be done in our lives when most of our time is spent at work. Work dominates the lives of all of us too much. As much as we may love it, most of us are out of balance with it, most by necessity rather than by choice. A society that demands that people sacrifice the major portion of their lives for the sake of other people's profit is not a nurturing or a healthy society.

When the rules of work begin to change at a larger societal level, life will become more balanced for all of us. But women may have to stimulate that larger change by making the point that they *can't* do it all. If we play by a rule, we reinforce it. Since our presence in the work force is becoming more economically important to businesses, women may be in a critical position of power to force change in the larger rules about how this society does business. If we learn to say "no" more often in a work setting, then we change the expectation that anyone, man or woman, can work singlemindedly without concern for relationships.

When our work environments can allow for more vacation time, child care, flexible work hours, job sharing and a shortened work day, we'll all feel differently about work. We'll get the message that perfection, competition, achievement, and production aren't the end goals of life itself, that they aren't the major measures of our value as people. We'll give up some of the drive to have "things" that feeds our imbalance with work. Work will have its important, but balanced, place in our lives, whether we're men or women. And as a result, we may get to be in better balance with ourselves.

12

GOOD MOTHERS, GOOD DAUGHTERS

——— ✳ ———

"You won't let me be myself." Sixteen-year-old Monica is tearful and frustrated with her mother, Gwen. "I can't even have a sad look on my face without you asking me, 'What's wrong, what's wrong?' "

Monica is Gwen's only child. Gwen has been divorced from Monica's father for four years. She confesses that her greatest fear has been that Monica would have "problems." She says to Monica, "When you think I'm trying to control your feelings, it's just that I'm worried. I keep feeling that I created your life and I'm responsible for it. What's so awful about my asking you what's wrong?"

Monica proceeds to tell us all the ways that she feels her mother "watches her like a hawk." Her major complaint is that Gwen disapproves of her boyfriend and some of the other friends she spends time with. But the catalog of complaints against Gwen is endless. "I'm not allowed to shut my bedroom door. You ask me all the time what I get in the mail. You pick up the extension when I'm on the phone, and you're always criticizing what I'm wearing and how much makeup I have on. You hate my friends, you think they're stupid; you don't like the way they look or the jobs they have. You're a real hypocrite, Mom, when you always tell me not to be judgmental about people."

Monica has responded to her mother's focus on her, predictably, by becoming more provocative. She wears outrageous outfits and stays away from home as much as possible. All Gwen has to do is raise an eyebrow and Monica flies into a rage.

Exploring the problem further made it fairly obvious that Gwen was doing too much for Monica as well as focusing on her too much. "I thought a job would teach Monica responsibility, so I arranged with the owner of the local coffee shop to hire her. The shop's only a short bike ride away, but I thought if I drove her there every day she wouldn't be late." When Monica had a sore throat, Gwen called in sick for her. Monica worked at the job for a very brief time and then just abandoned it.

"Gwen," we ask, "tell us more about your struggles to raise Monica by yourself. You're trying very hard with your daughter. What are your ideas about the job of being a mother?" As Gwen talked, Monica listened quietly, wiping an occasional tear from her eyes.

"Well, part of the problem for me was being left by my husband. Monica knows this story so I can talk about it. He left me for another woman. But, before he did, he was very bitter and spent most of his time telling me what an awful wife I was and how I was an awful mother. I *was* always the strict one. I'm real concerned to be a good mother. But he always told me I was too rigid. He would undermine everything I told Monica. Now that he's gone, he pays almost no attention to Monica at all. It's like he's rejecting her to get back at me. I feel like I'm all Monica's got, and really she's all the family I've got. I want to make things right for her. I want her to feel cared about. Growing up in my home back in Ohio wasn't so great. I want her to have a better growing up than I did."

It seemed that Gwen felt almost desperate to succeed as a mother. She somehow felt that it was her fault that Monica's father had abandoned her. Feeling like a failure as a wife had made her role as mother even more important to her. She also wanted Monica to have the kind of mother she felt she had missed. Yet all her good intentions were turning her daughter against her, and she felt totally out of control.

UNDERSTANDING GWEN'S DILEMMA

Imagine yourself in Gwen's position. You're a woman who began life as a good daughter, loyal to the needs of your parents, unclear about your own desires for yourself. Imagine now that you have a child, and think for a moment what that child might mean to you. Think about your hopes for that child.

Almost certainly if it has been important to you to be a good daughter, it will be even more important to you to be a good mother. You may think of your child as a visible symbol of your own goodness—having a child at all may confirm your compliance with the rule that women focus on someone other than themselves. If your own parents did fail to meet some of your developmental needs, you'll want to be sure you don't do the same. You'll want to give your child everything you lacked. And maybe you'll even hope to reclaim some part of your own lost self in your child.

Since you know it's your job to make relationships work, and since a mother's relationship with her child is viewed as the major influence on a child's development, you'll think of yourself as entirely responsible for your child's health and happiness. Since you know it's your role to nurture, you will expect yourself to do it perfectly. There will be a lot riding on the happiness and success of this child—in effect he or she will represent your own success or failure at being a good mother and thus a good woman.

Can any child really bear this burden of proof? Can any woman really live up to these impossible expectations of herself? The answer is obviously no. Yet we steadfastly try. Putting too much energy into our children often ends in their rebelling and being bad. Or they become "too good" themselves and go on to relate in the same ways to their own children. The Goodness Code gets passed along endlessly, as does the myth that women are responsible for it all.

And yet when it comes to being a mother, most of us feel that we're in a terrible bind. We sense or know that we're expected to be too responsible and then feel attacked for doing it.

Our culture assumes that every need of a child should be met all of the time and only by its mother.[1] Mothers are blamed for doing too much, but they are also blamed if they do too little. They're blamed if their child has any kind of problem, while fathers are assumed to have little impact on their children's development. Mothers can't win. The fact that a woman who's too good in other relationships is often told she's acting "like my mother" points to the fact that mothering is often a thankless and frustrating job at best, viewed with ambivalence and often hostility by men and adult children alike.

The "Mother, please, I'd rather do it myself" TV commercial that was so popular some years back was a commentary on this impossible bind of women—do too much and people become angry. Do too little and people become angry. Freud questioned many years ago, "What do women want?" But it might have been more pertinent to ask, "What do people want from women, particularly from mothers?" Since the answer to this question is represented in the Goodness Code, it's time for women to rethink their ideas about the requirements of womanhood in general and mothering in particular. Certainly new rules should be based on the premise that no woman is single-handedly responsible for the total well-being of her child.

Because while many women pour their hearts and souls into their children, many fathers somehow manage to default on their emotional obligations. They often take too little responsibility for the lives they've helped to create.

Let's look more closely at the balance of responsibility and goodness between parents and children from the perspective of women as mothers. And let's examine the problems of responsibility that come up when a woman is called on to take care of her aging parents as well as her growing child. Finally, where do men fit into this picture? Why, when it comes to children, does their presence seem no more well defined than that of a shadow in the pages of the family album?

THE AVIS MOTHER
BEING SECOND BEST, WE TRY HARDER

Gwen's relationship with Monica was troubled because of the deep shame and anxiety that surfaced for her when she felt that she'd failed to live up to the injunctions of the Goodness Code. Gwen questioned her attractiveness to men, she questioned her ability to make relationships work.

Monica's behavior had the power to define Gwen as a good or bad mother. As a result, their relationship was dominated by conflict, mistrust, and anger. The more Gwen tried to reinforce her sense of goodness by taking responsibility for Monica, the more pressured Monica felt and the more she fought back. The more Gwen did for her, the less Monica did for herself.

The relationship between Monica and Gwen illustrates the kind of breakdown that can occur when a mother puts too much energy into being good to her child. The child sometimes experiences that energy as an expectation and rebels.

The problem is heightened when our children let us know that, as much as we may do for them, it's their father's love and approval that feels more important. Monica, for example, would spend hours with Gwen talking about her father, maintaining an unrealistic idea that he truly loved her while Gwen's role in her life was to "give her grief." Male children, as they should, want a connection with the important male figure in their lives. Female children need that connection too, but they also learn that their value as a female is dependent on a male's, not a mother's, approval.

Mothers handle this anxiety about being fully responsible yet second best in different ways. Some of us do too much; others become afraid to get too emotionally involved with our children for fear of needing them too much. We don't feel secure that we can mother adequately, so we do too little. Many women in our mothers' generation dealt with their anxiety by seeking expert advice—so children in our generation were often raised according to the dictates of Dr. Spock.

We get more involved with some of our children than we do with others. Certain of our children take on special meaning for us. We may respond differently to them if they are sons rather than daughters. They are born, perhaps, just after the death of one of our parents and we hope they'll relieve the pain of that loss. They remind us of a beloved or a particularly troublesome sibling or parent. Perhaps they are born at a time when we feel less adequate in our roles as women in general. Or they may be an oldest child whom we depend on in the wake of a painful divorce. They may be the child who becomes a focus of attention in the midst of a painful conflict in our marriage. Or they may be handicapped by a physical or emotional problem.

In any one of these situations in particular and when raising children in general, we are constantly called on to question, what is appropriate responsibility for this child? What is good for this child? What is the difference between my ideas about mothering and what is really needed? What are the rules about goodness between mothers and children?

KNOWING WHEN GOOD IS TOO GOOD

In chapter 7 we talked about a new basic rule of appropriate responsibility: Never do something for another person that they can comfortably do for themselves. This rule applies equally to children and adults, taking age limitations into account. So the first question to ask yourself with regard to your children is, "Do I routinely do tasks for them that they could be doing for themselves? Do I expect them to care for their own physical well-being and for the well-being of the living space that we share?" If not, why not?

One of the forms that Gwen's overfocus on Monica took was that she did too much for her and expected Monica to do little for herself. At sixteen, Monica was competent to get herself a job and to ride a bicycle to get there. She didn't need Gwen to wash and iron all of her clothes and prepare every meal that she ate each day.

Gwen said, "I know I do too much for her. It's just my way of being sure that she's alright. If I take care of it, at least I know that it will get done. But I guess I'm doing all her thinking for her. I don't have anyone else to care for really. It's hard to give up that role. I guess I'm treating Monica like she's six instead of sixteen. I guess I've got to let her grow up."

Gwen had a mixture of feelings that ended in her doing too much for Monica. She wanted to be a caring mother, she wanted everything to be alright. She needed a focus for her nurturing energy, and without an intimate relationship in her life and without other outside interests, she tended to be too focused on what Monica was doing.

Monica, on the other hand, felt controlled and wanted to be more independent. Yet, as she gradually revealed, Gwen's tendency to do too much had left her feeling secretly frightened and incompetent to do the things she needed to do for herself.

As a first step in rebalancing the rules of goodness and responsibility in this relationship, Monica and Gwen decided that they would work out an agreement about what each of them was or wasn't to take care of. The agreement would change as Monica felt more competent and as Gwen felt more comfortable doing less.

Gwen was willing to let Monica take care of her own clothes. She agreed that Monica could fix dinner for herself at least twice a week, and that she would help clean up the house and take care of the kitchen. She agreed that Monica should take care of getting herself a job and that she should make her own arrangements to get there. Instead of focusing so much on doing *for* Monica, Gwen could now be concerned about how well the agreement was working. And the agreement assumed that it wasn't helpful to Monica to be too good.

Therapy sessions helped Monica and Gwen to talk about their expectations and assumptions about who was responsible for what. Gwen was surprised to learn that Monica really believed and accepted that she should take care of certain things for herself. Now, rather than rebelling, when Gwen did too much Monica was able to say, "You're not sticking to the agreement. This is up to me to take care of." Gwen could say to Monica, "I thought we agreed you'd take care of this—I'm feeling uneasy that you haven't done it." Gwen learned to voice her uneasiness *and* to let Monica handle the consequences of not taking care of things without going back to doing them for her.

These changes were difficult for both Gwen and Monica. Gwen's anxiety that Monica would be "bad" and thus render her a failure in her own eyes was painful for her. She was frequently tempted to go back to overdoing and often needed therapy sessions for support and reinforcement. Monica took every liberty to let things go, as if testing the new rules. But both were learning important lessons—Monica that she was increasingly expected to assume adult responsibility, and Gwen that her more important job as a parent was to prepare Monica to do just that. Gwen was learning that being a "good mother" sometimes meant doing less.

THE DIFFICULTY IN LIFE IS THE CHOICE

Gwen's difficulties with Monica were not just a matter of who did what. As we saw in the previous chapter, unbalanced rules in a relationship also reflect a deeper emotional imbalance between two people. When we take too much emotional responsibility for children, they don't learn how to make choices for themselves. They often don't develop good judgment, and they have a difficult time learning to be comfortable with their own feelings.

To take too much emotional responsibility means to protect a child's feelings, to undo or excuse the consequences of his behavior. It means to avoid discussing painful feelings and to handle situations yourself that may be emotionally difficult for her. It means to tell a child what he should feel or think. It means to make decisions for her without knowing what she thinks or feels herself.

In her effort to be protective of Monica, Gwen made many judgments for her about how she should dress, what kind of friends she should have, how she should or shouldn't spend her time. She didn't take the time to hear what Monica felt about these issues. Often Gwen felt she had to decide for Monica. As a mother, she felt that she knew what was best. And while, as an adult, her judgment certainly was better than Monica's, Monica wasn't likely to learn unless she had the opportunity to experience the consequences of her own decisions.

"What else am I supposed to do if I can't point things out to her?" Gwen asked. "Just sit back and watch while Monica gets pregnant or involved with the wrong crowd? Should I let her go out of the house looking like she buys her clothes at Army Surplus? How do you think that reflects on me?"

We know that adolescence is a difficult time for both a parent and a child to live through. It's never comfortable. Emotional ups and downs dominate. It's a time that often brings us face to face with the reality that our child is different from us and can't be depended on to act the way we expect.

But Gwen learned that she needed to focus less on the specifics of what Monica wore or on trying to monitor whom she saw and what she did with them. She needed to replace being too emotionally responsible for Monica with being firm and nurturing.

Gwen decided that in the interests of her own comfort, she could say to Monica, "I expect you to be in by a certain time. I expect you to call for a ride if people have been drinking. I expect you to tell me who you're with and where you'll be." In other words, she was clear with Monica about her expectations and limits rather than challenging Monica's decisions. Gwen talked seriously with Monica about birth control and safe sex, and insisted that she have a plan for taking care of both. She helped Monica with the names of doctors she could see, and she went with her to the appointment. She also told her she couldn't wear Army Surplus when the two of them were out together. But otherwise Monica made her own wardrobe decisions without Gwen's input.

Still, there were deeper issues to confront. Gwen and Monica had forgotten how to enjoy spending time together. They both had many leftover feelings about the divorce and the ongoing rejection by Monica's father. They never talked about it directly except when Monica rambled on about her father in a way that made Gwen resentful. In fact, Gwen had become so anxious that Monica might have a "problem" that she often forgot to just talk to Monica about everyday things. She knew little about how Monica really felt. The two had become strangers, and Monica missed feeling close to her mother. What might have been an intimate and satisfying bond between them had become blocked by Gwen's feelings of being overly responsible. Instead of being a nurturing emotional guide for Monica as she struggled through her adolescence, Gwen had become the Secret Police.

For Gwen, being more nurturing to Monica meant talking with her, trying to understand her experience, being supportive and encouraging when Monica felt upset. It sometimes meant talking to Monica about her own frustrations and pain. It meant not solving problems or making judgments for her, but offering guidance and allowing Monica to make decisions, good or bad, on her own.

Gwen learned to say things to Monica like, "Tell me what it felt like to be in that situation. It must have been upsetting, or fun, or exciting. Would you like my help? What do you think you'll do about this problem? I love you, I want you to have a good time. It's making me pretty anxious that things aren't going well for you right now, but I'm sure you'll handle it. I'll tell you my opinion if you want to hear it."

Being more nurturing to Monica made Gwen feel better about herself. She learned that being a "good" mother meant liking and enjoying and guiding Monica, not working hard to direct the outcome of her choices. Monica's job was to learn to live her own life. And Gwen's was to give up being too good.

The process wasn't an easy one because it involved much relearning and some painful moments for both of them. Gwen didn't feel good right away. At first she felt some emptiness and anxiety as she let go of her old ways of mothering. But after some hard work in therapy, Monica and Gwen really achieved a new relationship with one another. They often came to sessions laughing and comfortable together.

Gwen started to seek out new relationships and activities for herself. She liked what she called the "new me." She decided she wanted more closeness in her life, because achieving some of it with Monica had reminded her that it was a nice thing to have. And Monica was astounded when Gwen picked her up for her therapy session one day wearing a new Army Surplus jacket of her own.

DECIDING WHAT'S GOOD
ARE BOYS AND GIRLS REALLY DIFFERENT?

It's often difficult for us, as it was for Gwen, to know how much "doing" is appropriate for a given child. It's often hard, because of the kinds of anxieties that Gwen and all women feel about their children, to just let something go, even if we know it's in the interest of the child's learning to do so.

The other difficult issue is to decide how much to expect of our children. We often make assumptions about who's responsible for what based on their sex. While this was not the case for Gwen and Monica, many mothers expect a great deal of domestic help from their daughters but little from their sons. While daughters may routinely load the dishwasher, run the vacuum, clean the bathrooms and make meals, parents often look benignly on as the males in the family jump up from the table and leave everything behind undone. Teenage girls are often assumed to be experts on their own wardrobes, while mothers still shop for their teenage sons, who end up hard pressed to tell a plaid from a stripe.

As mothers, it's typical that we also have different emotional expectations of our daughters than we do of our sons. We expect our female children to intuitively know how to handle their feelings and how to relate to others effectively. We expect them to have absorbed, in utero, all the dictates of the Goodness Code. We often expect them to be more responsible, more concerned for their appearance, more competent, more flexible, more giving than their brothers. We may tend to give them less help.

We may endlessly "do for" our sons so that they become truly incompetent at tasks and come to expect service from others. In our sons we may tolerate insensitivity, selfishness, lack of responsibility. We tell ourselves "that's just the way men are." We don't expect them to talk about their feelings or to deal responsively with other family members, and we often make excuses for them when they make mistakes. We are hard on our daughters and easy on our sons emotionally.

Sexually we often perpetuate a double standard. We tell our daughters they are responsible for avoiding pregnancy, and we often tell our sons little at all. We end up with daughters who are too good and sons who expect the women in their lives to continue to make excuses and take too much responsibility for them. If the dictates of the Goodness Code are ever to change, sons and daughters must be expected to be equally responsible for the emotional development of their own lives. They must be expected to be equally responsible for the "details" of living.

These kinds of gender differences in the expectations we have of our children convey a message that women should keep doing too much. Families must always negotiate the assignment of chores and responsibilities. But if an underlying assumption exists that certain tasks are "women's work," male children will never learn to be responsible or even competent in certain aspects of their lives. Female children will keep hearing the message that they are somehow second-class citizens who are to be of service to the others in their lives. And even men who learn to take care of themselves in their bachelorhood may revert to a "service mentality" when there's a woman around to serve them.

THE <u>CONSEQUENCES</u> OF MOTHERING TOO WELL

When women parent too much, men parent too little. Women become identified as the sole nurturers of children, and men never learn how to nurture. There is a loyalty triangle implicit in this unspoken but historically ordained contract. Women and children are close and men are on the outside. Secretly children long for their fathers but feel disloyal to their mothers if they let on. Women long for more participation from their husbands but may not want to give up their special tie to the child. The child often seems openly close to mother but is secretly allied with father. And men may feel disloyal to their wives if they take their child's part in a family disagreement. Everyone is in an impossible position. Nobody is appropriately responsible, and everyone is emotionally deprived.

This triangle might have been more apparent when most women didn't work outside the home and roles in families were more polarized. But even as they pursue careers or work outside the home, women still assume or are issued, as a badge of womanhood, the primary emotional responsibility for children. With the majority of women and men working impossible hours, children may long for more contact with *both* parents, but their mother's attention is still thought to be more essential. And women may still not feel free to ask men to meet their own and their children's emotional needs. The old loyalty triangle is still very much alive and well, and is only beginning to change as men begin to realize how much they've missed by being the family outsider.

The Dodge family has struggled with this loyalty triangle for many years. It took the severe problems of a teenage daughter to begin to change it.

THE FATHER WHO DIDN'T UNDERSTAND

Marie and Robert Dodge have come to their therapy session to discuss the problems they've been having with their fifteen-year-old daughter. In the course of the discussion, Marie starts talking about her problems with her husband. Marie says she feels that she has been the only parent in the house.

MARIE: My anger is that when Marla asked you to be there for her recital, you didn't come. When I think back, you were not there for her grammar school play and you were not there for her middle school graduation. I thought, this is not the way I want to live. Then something hit me—a thought that shocked me. I realized that *I* feel guilty for not insisting that *you* be at your own daughter's recital. I feel responsible even for that. I am totally shocked at this.

ROBERT: I can't believe I'm hearing this. You know I have to travel on business.

MARIE: It's just that I came to realize that I didn't want to do it alone. I also didn't want to be holding the bag anymore with Marla.

ROBERT: I just can't communicate any more with that kid.

MARIE: No, don't give me that. Do you know that the last two trips you've been on, I've actually been afraid to be alone with her. Why couldn't I say to you, "Robert, I need you to be here, don't go on the trip"?

ROBERT: I came back a day early, didn't I?

MARIE: Yes, after you had finished most of your business. But the point was, I didn't even want you to go on that trip—I was in a very bad way. You said to me, "Do you want me to stay?" and I said to you, "I don't know." I didn't even have the nerve to say to you, "Don't go." When I told you this on the phone a week later, you said to me, "It's very important for me to take care of business." I didn't know what else to say. You always say to me, "Do you want me to . . ." in a way that makes me feel guilty if I say yes. I'm not strong enough to say, "Listen, this time, *I* want to come first."

ROBERT: (*Shaking his head*) I don't understand—I keep thinking you're strong.

In this dialogue, Marie was not referring to minor management problems with Marla. A physically large fifteen-year-old, Marla has violent outbursts of rage and has repeatedly threatened her mother, even pushing her against walls when Marie won't do what is asked. Marie relates to Marla in much the same way she does to Robert—she feels angry at her and guilty at the same time. She finds it difficult to say no, always convinced that she's depriving her of something important.

While Marie fears depriving Marla, the real deprivation in her own life is more hidden. It emerges in these last few pieces of dialogue between her and Robert.

ROBERT: I think in many ways our marriage used to work for us. I think we had adapted to each other's personalities. I think it's the tension with Marla, my inability to cope with her, that has brought up all these problems.

MARIE: I want us to stop talking about Marla now. I don't mean to keep harping on this, but this problem between us has been there for very long. It was two years ago when I first said to you I wanted you to make arrangements for us for the day of our anniversary. Before that I never asked you for anything. You always said you never understood what I wanted because I didn't say it outright. So, after all those months of therapy I finally learned. I came right out and said, "Robert, I want a gift, I don't want just a card, and I want you to make a reservation in a restaurant." I reminded you a week before, even two days before, to make sure that you wouldn't forget. Now how much more direct could I be? Still you didn't do it. There's no excuse for it.

ROBERT: It's no excuse. I just don't feel that anniversaries are that important. You've said it's not important to you.

MARIE: They're not important to you, but they're important to me. I said it's not always important that I get a gift. But I want some personal kind of acknowledgment. *You* didn't think to buy me a Christmas gift last year—you had your office wire me flowers.

ROBERT: I really don't understand, I just can't comprehend why two mature people need to make such a big deal out of events like anniversaries or Christmas.

MARIE: You want to know why, I'll tell you why it's important! (*Shouting*) Because I have always taken care of everything in that house— you, your daughter, the cleaning, the cooking, all of it. . . . I wanted to be taken care of on *one* day. I wanted you to make an effort and do something to take care of me. And it would be a token, a symbol that you can take the same kind of care—that you can write yourself a memo that it's an important day just the way you do when it's your business. I'm jealous of the business because what's important in business you don't forget.

What is ironic is that a woman who is so deprived of emotional responsiveness herself in her marriage should be so concerned to give to her child. Only after much therapy has she been able to break free from the belief that she is not "good" if she asks to have her needs met.

Had this belief not dominated their marriage for so many years, Robert might have been forced much sooner to learn how to be emotionally responsive. He might have been able to give up his image of himself as "good provider." He might have felt that the rewards of warmth and sharing in his relationships with his wife and child made competence at relating as important as competence at work.

Marie's efforts to be a good mother and Robert's absence in his efforts to be a good provider have left the whole family sadly disconnected. Neither is to blame—they are victims of the Goodness Code and the Code of Strength, as is our whole society. Marie did what she was taught was the "good" thing for a mother to do, and Robert assumed his sole task was to make a living.

This family has many days of struggle ahead of it. Marie needs to replace giving and doing with nurturing, particularly herself. And Robert needs to learn to be more present as a parent and as a partner to Marie. Marie's work as a woman is to demand more from Robert and to be firmer with her daughter. As Marie learns to embrace the principles of balance, she'll feel less deprived and less responsible to be a "good mother." Her husband and daughter will understand their own responsibilities in a new light. The rules of goodness in this family will be rebalanced.

BECOMING OUR MOTHER'S MOTHER

One rarely meets a woman over thirty-five who doesn't struggle with hard questions involving her relationship with an aging parent. Women in middle age are often referred to as the "sandwich generation." They're "sandwiched" between the demands of their own growing children and the needs of their aging parents. Often they struggle to meet the needs of both at the same time. Even if a woman is single, the problems of an aging parent can create both emotional and practical strains. It's in the face of these increasing demands to care for our own parents that the question of who's responsible for what can become even more difficult to answer.

Martha is a busy lawyer who struggles to balance her time with her family with her commitments to clients at work. On one recent weekend, she and her husband, Jim, were planning a two-day outing at a seaport town not far from their home with their twin girls. Martha's job at her current law firm was a relatively new one, and the family hadn't spent a weekend away together in quite a long while.

Martha's mother is widowed and lives alone in a town about two hours away from Martha. Just as the plans for the seaport weekend finally took shape and Martha started to look forward to getting away, her mother called. When she heard that Martha, Jim, and the girls were going away, she started complaining bitterly that she wouldn't see them that weekend. She told Martha, "I haven't seen you in a month. I'm older now and alone, and the time you manage to spend with me is just not enough. At least I'm honest about it."

Martha is normally a calm person who easily handles most problems in her life. But this confrontation left her in tears.

"No matter what I do, it never seems to be enough," she protested. "I love my mother. But I also love my husband and my kids. And what about myself? I used to feel pretty good about myself, but these days I feel like a selfish person most of the time. I don't know. Maybe I should have offered to take her with us. I probably should, but I don't want to. We need some time to be together ourselves. *I* need some time away, damn it!"

Martha went on to say that nobody, not even Jim or the kids, had the power to get her as upset as her mother did. She wondered why she always felt so much guilt and anger about her mother's demands. Her brother, who lived about the same distance away, saw her mother much less and that seemed to be acceptable. It was always Martha who was expected to "be there."

"Why is it," Martha went on to question, "that no matter what I do, my mother never approves of me? Do you know that she still sends me articles from the paper about how to raise my children? That she still tells me that I don't use the right laundry detergent or that I don't pay enough attention to Jim? And then when I do take the time to be with him, she complains that I don't see her. Jim kids me. He says maybe to make her happy, I should just go back to live with her and give up him, the kids, and my job. When he puts it that way, I see how crazy my reactions are. Do all mothers and daughters go through this?"

We tried to help Martha salvage her weekend without having it dominated by guilt. We told her that it was quite OK not to take her mother along. But in response to the question, "Can a daughter ever get a mother's approval," we had no easy answers.

Along with other writers on the subject,[2] we think that many women feel so pressured to be good and feel so inadequate to live up to the Code of Goodness that they transfer their perfectionistic expectations of themselves to their daughters. Most mothers seem intent on helping their daughters to be good women. What we experience as "impossible" demands and expectations from our mothers only reflect the impossible expectations of the code itself.

Martha's struggle with her mother is probably a familiar one to most of us. At least Martha's mother was direct about her expectations and claims on Martha's time. Often it's only when we're greeted with hostility or stony silence that we know we've disappointed our parents. When a parent's anger is indirect in this way, it can make us feel even more responsible, although we're not sure for what.

Expectations between mothers and daughters are complex. Mothers from more traditional families sometimes feel emotionally deprived. They've cared for their families and feel they've had little emotional caring for themselves. In old age, when the ability to connect with friends and resources outside the family is sometimes diminished, a mother's natural tendency is to expect increased loyalty and support from her daughter. There is an emotional ledger to be balanced: "I took care of you, now you take care of me."

For Martha there were two issues. One was the set of concrete questions: "Should I take her along? Should I be responsible for her feelings of loneliness? What is my real responsibility?" The second issue was the emotional one: "How can I stop being so upset when my mother is angry that I don't meet her demands? How can I stop giving her so much emotional power?"

HANDLING THE GUILT ABOUT GIVING UP GOODNESS

Martha felt guilty that she was leaving her mother alone, but she also felt guilty that she didn't want to visit her mother that weekend. She felt guilty that she wanted to do something for herself. Martha told herself that if she loved her mother, if she were a "good" daughter, she wouldn't feel inconvenienced by her mother's needs.

Martha also felt let down by her mother. She felt that her mother could have given more to *her* emotionally. She felt second to her brother in her mother's affection. She resented having to give to her mother now when her mother had seemed unresponsive to her in the past. These reactions reflected long-standing resentments in the relationship. By now, you can probably guess that Martha is apt to "prove" her goodness by overdoing for her mother, and then continue to feel angry and guilty.

Martha needed to find some new premise about goodness in her relationship with her mother. She was facing an ongoing goodness "crisis" and she had decided she wanted to change. On one level she'd already said no to her mother, but she needed to do the emotional work that would help her feel a sense of strength and certainty about her decisions. What she knew ultimately was that she didn't want guilt and bad feeling to be an ongoing and chronic part of her life.

Let's follow the steps of the change process: Before Martha could understand her crisis thoroughly, she needed to observe and understand the family patterns that dictated how people in her family responded to the crisis of aging. Were women always expected to be caretakers? What functions did men typically take care of? What had Martha's mother's role been with her own mother? How close, in general, did people in the family stay to one another? Was the fact that Martha lived two hours from her mother typical for adult children in her family, or was greater contact or even greater distance the norm? Did Martha's involvement with her career represent a change, or had other women in the family defined work outside the home as important? How likely was it that family members would look outside the family for help during times of stress?

Doing this work would give Martha some objective information about the family's attitudes. Were the aging parents of other family members expected to remain as independent as possible, for instance, or was it a norm that adult children were overly responsible? Knowing the family background would help her to understand her mother's reactions and not to personalize her criticisms. Seeing the family patterns more clearly would also help her to anticipate the effects of her decisions.

Since the rules about responsibility with aging parents pose special problems, Martha needed to take some other factors into account. She needed to examine the ideas of limitation and of choice. To be appropriately responsible is to make choices about one's life and that's no less true for an aging parent.

Martha realized that maybe her mother needed to make some different decisions. Maybe she needed to choose a place to live that would give her more contact with people. Maybe she needed to call Martha's brother more often. Maybe she needed to invite Martha and the family to have Sunday dinner occasionally and not just assume that it was Martha's obligation to visit. Martha began to see that her mother needed to take care of her own loneliness.

But, like Martha, when any of us confronts the fact that our parents too have choices, we run up against the major roadblock to our giving up being too good. It's typical that both we and our parents have difficulty accepting the concept of limitation.

We forget that our response to our parents' needs must be limited by our commitments to the other people in our lives, including ourselves. Our parents forget that their decisions are limited by the process of aging itself. Their physical capacities are diminished. Their lives are more constrained, and they often find it difficult to accept that fact.

But, since limitation reminds us of loss, we often have difficulty accepting that our choices are limited. Martha's mother may spend time trying to relate to her family as she did when her husband was alive and her children were more involved in her life. She may avoid making choices that acknowledge that this part of her life is gone. Martha may try to serve too many people at once and leave everyone, including herself, dissatisfied in the process. When she makes a choice to spend a weekend with her family, she may ruin it with guilt about her mother because she can't accept that her resources are limited and that she can't be all things to all people. Many women never accept that taking time for themselves is a legitimate and responsible choice.

But what about Martha's feelings toward her mother? Even if she doesn't overdo for her, and acknowledges her own and her mother's limitations, is she doomed to feel chronic resentment, distance, and guilt? Martha decided to have a series of long and direct talks with her mother. Over the course of many conversations, these were some of the things she said:

"Mom, I know that it's upsetting that you and I don't see each other more. But I have a very busy life and my time is limited. And sometimes I just need to do things for myself. I know that you want me to be happy and that you understand that. I care about you a lot and I plan to see you as much as I can, but that may not be as much as you would like. Sometimes I'd feel good if you would think about my needs a little more. I'd like you to invite us for a meal sometimes. Or I'd like it if you called to see how things are going when you know we're under stress here. I know you do that with my brother, and I'd like it if you cared about me in that way too. I think Granny always expected you to be her helper and her caretaker, but I'd like us to have a different kind of relationship.

"I'll always be here for you when you really need something. But I need to know what your thinking has been about about some important issues in your life. What are your plans for yourself as you get older? What would you hope to have me do for you? How would you like to see things handled if you become disabled? What kind of financial arrangements have you made for yourself? Does it frighten you to think about getting older and possibly getting sick? What ways have you thought of to handle your loneliness? How did you feel about her as Granny got older?"

In a responsive way, Martha let her mother know that she expects her to be responsible for herself. She clarified what her mother expects. She acknowledged her mother's needs and probable fears. She indicated a willingness to provide support, connection, and whatever appropriate help she could. She stated her position with her mother firmly but kindly. And she also asked directly for what she wanted from her mother. Martha didn't need to justify her position. She had begun to feel more certain that it's appropriate for her to be responsible to the other people in her life, including herself.

While Martha has stated her limitations, she needs to realize that it may take her mother awhile to accept them. By being direct with her mother about all the important issues between them, Martha has violated the hidden rule that exists in many families that people never say what's on their minds, especially not to an aging parent who's assumed to be too fragile to handle it. Martha's mother may resist the message or have to be told many times again. But being direct was exactly what Martha needed to do to begin to feel good about herself. If she can remain calm through her mother's reactions, the two stand a chance of having a less strained relationship with one another.

How did Martha feel as a result of her talks with her mother? "I truly felt that I had regained some balance with myself. I knew that the things I was saying were right for me so that they'd ultimately be right for her too. I didn't feel so guilty or angry anymore, I felt a sense of strength. Also, I felt closer to my mother for the first time in a while. We both cried a bit. But I felt she understood where I was coming from and that she knew I cared about her. The funny thing is that within a week she'd made a decision to move closer to her sister, and suddenly I could never reach her when I called on the phone. She'd started socializing with some of her neighbors. Now *I* feel slightly put out when I can't get through to her."

A FINAL NOTE ABOUT FAMILY RESPONSIBILITY

Even though questions of goodness are more difficult as we struggle to be responsive and nurturing to our aging parents, we can go back to the new premise about responsibility as a guide. Even if the person you're concerned about is an aging or ill parent, a general rule of thumb still applies: Don't do anything for them that they can reasonably do for themselves. Being too good never helps. The more you do for someone, the less they do for themselves. In the case of an aging parent, doing too much may foster a premature disability and dependence that robs them of self-worth and the opportunity to make important decisions about the ending phases of their life.

As we free ourselves from the Goodness Code, we'll be better able to make decisions about our children and our parents, decisions that respect their needs at the same time that we respect our own. To do otherwise is to invite anger, resentment, and damaged relationships.

13

FROM GOODNESS
TO WHOLENESS

———— ✳ ————

The Deeper Levels of Change

As the dictates of goodness give way to the concept of balance in the important relationships of our lives, we're ready to embrace change at a deeper level. We're ready to do the real work of nurturing ourselves. Taking small steps to change frees us to experience an enhanced sense of our own power. Being less responsible for others and more focused on ourselves sets us on a course in which we more deeply appreciate the power of choice.

The words of one of our therapy group members repeated from the end of chapter 1 begin to convey some sense of the power of change: "For the first time in my life I'm beginning to feel good about myself. I feel more alive and I feel more real . . . I feel more in charge of my life and, to myself, I seem to make much more sense. I know that I really am my own person now and nobody can take that away."

One small experience or many painful ones may start us on the process of change. But the end result is that we experience ourselves at a new level of strength and integration. We are no longer so hypnotically a prisoner of the trance of goodness. Our beliefs change, our feelings change, our behavior changes, and we gain a sense of certainty in the rightness of our own decisions. We develop a new appreciation of our own worth.

We may have started the process of change with only an idea, an image in our imagination, of the different person we hoped to be. But

207

as we do the work of expressing and affirming the self we hold in our imaginations and in our dreams, the more real we become to ourselves and to others. We rewrite our life scripts, retell our own stories, and in the process we experience the deep power of giving voice to our inner feelings.

A LAST STORY FROM CLAUDIA

Several years ago I went to a seminar on burnout. The workshop was meant to teach therapists skills to avoid becoming too responsible and overburdened with their work—an easy thing for a therapist to do, especially if she's a woman.

At one point, the workshop leader asked us to relax and then to allow our minds to playfully see ourselves in whatever environment we'd most enjoy being in. We were to imagine ourselves doing an activity that would be a metaphor for work. In other words, we were to envision ourselves working, but in some different, playful, enjoyable way.

I had just come back from a vacation on a Caribbean island. My mind resisted the notion of working at all. After all, the instructor had said "play." Convinced I was doing the exercise wrong, I took myself to the white sand beach that I had been on only days before. As the atmosphere in the auditorium became more and more quiet and as the group became more relaxed, each of us slipping into a light trance, my mind evolved its own imagery in a very unexpected way.

I began to reexperience, with even greater intensity than when I was there, my every response to the beauty of the beach. I felt the warm sun heat the sand almost to burning, and I felt the cool breezes from the water as they rustled through palm trees at the back of the beach. I felt the quiet—the few people, the lack of noise, clutter, and distraction. I was aware of the cloudless blue sky over me—of sun that seemed to warm the stress out of me. And with a kind of vividness that bordered on longing, I saw the clear, crystalline turquoise color of the ocean as it rolled gently onto the sand.

Before I could stop it, my mind had me in the water and, with a shock of pleasure, I felt myself dive to the coral reef just offshore to watch the many fish there.

On my vacation, I had discovered the joys of snorkeling. It had taken hold in my consciousness so that it now formed the framework for a powerful imaginative experience. In my imaginary journey I was underwater, feeling the contrast of the cool water on my body with the heat of the sun that now broke through the water in sharp points of light. The fish themselves astounded me. I had the experience that I was in an entirely new world—one that was almost unreal and unimagined before this dive to the coral reef.

I sensed the immense power and intelligence of a universe around me that could create so many colors, so many distinct forms and patterns, such beauty.

The fish were alive and teeming—there were more species than I could count or even remember to identify. This underwater world seemed so abundant with life that I felt I'd made some magical discovery and that my whole life was suddenly changed in some way because of it.

Now, in fantasy, I was compelled to leave the water and let somebody know what I'd seen. I struggled away from the reef, back onto the beach. I walked toward a small group of people whose faces were indistinct and I started, wildly excited, to tell them about the fish. But what I was telling them was not really about fish. I was trying to tell them about this experience of magic, of wonder, of being a suddenly changed person because more of the world had been opened to me. I was asking them to see the beauty that I saw, asking them to look deeper and understand my experience. I needed them to understand that there was more of life than they thought, perhaps there was more to me than they saw. On some deep level, I was trying to communicate with them, to share this very meaningful experience, to share something of myself. I was certain they would understand what I meant.

Unfortunately, the people on the beach looked at me blankly and turned away.

In the auditorium around me, other people began to sigh and stretch as if they were waking from a deep sleep. The instructor asked us gently to end our fantasy. As I opened my eyes, I was aware that I was crying. I wondered how I had gone from a workshop on work to a white sand beach and then to this experience of painful alienation.

GOODNESS VERSUS THE AUTHENTIC SELF

I was to learn that I wasn't the only one whose experience in their fantasy had been painful. Told to be playful and in a place we enjoyed to do our work, most of us, surprisingly, had gone to beaches or water. Most quickly slipped into doing something other than work. Many saw images of pleasure, relaxation, comfort, relief. In the privacy of our fantasies that day, most of us had images of our more playful, real selves. Most of us had made an attempt in our fantasy to feel connected with other people in some deeply meaningful way and had realized our true lack of connection in the process.

Many of us in the workshop came to the realization that in reality our work, all our frantic striving to achieve and overdo, was really a misplaced attempt to be deeply connected to others and to express ourselves in a clear and powerful way. In our fantasies, each of us was given a message about our true motivations, and we learned lessons about the deeper longings that lay, like the fish on the reef, just beneath the surface of our busyness. As people trying to help others, knowing what often motivated us was a desire to be connected helped give us some different perspective on our work.

My fantasy told me that my real need was to know and be known by those people on the beach. And the real lesson for me was that being too good often left me feeling frustrated and alone. My real "life" work was to find my own voice, articulate my inner feelings, share that experience with others, and listen to the experience of others in turn. This is what we call intimacy. It's what most of us strive for, what we all most want, and what the effort to be good and overresponsible most blocks.

As I explored the meaning of my fantasy further, I realized what had made me so sad. The blank-faced people on the beach really represented my family. Often my work and overdoing was a disguised struggle to have my family see that I had value. That struggle often failed, both with them and with the other people in my life. I needed to do the work of valuing myself.

I decided that I would refocus on the truer image in that fantasy, the one of the person who had intense feelings of excitement and enjoyment and wonder at the universe. That seemed the truer "voice" in me. Somehow I knew that if I really put those feelings into my work, I would work better. I would feel both more connected to others and more connected to myself.

MAKING DIFFERENT CHOICES

Any small change in our behavior sets the stage for deeper change. When we identify problems and try out new behaviors in our interactions with others, we begin to think differently about ourselves. We know and see with greater clarity how we want to change broader life goals, what larger themes in our lives we want to restate or alter. We re-envision ourselves, and in the process we gain important information about our true wants and needs.

Claudia, for instance, made a decision that, rather than focusing so much on the impulse to help and take care of people (her way of being good), she would refocus her work and her interactions with people on communicating and expressing her feelings more, activities that were much more enjoyable to her. Her imaginary journey had given her a powerful insight into the common themes of all her dreams and fantasies. It put her in touch with many of the negative feelings that resulted from blocking her own impulses. She knew she could gain the positive sense of connection with people she wanted by changing.

Our fantasies and journeys through imagery are guides to our real selves. And unless we're acting on the basis of those fantasies and images, chances are we're not taking appropriate responsibility for ourselves. It's in this sense that the old saying, "The child is the father of the man (or woman)" makes sense. Unless we allow the child in us to direct our lives, unless we allow our dreams and passions to emerge, shaped by the realistic limits of our lives, we numb ourselves by being too responsible, too much a serious adult. In this state we usually become focused on acting in a parental way toward everyone else. Instead of following our dreams, we take responsibility for theirs. We generally feel frustrated and stuck as a result.

Often we're blocked from making new decisions because we're reluctant to face the consequences of our choices. We won't change our jobs because we know we'll make less money. We don't relocate to a more desirable environment because we don't want to give up a comfortable house or a network of friends. We don't leave a destructive relationship because we have no guarantee that we'll meet someone else. If our lives are dominated by a series of statements that "I could or would do that if only . . . ," we may be avoiding the risks and the losses that are inherent in any real change.

On the other hand, following our impulses without first exploring and being willing to accept the consequences will usually make us even more unclear about the rightness of our decisions. We act impulsively and pick up the pieces later. We create more confusion for ourselves. This is a case of the child in us wanting to overpower the adult.

Often truly pursuing our fantasies and dreams will affect other people in our lives negatively. Many women avoid making changes or decisions because they feel they can't bring themselves to hurt someone else. Hurting others at times is a reality of real relationships. We can't be wholly involved and engaged with another person without sometimes hurting them because inevitably two people's needs and impulses are different and conflict. We do have a responsibility to consider the relational effects of our decisions. A basic human dilemma is to find a balance between pursuing our own desires and sustaining the relationships that are important to us.

But the bottom line is that unless we feel that the decisions we make are based in values that we've defined for ourselves, unless we feel that we're truly being responsive to our own needs and wants, then our relationships are likely to suffer anyway. They'll suffer from our being too focused on our partner, and they'll suffer from the underlying anger and resentment that we feel because we're not pursuing our own goals. We can't be responsive unless we're responsible to ourselves first. We can't be nurturing unless we experience the certainty of being directed by our own most powerful feelings. And the biggest block to acting on our true feelings is the fear of not being good.

✳IMAGINING DIFFERENT CHOICES

Find a quiet corner for yourself at a quiet time of day. Sit in a comfortable chair, or perhaps even lie down. Gradually let all the muscles in your body relax, as if someone were giving you a gentle massage. Now let your mind relax. Let your thoughts wander in and out; accept whatever goes through your mind without judging it. When you feel calmer and more quiet, begin to imagine yourself in a place where you'd love to be. Make it an ideal, wonderful place that is comforting, soothing, exciting. Make it a place where all your current needs can be met. Begin to envision doing something that you'd love to do there. There are no limits, there are no rules; anything you choose is what you may do. See yourself engaged in this activity, feel the feelings that go along with doing it. Your only goal is to feel free, to feel good about yourself.

Either continue with the fantasy until you're ready to have it end or, once you feel engaged with an activity, have one or many other people join you. Relate to these people in a way that would be satisfying and enjoyable. See yourself doing something with them that would be nurturing, comforting, exciting. Experience as much pleasure with them as you can. Say goodbye to each of them before you leave the fantasy.

Give yourself a few minutes to enjoy the good feelings that this imagery may have aroused. If a painful feeling comes up, put it aside for a moment and allow yourself to relax and be comfortable again.

When you feel that you're ready, ask yourself some questions:

- What was the enjoyable activity that I was doing?
- What was enjoyable about it?
- What good feelings did doing this activity stir up for me?
- Is this something I do in my current life? If not, why not?
- What part of me was I trying to express in this fantasy?
- What need of mine got met in this fantasy?
- If sad feelings came up, what made me sad?
- What could I have done differently in the fantasy not to be sad?
- What people were in my fantasy? What were they like? What did I want to do with them? What did I want *from* them?
- Do I do these things with any people in my current life? Do I get these things from any people in my current life? If not, why not?
- What does my fantasy tell me about the ways I would like my life to be different?
- What objections am I giving myself about why I can't make my fantasy real?

Try writing down your thoughts about the experience.

Over time, as you practice this exercise on different days and in different moods, you'll be teaching yourself about your own inner self. The feelings may often be good ones, and they may sometimes be quite painful. But if you are truly letting yourself feel free, they will always be powerful feelings. Often you'll experience actual physical responses. Your heart rate may speed up; you may feel sexual excitement; you may experience feelings of warmth all over your body. Sometimes you'll fall asleep: Pay attention to the events and stories in your images and fantasies that arouse these feelings—they're the guides to understanding who you are and what you want and need. Decisions need to be based on this very important information that comes to you from your deeper self. No external form of reward for "goodness" can ever compare with the inner satisfaction to be reaped when we act on those powerful currents of thought and feeling.

MOVING INTO COMMUNITY

Paradoxically, the more we go inward in the search for wholeness and self-definition, the more we want to be deeply connected to others. As we become less concerned with being good and being right, the more we want others to know and accept us as we are. As we become more engaged with other people, we learn that we're all more similar than different. We learn to be responsive and nurturing. We learn about our own uniqueness. We learn the value and the limits of intimacy. And we learn that we don't need to feel ashamed of being imperfect.

Change is a difficult process, and it's rare for someone to accomplish it alone. We need others' support to overcome our own objections to change. Often we need others to help us see the concrete steps necessary to realizing our fantasies. We need other people who know us well enough to keep us on track when we seem to be following a destructive rather than a positive impulse. We need other people to nurture us and to allow us to nurture them. This sharing in community is one of the most satisfying forms of good feeling that most of us can achieve.

Community means different things for each of us. Some may find community in our families. Some of us find it in church. Others find an informal community that grows right in our neighborhood. Women often form their own support groups, or they have supportive networks of friends who meet regularly or spontaneously to maintain ongoing connections. The self-help programs of AA, Al-Anon, and Adult Children of Dysfunctional or Alcoholic Families are popular forms of community in our culture. Isolation can kill, and community is healing and growth-enhancing. The common thread among all types of communities is that people are supported and nurtured in their growth. They are helped to change and to weather the consequences of change. In community people feel accepted, supported, validated. They know they don't have to wear a false mask of goodness in order to be valued and cared for. They become a part of something larger than themselves. To be a part of community is to feel good.

If you feel that you lack a network of supportive and caring people, create one or join an existing one. The local newspapers of most towns list support groups designated by almost any interest or concern a person could have. Seek community with people who enjoy doing the activities that you enjoy, or who share the same religious or political values that you share. There is no good reason for anyone to be isolated and alone in a world that is alienating yet increasingly aware of the need for community. The most self-proclaimed loner among us needs the support of other people. To deny that reality suggests that one is stuck in a cycle of shame.

And remember that moving into community takes time. It's both an outgrowth of and a stimulus for change. The more you achieve it, the better you'll feel.

ACHIEVING CREATIVITY AND BALANCE

"The problem is not merely one of Women and Career, Women and the Home, Women and Independence. It is more basically: how to remain whole in the midst of the distractions of life; how to remain balanced, no matter what centrifugal forces tend to pull one off center; how to remain strong, no matter what shocks come in at the periphery and tend to crack the hub of the wheel."[1]

This quote from Anne Morrow Lindbergh's *Gift from the Sea* speaks to the ever-present dilemma of a woman's being pulled in many different directions by the injunctions that she be a hub of relatedness for others while trying to maintain the equilibrium of her own self-definition. In her book, Lindbergh describes a vacation away from the demands of her roles as wife, mother of five children, and person of high social visibility in her community. She goes to a secluded beach and stays there alone. She explores and expresses a deep awareness of change and a search for balance through the vehicle of her writing. She suggests that, at least for herself, a woman finds integration of the many diverse pieces of herself in the act of creative expression.

Lindbergh's work suggests that the way we consolidate change is to creatively express ourselves, to make something new out of the diverse pieces of our life experience. Taking creative control may be the ultimate form of being responsible for self—of making a mark on the world, of giving a voice to the self. There is nothing so absorbing and so powerful as creative work. There is little else that can make us feel so good. Creativity is a way of nurturing ourselves and others at the same time.

In therapy we work with women who struggle painfully with many conflicts in their lives. Often in the midst of their work, as if recovering some dim memory of themselves, they tentatively mention the journal they used to keep, the poem that was rejected by a magazine ten years ago, the paintings that sit collecting dust in the attic. They have little awareness that by shutting off or ignoring the flow of their creative energy, they've essentially told themselves that what they have to say, in effect who they *are,* is not important.

When we block ourselves from giving voice to our inner selves, we become alienated from ourselves and we feel bad. We often look for external reasons to explain our discontent. But the bottom line is that we've become involved in a process of disowning ourselves, and we begin to live our lives out of touch with the inner resources that can make us feel good.

Often we ask women in treatment, "Tell me about a part of yourself that you've left behind—something that you used to enjoy doing that you don't do anymore." We discover the most remarkable talents that have simply been left, abandoned: women who studied piano for years who never touch a keyboard; women who were told they "had a talent" for drawing or writing who never put pen to paper except to pay their bills; women who loved to explore the out-of-doors who rarely even take a walk.

These are incredibly sad losses of ourselves, losses of the creative child in us who is naturally responsive and expressive. But we live in a society that discourages women from being focused on their inner lives. Given the constricting ways that women's roles are defined, the miracle is that any women have emerged to do creative work at all.

In spite of the gains of the last few years, women who do creative work still tend to find that work given less attention and to be valued less than the work of men. As a result our society suffers from a skewed definition of its reality. The lack of attention given to women's experience prevents us from offering as much as we might to the re-creation and renewal of our social life.

Creativity isn't confined to the performing or expressive arts. Women have all kinds of creative power that can express itself in any of the jobs and tasks that they decide to pursue in life. Creativity can express itself in a hobby, in an interest that one pursues and develops just for the enjoyment of it. One can raise children creatively, one can practice law or medicine creatively. One can manage people in a creative way; one can develop new and innovative ideas for a business. The question each of us needs to ask is, Is the job or work I do in some way an expression of myself—of my own ideas, of my own way of seeing the world? Do my inner beliefs, feelings, needs get expressed? Am I helping to produce something that I would want to see created in the world? Do I allow myself to be totally defined and structured by external expectations, or can I put something of myself into what I do in some part of my life?

THE NECESSARY CONDITIONS OF CREATIVITY

If we're to be creative—an essential aspect of wholeness and of feeling good—we need to do four things to make it possible. First, we have to provide ourselves with the time and the solitude to be in touch with creative impulses. We need to be alone, and we need to take the time to play and have recreation. If our days are filled with the endless details of living and of meeting our obligations and responsibilities, our true feelings will never emerge and our true sensitivities will become dulled. We'll lose touch with the rhythms of our inner world. As Lindbergh put it, "Women need solitude in order to find again the true essence of themselves." [2]

Second, we need to recapture the resourcefulness and curiosity of our childhood. Think back to the way you played as a child. What games did you enjoy? How did you imaginatively cope with pain and fear? How did you fill your time? What activities did you pursue? Did you study and learn a skill that you've dropped? What happened to the child who loved to play, perform, paint pictures, tell stories?

When we ask women in therapy, we often discover that as children they were engaged in some creative pursuit constantly. They created dramas, made up dances, published neighborhood newspapers, made things up from scraps of junk in their basements or attics, and otherwise lived in a highly imaginative world that often helped them survive even traumatic and abusive situations. Creativity as an adult requires a recapturing of those patterns of play that became themes in our childhood.

We need to do what we enjoy doing without judging it and without requiring that it have a purpose or be judged acceptable by others. In other words, we have to create for the joy of it, not for a painting to hang in a gallery or a poem to be published. If those things happen, that's wonderful. But if they become our chief aim, then we constrict our own creation by trying hard to force it to meet external standards. The important thing is the enjoyment of the activity, the expression of the self.

Finally, we need to take our creative lives seriously. We need to act as if our creativity is as important to our health and well-being as it truly is. We need to not make excuses about why we can't write a poem, paint a picture, or do the needlework we've been longing to get to for months. If our jobs don't allow us creativity, we need to think seriously about changing them. If we know we need time to develop an idea or a project, we need to make the time to do it. If we question whether it's legitimate to take time to work on a project because we won't achieve the success of a "true" artist, or because others in our lives want our time and attention, we need to reexamine our assumptions. We need to be creative for no other reason than that it centers us in our own experience, nourishes us, and makes us feel good.

FINDING THE SPIRITUAL

If we truly do the work of going inward and knowing ourselves in solitude and in community, we quite naturally come to ask ourselves questions about the ultimate purpose of our lives. In learning to value ourselves, we learn a new respect and regard for the life process itself. We sense that there's some mystery to our being, some overriding purpose or intelligence that informs our experience.

In response to the daily struggles that cause them pain, women often redefine their ideas about the larger meaning of their lives. A therapeutic struggle to change often becomes a search to answer questions such as, "Why is this happening to me? What am I meant to learn from this experience? Is there a point to my struggling to change and grow?"

All truly effective change takes place within a strong framework of belief. We seem to have the most energy for change when we hold some basic faith that there is a spiritual dimension to life, when we believe that we're a part of something larger than ourselves. We feel best when we operate from a strong set of values that direct our behavior. We feel even better when that set of values is our own and not just a response to beliefs that are imposed by others.

At the end of her stay on the beach, Anne Morrow Lindbergh emerges with a renewed sense of her own values. Those values are ones that she reshapes and reaffirms in response to her experience of the natural rhythms of the environment around her. She decides that she needs greater simplicity to help restore and maintain her awareness of life. She recognizes the need to find a balance of "physical, intellectual, and spiritual life." She decides that there should be "space for significance and beauty. Time for solitude and sharing. Closeness to nature to strengthen understanding and faith in the intermittency of life." [3]

One has the sense that she emerges from her time alone with herself having creatively struggled with the many levels at which, as women, we must all live our lives. She leaves feeling whole and with a renewed sense of her place in the larger stream of life.

We all seek some larger sense of meaning in our lives. All too often, we lose track of that meaning or we forget to look for it in the endless pressures of making money, managing our relationships, raising our children, dealing with the clutter of our lives. And yet, unless we have that larger sense of meaning, a framework of principles and values for directing our experience, the normally painful events of our lives become ones of suffering rather than ones of shared pain. Without belief, our conflicts seem empty and alienating. We're unable to bring good out of the more negative experiences of life. We're not motivated to change because change itself has no meaning.

Like community and like creativity, a sense of the spiritual can be different for each of us and can be achieved in many diverse ways. Few of us totally give up some observance of the religious rituals of our childhoods, even though we may modify them to meet our more adult sense of value and belief. Some of us turn to Eastern forms of spirituality. We meditate or pursue the principles of New Age thinking and practice. Some of us embrace the spiritual structure of the twelve-step self-help programs in which an awareness of the spiritual becomes a major part of the program of self-healing.

Many of us embrace a specifically feminist spiritual framework in which we seek to define a sense of larger meaning in a way that's affirming of a female or "goddess"-centered sensibility. We reject old patriarchal religious structures and in community with other women, we seek to create new rituals and principles that celebrate the deep, archetypal power of the feminine in our lives. Instead of conventional religious holidays, we may celebrate the summer or winter solstice or the waxing and waning of the moon. We affirm our deep connection to the natural world around us.

Finally, a framework of meaning may take the form of commitment to larger social and political change. It may express itself in a life devoted to art and creative work. Some of us may integrate all of these efforts at finding meaning. Whatever their expression, the spiritual values we embrace help us to feel whole and balanced because they provide us with an experience of our correct relationship to the universe. We sense that we're part of some larger whole and that our individual choices have the power to radically affect the integrity of that larger system. Being part of something larger, we share meaning with others and we learn that we're not alone.

CELEBRATING THE SELF

The deepest affirmation of our faith in life and a larger life process is celebration. Most of our religious ritual is motivated by a need to mark and celebrate the recurring passages and changes of life. In fact, most of our rituals really celebrate, paradoxically, the continuity of change. Each year we mark birthdays, anniversaries, changes of season, achievements of growth. The occasions are the same, but each one of them finds us at a different point in our development, changed since the previous celebration.

Nurturing environments, whether at work or at home, encourage celebration. It's not by mistake that most of our major holiday rituals involve food—celebration is meant symbolically to nurture the spirit, to nurture our ongoing life in community.

If one fails to take the time in life to celebrate it, to affirm both life and oneself, one doesn't totally feel good. Celebration salutes change. It affirms our choices to continue to live and grow; it brings us together in a community of people with whom we share meaning and usually history; it requires a creative act, the creation of a party, a ritual, an event; and it affirms something larger and even more ongoing than ourselves. Celebration marks beginnings, endings, comings, and goings. Without it we feel emptiness and alienation in our lives.

If it's been awhile since you've been a part of a satisfying celebration, plan one. Give yourself or someone else a party to mark an occasion. Celebrate the first day of spring or the last day of summer. Plan a family reunion. Invite your therapy group to dinner. Chances are that you'll feel good and other people will feel closer. Most importantly, remember to talk to others about the evolving state of your spiritual life. Talk about what you believe and why. Ask others the same questions and, if you find you share certain beliefs, celebrate them together.

FINALLY, FEELING GOOD

We've suggested that the real work of feeling good for women not only involves the process of shifting behavior, but extends to deeper levels where we integrate new choices, define spiritual values, achieve deeper connection to others, act with creativity, and celebrate change. In the process we become more comfortable with ourselves. When we make choices and define our own values, we act with directness and firmness.

When we are creative and connected, we're also responsive and nurturing. All our old tendencies to be good seem irrelevant, as if they somehow miss the point. Wholeness and balance feel much better than being too good. Finally we behave based on what's within ourselves rather than being trapped by what's imposed from without.

There is no more privileged or more inspiring role than to be a witness to another person's change. The forces that can keep all of us unbalanced and mired in bad feelings are so compelling that what therapists witness every day in their offices are truly small triumphs of the soul. It takes great strength and determination for any woman to throw off the burdens of goodness. And yet as therapists we watch that process go on each day in small and painstaking ways. We see people making small but important choices that literally change their lives.

Feeling good, powerful, and whole is a state that we achieve when we've worked through the many levels of the process of change. Change requires work. It's work that many women undertake with enormous courage, energy, and commitment. And it's not as if feeling good is the end point of a cycle that doesn't continue. Having awakened from our trance of goodness and responsibility one day, on the next we may find ourselves hypnotically pulled back into it again at a different level for a different reason. Each time we're confronted with a new crisis or a bad feeling, we become engaged with the change process all over again. We never change ourselves perfectly.

This is the most important lesson that change has to teach. We don't change in order to get to perfect, because that's not achievable. We only change in order to get to good. Not *being good,* which is only another way of saying "perfect," but *feeling good,* which is another way of saying, "I'm OK and it's alright."

The message of change is that we naturally seek wholeness. Every time we succeed in recovering from an addiction, freeing ourselves from abuse, or simply changing the unworkable rules of a relationship, we affirm the deep power of our inner need for self-definition and balance. When we give up being too good for others, we do the work of empowering ourselves.

We are challenged by our own discomfort to do the work of change. Feeling bad is our greatest opportunity. Only by having been too good for her own good does a woman understand the high price that she pays for focusing on others at the expense of herself. That price is too high a one to pay. Breaking free from the burdens of female goodness is the hardest and most important work any woman may ever do.

QUESTIONS WOMEN ASK
ABOUT GIVING UP GOODNESS

———— ✳ ————

Once you've begun the process of changing goodness patterns, you're likely to feel some confusion about what behavior is too responsible or too good and what's not. It's very easy to confuse being too good with simple caring or concern. You find that, at first, you go to extremes and fear doing anything for anybody.

You'll also find yourself having reactions to giving up certain forms of goodness that have felt comforting to you and seem somehow "right." This confusion and discomfort is a natural part of the change process. Inevitably you'll feel that there must be exceptions to the revised rules of goodness. You may also have difficulty knowing how to apply new rules in situations that we haven't talked about specifically.

The questions that follow are samples of the ones women most often ask us as they struggle to give up goodness. Some of the questions reflect a discomfort with violating the old rules of goodness. Others suggest the difficulty of understanding at all times and in all circumstances what appropriate standards of responsibility might be. And, in still other cases, women ask us questions that seem to reflect a confusion between being responsible and being responsive.

The questions aren't presented in any particular order. As you read them try to identify which injunctions of the Code of Goodness are operating behind the scenes. You might want to try coming up with your own answer to each question before you read ours.

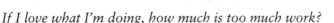

If I love what I'm doing, how much is too much work?

When you love your work, work seems like play and it's easy to get your life out of balance. No matter how much you love your work, too much of it will eventually lead to burnout. Good creative work is fueled by other interests. Loving your work may or may not mean that other areas of your life are suffering. One rule of thumb is to ask yourself whether other people in your life complain that you leave no time for anything else, in particular them. And it's important to examine in what ways working too much may be leaving you little time to take care of other needs of your own, such as those for recreation, intimacy, or basic physical needs for a healthy diet and exercise.

My child is handicapped and can't do certain things for himself. What's appropriate to do for him?

Having a handicapped child is guaranteed to pull all of your responsibility strings. The usual rule applies: Never do anything for someone else that they are developmentally capable of doing for themselves, unless it is occasionally, they ask for it directly, and you experience it as a choice. A positive goal is to help your child to learn to live as independently as possible. Most women err in the direction of doing too much for a handicapped child because they feel guilty and responsible for the problem. Try raising your expectations of your child instead of your expectations of yourself.

My partner has a demanding job that requires a fair amount of travel. I work too, but I take on most of the details of caring for our life together. I don't feel that I have any choice.

You do have choices. You can discuss the situation with your partner and together make a decision to hire someone to do some of the other chores. You can take a position that your partner will have to limit his or her travel, if that's an option, or that he take responsibility for coming up with his own solution for handling his fair share of the chores. If it's agreed that it's his job to get the clothes to the cleaners, for instance, let him worry about it and don't do it yourself. The most important principle in a situation like this is not to assume that circumstances make you more responsible by default. Remember, your partner has choices too and has chosen a job that exonerates him from most of the mundane details of life. If you keep doing too much, in time the relationship will become unworkable. Your partner needs to assume responsibility for his fair share of the relationship, no matter what his work demands.

I feel that if I don't do it, it won't get done.

If you don't do it, it might not get done, might not get done on your timetable, or might not get done your way. Sometimes the "it" is critical. But at other times you might ask yourself how much it really matters if it doesn't get done. You might be surprised at how little in life is really critical to get done. If the task is clearly not your responsibility, you shouldn't be worrying about it anyway. If it's something that does affect you and it doesn't get done, you need to talk with your partner about his or her understanding of the rules for managing the tasks in your life together.

My children always come to me with their problems. Their father is rigid and punishes them if they so much as raise their voices. How can they have more of a relationship with him?

Encouraging your children to come to you with their problems reinforces their belief that they can't have a relationship with their father and reinforces his belief that he doesn't have to learn how to deal with his children's feelings. Say to your kids, "You have to talk to your dad from now on. I'm sure that you can figure out a way to do it. I'm not going to run interference anymore." Say to your husband, "You have to learn to deal with the kids without making them frightened of you. I know it's hard for you sometimes. But I trust that you will find a way to do it. I'm not going to take their side against you anymore. I know your relationships with them are important to you." Then do your best to leave them alone to work things out. Focus on doing something nurturing for yourself.

I really lost control the other day. My sixteen-year-old kept trying to get me to agree to let her go to a rock concert when she was grounded. I finally screamed at her and felt terrible afterward.

Unless screaming is a pattern, it's natural to lose your temper some-times. Letting others know you have emotional limits rather than always protecting their feelings is useful for them as well as for you. It's emotionally overresponsible to always Be a Lady. But as you look at the interaction with your daughter, were you as firm as you might have been in your position the first few times she asked? Were you feeling guilty about saying no? Children pick up our guilt and play on it. They push for us to get out of control. In the future, being clear about your position and communicating it firmly may help avoid a scene that makes you feel bad later on.

Is it overresponsible to do volunteer work for a community organization?

If you're doing volunteer work for an organization because you have the time and volunteering represents your values, that's terrific. It becomes a problem only when you do so much of the work over time that the organization fails to involve other people to share the load. If you consistently do more than your share, others will do less than their share. The more you do, the more you'll be asked to do.

I've been asked to serve on the board of my national professional organization at a time that it's facing a change of direction. I have particular expertise that would be very useful. I've said no, however, because it doesn't fit with my personal agenda. Am I being selfish or underresponsible?

Often we feel that, because we have the expertise to do something, we're obligated to offer our services when asked. But you say serving on the board would take you off track of your personal agenda right now. Stick to your position. The issue here isn't one of selfishness; it's one of being responsible to yourself first. Remember the paraphrase of the old saying: Many are called and all of them are exhausted.

If everybody's responsible for themselves, why do we help the homeless or the poor?

Questions of social responsibility are always complex ones. But just as it takes two people to create the rules of a two-person relationship, we have to assume that as a society we all participate in creating policies and behaving in ways that contribute to problems of poverty and homelessness. If one segment of a society is overfunctioning while another seems unable to care for themselves, we're all doing something to maintain that imbalance. We help the homeless and the poor because it's appropriate to help when others truly don't have the resources to care for themselves. It may be that they don't have those resources because for years they've been institutionalized. Perhaps we've created policies that made people too dependent on help rather than fostering responsibility. We know that many homeless are veterans of the Vietnam war who suffer from inadequate attention to the emotional scars left by that trauma. Without question, as a society we need to address these hard questions of our appropriate response to people in need and to look at the ways we've fostered that need. In the meantime, it's best to help in a way that respects and supports a person's need to become self-supporting and independent. Helping on this level becomes a matter of personal values, not necessarily one of being "too good."

You keep saying to keep the focus on myself. Isn't it selfish to focus on myself so much?

When we say, "keep the focus on yourself," what we're suggesting is that you maintain a clear sense of your own needs and feelings in any given situation rather than being overly concerned to do something about the feelings and responsibilities of others. It's never selfish to be responsible for yourself. As women, we only believe it is because we've been taught to ignore our own needs. When you're clear about what you need and what you will and won't do, you can make choices to be responsive and nurturing to others. This is different from believing that focusing on them at the expense of yourself is an act of unselfishness.

My mother has a serious disease and lives alone. I can't decide how much she really needs me to do for her and how much she can handle on her own. I feel guilty all of the time. She constantly tells me I don't do enough for her. Should I feel guilty?

What your mother needs and what she may want you to do may be two different issues. Even if she can handle many things on her own, she may want you to handle them for her. The other possibility is that it's your own sense of goodness that leads you to believe she has specific expectations of you. Maybe all she wants is the emotional support you can offer by discussing things with her. In any case, there is no resolution to this problem without your having a direct discussion with your mother. "Mom, sometimes I feel really guilty that I'm not there for you more. Could we talk about this? What are the things you feel you really need me to help you with? Do you have some resentment that I don't do more, or is that just in my head? When your mother was older, how did you handle the issue of how much time to spend with her and how much to do for her? How did your mother handle those issues in her life? What do you feel you really need from me at this time?"

The second part of this issue is your guilt. It's been our experience that inappropriate guilt usually disappears when one can talk frankly about the issues in a relationship. In all likelihood, your discussion will show you that some of her expectations of you were *your* expectations, not *her* expectations. If, on the other hand, she does admit that she's angry and resentful that you don't do more, you can assess whether her expectations are reasonable given the limitations on your time and on your willingness to be available. It's important to let your mother know clearly what you will and won't, can and can't do. Remember that doing things for her that she can do for herself is never helpful.

What do I do when my boss asks me to work overtime or to take on work that's really not my job?

Sometimes any job requires an above-and-beyond-the-call-of-duty effort. That's just reality. However, if you are consistently being asked to take on overtime work or work that's not in your job description, you need to take a firm position with your boss. You may decide to tell the boss that you will not do more work without a new job description and extra financial compensation. You may ask for compensatory time off. The point is that you need to advocate for your own rights. Your boss may be quite uninterested in your feelings, but he or she will need to respect you for taking a position. If nothing changes as a result of your position, you face different choices in terms of what to do about the job.

I'm a busy trial lawyer. I've been asked to work on a project that I don't really have time to handle. I fear it will hurt my career if I say no. What do I do?

Clarify the chances of damaging your career by discussing your situation with a trusted mentor. Often we think we will damage our careers by saying no to things, only to find that saying no seems to make us even more desirable and respected. Also get feedback and support from friends and family before and after you make your decision. Brainstorm other alternatives to giving up the project. For example, you might be able to negotiate a delay in beginning the project. Or there may be other activities in your life that you can put on hold for a while. You might be able to get more support for your other responsibilities for a while by hiring someone to do some of them.

But, if you decide to say no to the project, then even if that decision might hurt your career, it's probably more important to acknowledge limits than to overwork at the expense of your physical and emotional well-being. You need to reassess the importance of achievement in your life. Is the achievement for you or something you feel you have to do to be acceptable to others?

I've decided that my dieting over the years has only made me miserable. I seem to remain at about twenty-five pounds overweight no matter how much I diet and exercise. Is it a copout to simply accept my weight?

How do you define overweight? Many women unfortunately accept the cultural norms for weight without assessing what is a comfortable and healthy weight for them. There are an extraordinary variety of opinions and approaches to difficulties with food and weight and every situation is individual. However, it is our belief that "overcontrol" in the form of dieting and deprivation inevitably leads back to "out-of-control" eating or other "out-of-control" behavior. We suggest that you stop shaming yourself, read several of the excellent books on the market that deal with women's ideas about food from a feminist perspective (see the bibliography), and think through your relationship to food *for yourself* with the help of dialogue with other women. Ultimately, self-acceptance, becoming comfortable with your body as it is, is the first step in any process of change.

I could never tell my parents that my uncle molested me because it would kill them and damage all of our family relationships. Am I wrong to keep it a secret?

You may still be too influenced by the rule to Make Relationships Work. You forget that it is not your job to take care of other people's relationships in the family. It is your job to protect yourself and promote your own healing. Whatever helps you heal is right. That may mean disclosing the incest in a responsible, planned way, with the help of a professional's coaching. But you do need support in making your decision to disclose; if you decide to break the secrecy, your first disclosure should be made to friends or family members who will be certain to give you support. The choice between the short-term hurt of telling the truth and the long-term harm of keeping the secret is a choice that needs to be made carefully, thoughtfully, and with support. But ultimately we believe that secrets usually maintain our shame and damage families.

My twenty-two-year-old son has a drug problem and has asked me to pay for a rehabilitation program for the third time. How can I say no?

You can take a position that your son has to pay for this treatment program himself. If he has no means to do this, there are programs with beds for the indigent. We know that this may seem hard-hearted, but if you have paid for his first two efforts at rehabilitation, chances are that he thinks that you'll just continue to pay. The program will be more likely to be effective if he has to make a real commitment to it himself. In general, if you are overly invested in someone else's getting well, they tend not to be as invested themselves as they could be. Your continuing to pay his way communicates a message that there are no limits, that he's free to go back to using drugs because whenever he decides to get help, you'll be there to pay the bill. Paying for an adult child's treatment more than once is a way of being overresponsible.

I can't seem to get over the feeling that men won't approve of me if I don't have sex with them whenever they want it. What can I do about this fear?

A fear like this probably is rooted in some earlier experience in your life in which you learned that doing what someone else wanted was the price of love. It is a very painful fear to live with. You may have learned that women are to be submissive or that their sexuality is not their own to make decisions about. You should let those experiences see the light of day by discussing them with your therapist, your women's support group, or friends, and you should also talk with the women in your family—your sisters, mother, aunts, cousins—about their attitudes about men and sex.

Changing the attitude, once you've identified the source, involves changing your behavior first by not having sex with a man until you've built a friendship. Learn that it's being responsible to yourself to say no. Your feelings will change once you change your behavior. You may also want to share this feeling with the man you're involved with. Check out whether he really does expect sex. It is our experience that men often think they have to express affection and emotions by being sexual. Your partner may be quite relieved at the chance to talk about your mutual expectations. If a man is a potentially equal partner, he may be able to share some of his leftover attitudes about sex too.

For forty years I gave up many of my own plans because my husband didn't want me to travel on my own. I've recently realized the price I've paid by giving in. Isn't it unfair to change at this point?

It does seem unfair to change the rules late in life. But you're forgetting that the rule change will ultimately benefit your husband too. Discuss the rule change with him, acknowledge that it will be a frightening and somewhat difficult change for both of you, and make your first changes small ones. Also, ask him what rules he's been living by for forty years that he might like to change too.

In the corporate environment that I work in, it would be viewed as a sign of weakness to ask for help with a work problem. Everyone works too hard and that is the norm. How can I change within a structure that demands conformity?

Although the principle is that, if one person makes a change and can sustain it, the entire system will eventually change, it is foolhardy to take on an entire corporation. Test out your assumptions by discussing your work load with your boss and letting him or her know what you feel is reasonable. If overwork is the norm in this particular corporation, you will have some latitude in setting limits on how much you will work, but only some.

Not all corporate cultures are identical, however. You might have to assess the place of work in your life and maybe you will have to turn down the next job promotion in this corporation or even change your job.

It takes so much energy to force my husband to do things to help with the children that I'd rather just do it myself. What's wrong with this?

What's wrong is that you'll wake up one day totally depleted of energy, wanting to leave your marriage, and recognizing that your kids and your husband have little relationship. Better to spend the energy now. Also ask yourself if the energy expenditure is on getting him to do it or getting him to want to. Your job is to let him be involved with the kids. He won't want to initially, but after he does it successfully he will probably enjoy the added contact with them and feel good about himself.

I always got more attention in the family than my sister did. At family gatherings I try to downplay my achievements when she's there. Does this mean that I'm taking care of her feelings?

You may be taking care of her feelings, and you may also think you're protecting your relationship with her. You may not want to look like the achieving person you are for fear of losing her friendship. This is a common dilemma for women. Have a talk with her privately in which you acknowledge the favoritism you were shown as well as the conflict it caused for you. And start being yourself. You might be surprised to discover that she wouldn't trade places with you and live your hectic, demanding life on a bet.

My brother keeps asking me to lend him money. If I don't, I fear that his children will suffer. How can I say no?

It's always most difficult to set limits on goodness when children are involved. However, it's not your job to support your brother's children, and you should not do it unless you intend to support them for the rest of their lives. Your support now will only deprive your brother of the opportunity to find alternate solutions that would give his children what they need consistently. If he truly cannot support his children, maybe an alternative living arrangement needs to be made for them. Since you say your brother "keeps" asking you for money, apparently he isn't doing the work he needs to do to solve his own problem. Your continuing financial help may prevent him from taking appropriate responsibility for his own life.

I'm a single mother. How can I not take on the responsibility for every-thing when there is nobody else to do it?

There are no perfect solutions to the dilemmas of single parenting. But there are other people to help. There are friends who will help out in return for your doing the same for them. Service people can be hired to do some things. Community agencies offer support. Other family members are often willing to help. And your children are capable of taking on many tasks themselves. Children gain independence and a sense of satisfaction from helping out. As long as their basic needs for safety and emotional security are being met, it's not inappropriate to expect children to help. More important is to explore ways to meet your own needs. And is your ex-husband doing his fair share of the parent-ing?

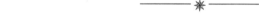

There is a novel I've been trying to write for ten years. I just never seem to find time for my own creative work. What's going on with me?

Your creative energy has been drained off into supporting everyone else's work. We suggest that you find other women who are trying to do serious creative work and discuss this issue with them. They are legion. Also, look in detail at the little distractions that murder your soul. For example, if you are a writer who writes in the morning, do not accept any phone calls until afternoon. No exceptions!

My husband invited his family for a visit, but he is working for part of the weekend. I feel really resentful that I'm going to have to do all the work. Any suggestions?

Talk with your husband and ask him what his thinking was about food, entertaining his family, and so forth. Agree on which responsibil-ities are his and which are yours. It has probably not occurred to him that it is his family and therefore his responsibility to plan for their visit. It probably never occurred to you either.

Whenever I say no, I get attacked and told I'm bad. Sometimes it's just easier to give in. How can I handle the other person's negative reactions? I don't like being told there's something wrong with me for wanting something different.

It's only easier to give in in the short run. First you need to take a position that you will not be criticized every time you say no. Then you need support from other friends to help you believe that you have the right to say no. Finally, are you saying no in a way that is firm, direct, clear, and kind? Or are you saying no in a way that blames and shames the other person for asking? If you're clear that you have a right to say no, you can say no kindly.

I don't want to be a bad mother. I feel that I have to meet all my children's needs or they'll end up neurotic and in therapy like me. What do you think?

Meeting all of your children's needs will practically guarantee that they'll have problems because they won't be very well prepared to deal with reality. The mythology surrounding motherhood has been very damaging to women. Good mothers sometimes meet the need of their children to learn to handle frustration when someone says no.

Sometimes I feel selfish and that, if I were honest, I'd never want to do what my partner wants. What does this mean?

You may be angry at having been too unselfish and too good for too long. Your interests, needs, and priorities may have changed. Often when we first give up being too good, we go to an extreme of being unwilling to compromise at all. This is normal for a time. But if, after a time—and perhaps with the perspective of therapy or a support group —you find that it's true that you never want to respond at all to the other person's needs, even when your partner has begun to be nurturing and responsive to you, then maybe you need to end the relationship. It's sad that some relationships are too damaged for the rules to be renego-tiated, but sometimes that's reality.

I'm a recovering alcoholic. I feel ashamed about the effects of my alco-holism on my friends and family. How can I make it up to them without being too good?

Your alcoholism was one sign that your life was out of balance. Staying out of balance by being too good won't resolve your guilt. Remember that *making amends* (step nine of the AA and Al-Anon pro-grams) means to *make changes*. If you change from being too good, which only sets you up to go out of control, and adopt the principles of balance *as they fit your own life,* you will be making changes that are good for everybody.

Is codependency the same as being too good?

Yes and no. Both women and men who are too good can probably identify with descriptions of codependent behavior. Codependency is one *name* for behavior that involves being too focused on others and too driven by the expectations of others. But codependency suggests sickness, and we don't believe all or even most women are sick. Most of us are too good because we've been influenced by the rules of goodness, because our sense of who is responsible for what is unbalanced. Code-pendency suggests extreme imbalance. All women who think of them-selves as codependent are probably too good in some way, but not all women who are too good are codependent.

My biggest fear is that if I start saying what I want or saying no to my partner's agenda we won't have a relationship anymore. How can I get past this fear?

You can only get past this fear by beginning to be emotionally honest about your own needs. You also have to be willing to compromise. That is part of having a relationship. Someone else's initial reaction to your honesty is not necessarily their final reaction. Remember that change is a process with several steps. Relationships are mutually created and sustained and always require readjusting as people's needs change from time to time in life.

Most of your primary partners (such as family members and friends) won't end a relationship just because you want to make it more equal and more honest. They might threaten to end it, as an initial reaction to change. But if you can hang in there with the process and be responsive to your partner's normal anxiety about change and your own anxiety as well, the vast majority of relationships are workable.

We're sure that you may have had many other questions as you've read and tried to apply the ideas in this book. We suggest that you make a habit of talking with other women about these ideas. When any situation arises that poses a "goodness crisis," you may also want to run through the following questions to help you clarify where you stand:

- Which goodness rule is being challenged by this situation?
- What responsibility do I need to take for myself?
- What responsibility do I need to take for someone else?
- Will "being good" by the old rules lead to "feeling good" in this situation, or will it lead to resentment?
- What would I tell someone else to do in this situation?
- If I take responsibility for someone else, what is it that I may be avoiding in my own life?
- What are my emotional needs in this situation?
- What can I do to feel good?

NOTES

---- ✳ ----

2. LIVING THE CODE
WOMEN'S WAYS OF BEING GOOD

1. Ellen Berman, "Going Shopping," *The Family Therapy Networker* (September/October 1989).
2. We originally learned about the Bacchantic Maidens and this piece of historical information in Marian Sandmaier's book *The Invisible Alcoholics* (New York: McGraw-Hill, 1980). This book is recommended reading for anyone who wants a better understanding of women's alcoholism.
3. Karen Horney, *Neurosis and Human Growth* (New York: W. W. Norton and Company, 1988).

3. LIVING THE CODE
WOMEN'S WAYS OF DOING GOOD

1. For a more in-depth discussion of a woman's sense that it's "moral" and necessary to give care to others, see Carol Gilligan's book *In a Different Voice* (Cambridge, Mass.: Harvard University Press, 1982).
2. Monica McGoldrick, "Reaching Mid-Career Without a Wife," *The Family Therapy Networker* (May/June 1987).
3. Arlene Rossen Cardozo's *Sequencing* (New York: Macmillan, 1986) describes the possibilities for women to time pregnancies, career, and other important life goals sequentially in ways that make maintaining relationships a priority.

4. Doreen E. Schecter, "Women in the Labor Force: Some Mental Health Implications," in *Psychiatry Opinion* (September 1979), 17–19. Dr. Schecter was an assistant clinical professor of psychiatry at Albert Einstein College of Medicine when she wrote this article.

4. IF I'M SO GOOD, WHY DO I FEEL SO BAD
BASIC FEMALE SHAME

1. For an excellent discussion of women's depression, see Lois Braverman's chapter, "The Depressed Woman in Context: A Feminist Family Therapist's Analysis," in *Women and Family Therapy,* edited by Marianne Ault-Riche (Rockville, Md.: Aspen Systems, 1986).
2. This quote from Aristotle appears in the introduction to Simone de Beauvoir's *The Second Sex* (New York: Alfred A. Knopf, 1952).
3. Merle Fossum and Marilyn Mason, *Facing Shame* (New York: W. W. Norton, 1986), 5. See this excellent book for a discussion of shame in addictive families.
4. Ernest Kurtz, "Why AA Works: The Intellectual Significance of Alcoholics Anonymous," *Journal of Studies on Alcohol* 41 (1982).
5. See *Facing Shame* for a furthur discussion of "shame-bound" families or identities. For other discussions of shame see John Bradshaw's *Healing the Shame That Binds You* (Deerfield Beach, Fla.: Health Communications, 1988) and Gershen Kaufman's *The Psychology of Shame* (New York: Springer Publishing Co., 1989).
6. See Lenore Walker's book *Terrifying Love* (New York: Harper & Row, 1989) for a penetrating discussion of the battered woman syndrome as well as the concept of "learned helplessness" that is so critical to an understanding of women's experience of abuse.
7. Carolyn Heilbrun, *Writing a Woman's Life* (New York: W. W. Norton, 1988), 15.
8. *Neurosis and Human Growth.*
9. The concept of a "shame cycle" is derived from our previous work *The Responsibility Trap* (New York: Free Press, 1985), where we referred to the same process as a "pride cycle." Fossum and Mason discuss a similar concept in *Facing Shame.*

5. THE HIGH COST OF GOODNESS

1. For a more thorough discussion of the current understanding of the concept of alcohol addiction, see James Royce's *Alcohol Problems and Alcoholism* (New York: Free Press, 1981). If you feel concerned about your own drinking behavior, contact the local chapter of the National Council on Alcoholism,

your local mental health center, or any local hospital that has an alcoholism treatment unit. Any of these resources will provide you with information without requiring a commitment to treatment. You'll also find a number in your phone book for Alcoholics Anonymous, and you'll generally find a list of meetings in your local paper.

2. Oscar Hammerstein wrote the lyrics to "Can't Say No" in 1943. Refer to Williamson Music, Inc., for any additional information.

3. These ideas are more thoroughly developed in our book *The Responsibility Trap.* Also see Claudia Bepko's chapter "Disorders of Power: Women and Addiction in the Family," in *Women in Families,* by Monica McGoldrick, Carol Anderson, and Froma Walsh (New York: W. W. Norton, 1989).

4. The research of Dr. Sharon Wilsnack is perhaps the most compelling in connecting drinking and possibly other addictions to women's sense that they fail to live up to the dictates of the code. Wilsnack found that women drink to feel more "womanly," and that in fact when they drink they feel more able to be warm, loving, sexy—all traits that put them more in line with the expectations of the Goodness Code. Other research finds that when women talk about the stresses that precipitate their drinking, they are typically life events that in some way challenge their sense of being an adequate woman—such as divorce, miscarriage, reproductive problems, failures with their children. See Wilsnack's paper "Sex-Role Identity in Female Alcoholism," *The Journal of Abnormal Psychology* 82 (1972): 253–261.

For further discussions of the dilemmas faced by women alcoholics, see John and Dolores de Nobrega Langone's *Women Who Drink* (Reading, Mass.: Addison-Wesley, 1980). Also see Harriet Braiker's chapter "Therapeutic Issues in the Treatment of Alcoholic Women," part of the excellent text on alcoholism and women in *Alcohol Problems in Women,* edited by Sharon Wilsnack and Linda Beckman (New York: Guilford Press, 1984).

5. Because women who become addicted feel so ashamed, it's intensely difficult for them to acknowledge that they need help. Much of the research that's been done on female alcoholism and addiction reflects an attitude that women who drink or are compulsive in some way are "sicker" than men who do the same thing. Women internalize this attitude and logically feel uncomfortable admitting they have a problem. See the references above for further discussion.

6. There are many books available on the subject of codependency. For an overview, see Anne Wilson Schaef's *Co-Dependence: Misunderstood—Mistreated* (New York: Harper & Row, 1986).

6. GOODNESS THAT LEADS TO FEELING GOOD
THE NEW CODE OF BALANCE

1. See Judith Jordan's "Empathy and Self Boundaries," a paper published in 1984 as number 16 of the series *Works in Progress* published by the Stone

Center, Wellesley College, Wellesley, Massachusetts. The work of women at the Stone Center has enormous importance to evolving concepts of female psychology. See the papers of Dr. Jean Baker Miller, also part of the Stone Center, as well as her book *Toward a New Psychology of Women* (Boston: Beacon Press, 1976).

2. From *Webster's New Twentieth Century Dictionary*, Unabridged Second Edition, World Publishing Company.

7. GOODNESS EQUALS RESPONSIBILITY
CHANGING THE EQUATION

1. The original concept of over- and underresponsibility as it evolves in family relationships can be found in the work of Murray Bowen, particularly in his book *Family Therapy in Clinical Practice* (New York: Jason Aronson, 1978). Some of our comments in this chapter reflect our elaboration of his work. These original ideas can be found in our own book *The Responsibility Trap*. The Responsibility Wheel is another version of the Pride Wheel from that book.

2. Harriet Goldhor Lerner, *The Dance of Anger* (New York: Harper & Row, 1985), 1. See also Lerner's *The Dance of Intimacy* (New York: Harper & Row, 1989).

8. FROM THE PAST INTO THE PRESENT
UNRAVELING THE RULES OF GOODNESS

1. For an entertaining and thought-provoking discussion of family stories, see Elizabeth Stone's *Black Sheep and Kissing Cousins* (New York: Times Books, 1988). Family therapist Joan Laird has demonstrated the importance of story in work with families. For a discussion of women and story see her chapter "Women and Stories: Restorying Women's Self-Constructions," in McGoldrick, Anderson, and Walsh's *Women and Families*. Laird's chapter, with Ann Hartman, "Women, Rituals, and Family Therapy," in Lois Braverman's collection *Women, Feminism and Family Therapy* (New York: Haworth Press, 1988) is another important resource.

2. For a more in-depth discussion of the concept of ritual in families, see Evan Imber-Black's chapter "Rituals of Stabilization and Change in Women's Lives," in *Women, Feminism, and Family Therapy*, as well as *Rituals in Families and Family Therapy*, by Evan Imber-Black, Janine Roberts, and Richard Whiting (New York: W. W. Norton, 1988).

3. The original concept of the triangle in a family system is generally credited to Salvador Minuchin in his book *Families and Family Therapy* (Cambridge, Mass.: Harvard University Press, 1974). The concept is also central to Murray

Bowen's work. When we use the term "loyalty triangle" and when we talk about the "ledger of justice" on page 124, we also refer to the work of Ivan Boszormenyi-Nagy and Geraldine Spark in *Invisible Loyalties* (Hagerstown, Md.: Harper & Row, 1973).

4. Jane Middelton-Moz and Lorie Dwinell, *After the Tears* (Deerfield Beach, Fla.: Health Communications, 1986). The book describes the process of recovery from the damaging effects of the losses we experience when, as children, our basic developmental needs go unmet.

5. "Coaching" is a technique used by family therapists who work with people to change family relationship patterns by guiding them to talk directly with family members and making direct changes in their patterns of relating to them. The "conversations" Martha has with her mother in chapter 12 are an example of this work. To better understand this concept, see Harriet Goldhor Lerner's *The Dance of Anger* and *The Dance of Intimacy*. Also see Betty Carter and Monica McGoldrick's chapter "Family Therapy with One Person and the Family Therapist's Own Family," in *Family Therapy in Clinical Practice*.

11. DEEPER DILEMMAS
WOMEN AND MEN, WOMEN AND WOMEN, WOMEN AND WORK

1. For an in-depth discussion of the male dilemma, see Mark Gerzon's book *A Choice of Heroes* (Boston: Houghton Mifflin, 1982).

2. For a further discussion of the dilemmas of working women see Diane Holder and Carol Anderson's chapter, "Women, Work, and the Family," in *Women in Families*.

3. See Matina Horner's chapter "Towards an Understanding of Achievement-related Conflicts in Women," and Michele Paludi's rebuttal to it, "Psychometric Properties and Underlying Assumptions of Four Objective Measures of Fear of Success," in *The Psychology of Women*, edited by Mary Roth Walsh (New Haven, Conn.: Yale University Press, 1987).

4. Colette Dowling discusses this idea in *Perfect Women* (New York: Simon and Schuster, 1988).

12. GOOD MOTHERS, GOOD DAUGHTERS

1. Dorothy Dinnerstein develops this idea in her important book *The Mermaid and the Minotaur* (New York: Harper & Row, 1976).

2. See especially Paula Caplan's excellent book *Don't Blame Mother* (New York: Harper & Row, 1989).

13. FROM GOODNESS TO WHOLENESS
THE DEEPER LEVELS OF CHANGE

1. Anne Morrow Lindbergh, *Gift from the Sea* (New York: Random House, 1955), 29.

2. *Gift from the Sea,* 50.

3. *Gift from the Sea,* 120.

SELECTED BIBLIOGRAPHY

———— ✳ ————

Ault-Riche, Marianne, ed. *Women and Family Therapy*. Rockville, Md.: Aspen Systems, 1986.

De Beauvoir, Simone. *The Second Sex*. New York: Alfred A. Knopf, 1952.

Bepko, Claudia, with Jo-Ann Krestan. *The Responsibility Trap: A Blueprint for Treating the Alcoholic Family*. New York: Free Press, 1985.

Boszormenyi-Nagy, Ivan, and Geraldine Spark. *Invisible Loyalties*. New York: Hagerstown, Md.: Harper & Row, 1973.

Bowen, Murray. *Family Therapy in Clinical Practice*. New York: Jason Aronson, 1978.

Bradshaw, John. *Healing the Shame That Binds You*. Deerfield Beach, Fl.: Health Communications, 1988.

Braverman, Lois, ed. *Women, Feminism and Family Therapy*. New York: Haworth Press, 1988.

Brodsky, Annette, and Rachel Hare-Mustin, eds. *Women and Psychotherapy*. New York: Guilford Press, 1980.

Caplan, Paula J. *Don't Blame Mother: Mending the Mother-Daughter Relationship*. New York: Harper & Row, 1989.

Cardozo, Arlene Rossen. *Sequencing*. New York: Macmillan, 1986.

Carter, Elizabeth, and Monica McGoldrick. *The Changing Family Life Cycle*, second ed. Needham Heights, Mass.: Allyn and Bacon, 1988.

Clunis, D. Merilee, and G. Dorsey Green. *Lesbian Couples*. Seattle, Wash.: Seal Press, 1988.

Dinnerstein, Dorothy. *The Mermaid and the Minotaur*. New York: Harper & Row, 1976.

Dowling, Colette. *Perfect Women*. New York: Simon and Schuster, 1988.

Eichenbaum, Luise, and Susie Orbach. *What Do Women Want: Exploding the Myth of Dependency*. New York: Coward-McCann, 1983.

Elkin, Michael. *Families Under the Influence: Changing Alcoholic Patterns*. New York: W. W. Norton, 1984.

Fossum, Merle, and Marilyn Mason. *Facing Shame*. New York: W. W. Norton, 1986.

Freedman, Rita. *Bodylove*. New York: Harper & Row, 1989.

Friedan, Betty. *The Feminine Mystique*. New York: W. W. Norton, 1963.

Gerzon, Mark. *A Choice of Heroes*. Boston: Houghton Mifflin, 1982.

Gilligan, Carol. *In a Different Voice*. Cambridge, Mass.: Harvard University Press, 1982.

Guerin, Philip, ed. *Family Therapy: Theory and Practice*. New York: Gardner Press, 1976.

Heilbrun, Carolyn. *Writing a Woman's Life*. New York: W. W. Norton, 1988.

Hirschmann, Jane, and Carol Munter. *Overcoming Overeating: Living Free in a World of Food*. Reading, Mass.: Addison-Wesley, 1988.

Hochschild, Arlie. *The Second Shift*. New York: Viking Press, 1989.

Horney, Karen. *Neurosis and Human Growth*. New York: W. W. Norton, 1950.

Imber-Black, Evan, Janine Roberts, and Richard Whiting. *Rituals in Families and Family Therapy*. New York: W. W. Norton, 1988.

Kaufman, Gershen. *The Psychology of Shame*. New York: Springer Publishing Company, 1989.

Langone, John, and Dolores de Nobrega. *Women Who Drink*. Reading, Mass.: Addison-Wesley, 1980.

Lerner, Harriet Goldhor. *The Dance of Intimacy*. New York: Harper & Row, 1989.

———. *Women in Therapy*. New York: Harper & Row, with Jason Aronson, Inc., 1988.

———. *The Dance of Anger*. New York: Harper & Row, 1985.

Leupnitz, Deborah. *The Family Interpreted: Feminist Theory in Clinical Practice*. New York: Basic Books, 1988.

Lindbergh, Anne Morrow. *Gift from the Sea*. New York: Random House, 1955.

McGoldrick, Monica, Carol Anderson, and Froma Walsh. *Women in Families*. New York: W. W. Norton, 1989.

Middelton-Moz, Jane, and Lorie Dwinell. *After the Tears*. Deerfield Beach, Fl.: Health Communications, 1986.

Miller, Jean Baker. *Toward a New Psychology of Women*. Boston: Beacon Press, 1976.

Minuchin, Salvador. *Families and Family Therapy*. Cambridge, Mass.: Harvard University Press, 1974.

Olson, Tillie. *Silences*. New York: Delacorte Press/Seymour Lawrence, 1965.

Papp, Peggy. *The Process of Change*. New York: Guilford Press, 1983.

Pittman, Frank, III. *Turning Points: Treating Families in Transition and Crisis*. New York: W. W. Norton, 1987.

Royce, James. *Alcohol Problems and Alcoholism*. New York: Free Press, 1981.

Sandmaier, Marian. *The Invisible Alcoholics*. New York: McGraw-Hill, 1980.

Schaef, Anne Wilson. *Co-Dependence: Misunderstood—Mistreated*. New York: Harper & Row, 1986.

Stone, Elizabeth. *Black Sheep and Kissing Cousins*. New York: Times Books, 1988.

Walker, Lenore. *Terrifying Love: Why Battered Women Kill and How Society Responds*. New York: Harper & Row, 1989.

Walsh, Mary Roth. *The Psychology of Women*. New Haven: Yale University Press, 1987.

Walters, Marianne, Betty Carter, Peggy Papp, and Olga Silverstein. *The Invisible Web*. New York: Guilford Press, 1988.

Wilsnack, Sharon, and Linda Beckman, eds. *Alcohol Problems in Women*. New York: Guilford Press, 1984.

INDEX

———— ✳ ————

Regular loan : 2 weeks
A daily fine is charged for each overdue book.
Books may be renewed once, unless reserved
for another patron.
A borrower is responsible for books damaged
or lost while charged on his card